Lecture Notes in Computer Science   2283

Edited by G. Goos, J. Hartmanis, and J. van Leeuwen

Springer
Berlin
Heidelberg
New York
Barcelona
Hong Kong
London
Milan
Paris
Tokyo

Tobias Nipkow   Lawrence C. Paulson
Markus Wenzel

Isabelle/HOL

A Proof Assistant for Higher-Order Logic

Springer

Series Editors

Gerhard Goos, Karlsruhe University, Germany
Juris Hartmanis, Cornell University, NY, USA
Jan van Leeuwen, Utrecht University, The Netherlands

Authors

Tobias Nipkow
Markus Wenzel
Technische Universität München, Institut für Informatik
Arcisstraße 21, 80333 München, Germany
E-mail: {nipkow,wenzelm}@in.tum.de

Lawrence C. Paulson
University of Cambridge, Computer Laboratory
JJ Thomson Avenue, Cambridge CB3 0FD, UK
E-mail: lcp@cl.cam

Cataloging-in-Publication Data applied for

Die Deutsche Bibliothek - CIP-Einheitsaufnahme

Nipkow, Tobias:
Isabelle, HOL : a proof assistant for higher order logic / Tobias Nipkow ;
Lawrence C. Paulson ; Markus Wenzel. - Berlin ; Heidelberg ; New York ;
Barcelona ; Hong Kong ; London ; Milan ; Paris ; Tokyo : Springer, 2002
  (Lecture notes in computer science ; Vol. 2283)
  ISBN 3-540-43376-7

CR Subject Classification (1998): F.4.1, I.2.3, F.3.1, D.3.1, D.2.1

ISSN 0302-9743
ISBN 3-540-43376-7 Springer-Verlag Berlin Heidelberg New York

Springer-Verlag Berlin Heidelberg New York
a member of BertelsmannSpringer Science+Business Media GmbH

http://www.springer.de

© Springer-Verlag Berlin Heidelberg 2002
Printed in Germany

Typesetting: Camera-ready by author, data conversion by Boller Mediendesign
Printed on acid-free paper   SPIN: 10846296   06/3142   5 4 3 2 1 0

In memoriam

ANNETTE SCHUMANN

1959 – 2001

Preface

This volume is a self-contained introduction to interactive proof in higher-order logic (HOL), using the proof assistant Isabelle 2002. Compared with existing Isabelle documentation, it provides a direct route into higher-order logic, which most people prefer these days. It bypasses first-order logic and minimizes discussion of meta-theory. It is written for potential users rather than for our colleagues in the research world.

Another departure from previous documentation is that we describe Markus Wenzel's proof script notation instead of ML tactic scripts. The latter make it easier to introduce new tactics on the fly, but hardly anybody does that. Wenzel's dedicated syntax is elegant, replacing for example eight simplification tactics with a single method, namely *simp*, with associated options.

The book has three parts.

- The first part, **Elementary Techniques**, shows how to model functional programs in higher-order logic. Early examples involve lists and the natural numbers. Most proofs are two steps long, consisting of induction on a chosen variable followed by the *auto* tactic. But even this elementary part covers such advanced topics as nested and mutual recursion.
- The second part, **Logic and Sets**, presents a collection of lower-level tactics that you can use to apply rules selectively. It also describes Isabelle/HOL's treatment of sets, functions, and relations and explains how to define sets inductively. One of the examples concerns the theory of model checking, and another is drawn from a classic textbook on formal languages.
- The third part, **Advanced Material**, describes a variety of other topics. Among these are the real numbers, records, and overloading. Esoteric techniques are described involving induction and recursion. A whole chapter is devoted to an extended example: the verification of a security protocol.

The typesetting relies on Wenzel's theory presentation tools. An annotated source file is run, typesetting the theory in the form of a LATEX source file. This book is derived almost entirely from output generated in this way. The final chapter of Part I explains how users may produce their own formal documents in a similar fashion.

Isabelle's web site[1] contains links to the download area and to documentation and other information. Most Isabelle sessions are now run from within David Aspinall's wonderful user interface, Proof General[2], even together with the X-Symbol[3] package for XEmacs. This book says very little about Proof General, which has its own documentation. In order to run Isabelle, you will need a Standard ML compiler. We recommend Poly/ML[4], which is free and gives the best performance. The other fully supported compiler is Standard ML of New Jersey[5].

This tutorial owes a lot to the constant discussions with and the valuable feedback from the Isabelle group at Munich: Stefan Berghofer, Olaf Müller, Wolfgang Naraschewski, David von Oheimb, Leonor Prensa Nieto, Cornelia Pusch, Norbert Schirmer, and Martin Strecker. Stephan Merz was also kind enough to read and comment on a draft version. We received comments from Stefano Bistarelli, Gergely Buday, and Tanja Vos.

The research has been funded by many sources, including the DFG grants Ni 491/2, Ni 491/3, Ni 491/4 and the EPSRC grants GR/K57381, GR/K77051, GR/M75440, GR/R01156/01, and by the ESPRIT working groups 21900 and IST-1999-29001 (the *Types* project).

---

[1] http://isabelle.in.tum.de/
[2] http://www.proofgeneral.org/
[3] http://www.fmi.uni-passau.de/~wedler/x-symbol/
[4] http://www.polyml.org/
[5] http://cm.bell-labs.com/cm/cs/what/smlnj/index.html

Table of Contents

Part II. Logic and Sets

Part I

Elementary Techniques

1. The Basics

1.1 ntro uction

This book is a tutorial on how to use the theorem prover Isabelle/HOL as a specification and verification system. Isabelle is a generic system for implementing logical formalisms, and Isabelle/HOL is the specialization of Isabelle for HOL, which abbreviates Higher-Order Logic. We introduce HOL step by step following the equation

$$HOL = Functional\ Programming + Logic.$$

We do not assume that you are familiar with mathematical logic. However, we do assume that you are used to logical and set theoretic notation, as covered in a good discrete mathematics course [31], and that you are familiar with the basic concepts of functional programming [5, 13, 27, 32]. Although this tutorial initially concentrates on functional programming, do not be misled: HOL can express most mathematical concepts, and functional programming is just one particularly simple and ubiquitous instance.

Isabelle [26] is implemented in ML [17]. This has influenced some of Isabelle/HOL's concrete syntax but is otherwise irrelevant for us: this tutorial is based on Isabelle/Isar [33], an extension of Isabelle which hides the implementation language almost completely. Thus the full name of the system should be Isabelle/Isar/HOL, but that is a bit of a mouthful.

There are other implementations of HOL, in particular the one by Mike Gordon *et al.*, which is usually referred to as "the HOL system" [10]. For us, HOL refers to the logical system, and sometimes its incarnation Isabelle/HOL.

A tutorial is by definition incomplete. Currently the tutorial only introduces the rudiments of Isar's proof language. To fully exploit the power of Isar, in particular the ability to write readable and structured proofs, you need to consult the Isabelle/Isar Reference Manual [33] and Wenzel's PhD thesis [34] which discusses many proof patterns. If you want to use Isabelle's ML level directly (for example for writing your own proof procedures) see the Isabelle Reference Manual [23]; for details relating to HOL see the Isabelle/HOL manual [22]. All manuals have a comprehensive index.

T. Nipkow, L.C. Paulson, and M. Wenzel: Isabelle/HOL, LNCS 2283, pp. 3-8, 2002.
© Springer-Verlag Berlin Heidelberg 2002

1.2 Theories

Working with Isabelle means creating theories. Roughly speaking, a **theory** is a named collection of types, functions, and theorems, much like a module in a programming language or a specification in a specification language. In fact, theories in HOL can be either. The general format of a theory T is

> **theory** T = B$_1$ + $\cdots$ + B$_n$:
> *declarations, definitions, and proofs*
> **end**

where B$_1$, ... , B$_n$ are the names of existing theories that T is based on and *declarations, definitions, and proofs* represents the newly introduced concepts (types, functions etc.) and proofs about them. The B$_i$ are the direct **parent theories** of T. Everything defined in the parent theories (and their parents, recursively) is automatically visible. To avoid name clashes, identifiers can be **qualified** by theory names as in T.f and B.f. Each theory T must reside in a **theory file** named T.thy.

This tutorial is concerned with introducing you to the different linguistic constructs that can fill the *declarations, definitions, and proofs* above. A complete grammar of the basic constructs is found in the Isabelle/Isar Reference Manual [33].

HOL's theory collection is available online at

http://isabelle.in.tum.de/library/HOL/

and is recommended browsing. Note that most of the theories are based on classical Isabelle without the Isar extension. This means that they look slightly different than the theories in this tutorial, and that all proofs are in separate ML files.

! HOL contains a theory Main, the union of all the basic predefined theories like
• arithmetic, lists, sets, etc. Unless you know what you are doing, always include Main as a direct or indirect parent of all your theories.

There is also a growing Library [4] of useful theories that are not part of Main but can to be included among the parents of a theory and will then be loaded automatically.

1.3 Types, Terms, an Formulae

Embedded in a theory are the types, terms and formulae of HOL. HOL is a typed logic whose type system resembles that of functional programming languages like ML or Haskell. Thus there are

base types, in particular *bool*, the type of truth values, and *nat*, the type of natural numbers.

type constructors, in particular `list`, the type of lists, and `set`, the type of sets. Type constructors are written postfix, e.g. `(nat)list` is the type of lists whose elements are natural numbers. Parentheses around single arguments can be dropped (as in `nat list`), multiple arguments are separated by commas (as in `(bool,nat)ty`).

function types, denoted by $\Rightarrow$. In HOL $\Rightarrow$ represents *total* functions only. As is customary, $\tau_1 \Rightarrow \tau_2 \Rightarrow \tau_3$ means $\tau_1 \Rightarrow (\tau_2 \Rightarrow \tau_3)$. Isabelle also supports the notation $[\tau_1,\ldots,\tau_n] \Rightarrow \tau$ which abbreviates $\tau_1 \Rightarrow \cdots \Rightarrow \tau_n \Rightarrow \tau$.

type variables, denoted by `'a`, `'b` etc., just like in ML. They give rise to polymorphic types like `'a` $\Rightarrow$ `'a`, the type of the identity function.

! Types are extremely important because they prevent us from writing nonsense.
• Isabelle insists that all terms and formulae must be well-typed and will print an error message if a type mismatch is encountered. To reduce the amount of explicit type information that needs to be provided by the user, Isabelle infers the type of all variables automatically (this is called **type inference**) and keeps quiet about it. Occasionally this may lead to misunderstandings between you and the system. If anything strange happens, we recommend that you set the flag `show_types`. Isabelle will then display type information that is usually suppressed. Simply type

    ML "set show_types"

This can be reversed by `ML "reset show_types"`. Various other flags, which we introduce as we go along, can be set and reset in the same manner.

Terms are formed as in functional programming by applying functions to arguments. If `f` is a function of type $\tau_1 \Rightarrow \tau_2$ and `t` is a term of type τ_1 then `f t` is a term of type τ_2. HOL also supports infix functions like `+` and some basic constructs from functional programming, such as conditional expressions:

`if b then` t_1 `else` t_2 Here `b` is of type `bool` and t_1 and t_2 are of the same type.

`let x = t in u` is equivalent to `u` where all occurrences of `x` have been replaced by `t`. For example, `let x = 0 in x+x` is equivalent to `0+0`. Multiple bindings are separated by semicolons: `let` x_1 `=` t_1`; ... ;` x_n `=` t_n `in u`.

`case e of` $c_1 \Rightarrow e_1$ `| ... |` $c_n \Rightarrow e_n$ evaluates to e_i if `e` is of the form c_i.

Terms may also contain λ-abstractions. For example, $\lambda x.\ x+1$ is the function that takes an argument `x` and returns `x+1`. Instead of $\lambda x.\ \lambda y.\ \lambda z.\ t$ we can write $\lambda x\ y\ z.\ t$.

Formulae are terms of type `bool`. There are the basic constants `True` and `False` and the usual logical connectives (in decreasing order of priority): $\neg$, $\wedge$, $\vee$, and $\longrightarrow$, all of which (except the unary $\neg$) associate to the right. In particular $A \longrightarrow B \longrightarrow C$ means $A \longrightarrow (B \longrightarrow C)$ and is thus logically equivalent to $A \wedge B \longrightarrow C$ (which is $(A \wedge B) \longrightarrow C$).

Equality is available in the form of the infix function `=` of type `'a` $\Rightarrow$ `'a` $\Rightarrow$ `bool`. Thus t_1 `=` t_2 is a formula provided t_1 and t_2 are terms of the same type. If t_1 and t_2 are of type $bool$ then $=$ acts as if-and-only-if. The formula $t_1 \neq t_2$ is merely an abbreviation for $\neg(t_1 = t_2)$.

Quantifiers are written as $\forall x.\ P$ and $\exists x.\ P$. There is even $\exists! x.\ P$, which means that there exists exactly one x that satisfies P. Nested quantifications can be abbreviated: $\forall x\ y\ z.\ P$ means $\forall x.\forall y.\forall z.\ P$.

Despite type inference, it is sometimes necessary to attach explicit **type constraints** to a term. The syntax is $t::\tau$ as in $x < (y::nat)$. Note that $::$ binds weakly and should therefore be enclosed in parentheses. For instance, $x < y::nat$ is ill-typed because it is interpreted as $(x < y)::nat$. Type constraints may be needed to disambiguate expressions involving overloaded functions such as $+$, $*$ and $<$. Section 8.4.1 discusses overloading, while Table A.2 presents the most important overloaded function symbols.

In general, HOL's concrete syntax tries to follow the conventions of functional programming and mathematics. Here are the main rules that you should be familiar with to avoid certain syntactic traps:

- Remember that $f\ t\ u$ means $(f\ t)\ u$ and not $f(t\ u)$!
- Isabelle allows infix functions like $+$. The prefix form of function application binds more strongly than anything else and hence $f\ x + y$ means $(f\ x) + y$ and not $f(x{+}y)$.
- Remember that in HOL if-and-only-if is expressed using equality. But equality has a high priority, as befitting a relation, while if-and-only-if typically has the lowest priority. Thus, $\neg\ \neg\ P = P$ means $\neg\neg(P = P)$ and not $(\neg\neg P) = P$. When using $=$ to mean logical equivalence, enclose both operands in parentheses, as in $(A \wedge B) = (B \wedge A)$.
- Constructs with an opening but without a closing delimiter bind very weakly and should therefore be enclosed in parentheses if they appear in subterms, as in $(\lambda x.\ x) = f$. This includes if, let, $case$, λ, and quantifiers.
- Never write $\lambda x.x$ or $\forall x.x{=}x$ because $x.x$ is always taken as a single qualified identifier. Write $\lambda x.\ x$ and $\forall x.\ x{=}x$ instead.
- Identifiers may contain the characters _ and ', except at the beginning.

For the sake of readability, we use the usual mathematical symbols throughout the tutorial. Their ASCII-equivalents are shown in table A.1 in the appendix.

! A particular problem for novices can be the priority of operators. If you are **•** unsure, use additional parentheses. In those cases where Isabelle echoes your input, you can see which parentheses are dropped — they were superfluous. If you are unsure how to interpret Isabelle's output because you don't know where the (dropped) parentheses go, set the flag $show\_brackets$:

```
ML "set show_brackets"; ...; ML "reset show_brackets";
```

1.4 Variables

Isabelle distinguishes free and bound variables, as is customary. Bound variables are automatically renamed to avoid clashes with free variables. In addition, Isabelle has a third kind of variable, called a **schematic variable** or **unknown**, which must a *?* as its first character. Logically, an unknown is a free variable. But it may be instantiated by another term during the proof process. For example, the mathematical theorem $x = x$ is represented in Isabelle as *?x = ?x*, which means that Isabelle can instantiate it arbitrarily. This is in contrast to ordinary variables, which remain fixed. The programming language Prolog calls unknowns *logical* variables.

Most of the time you can and should ignore unknowns and work with ordinary variables. Just don't be surprised that after you have finished the proof of a theorem, Isabelle will turn your free variables into unknowns. It indicates that Isabelle will automatically instantiate those unknowns suitably when the theorem is used in some other proof. Note that for readability we often drop the *?*s when displaying a theorem.

! For historical reasons, Isabelle accepts *?* as an ASCII representation of the
• ∃ symbol. However, the *?* character must then be followed by a space, as in
? x. f(x) = 0. Otherwise, *?x* is interpreted as a schematic variable. The preferred
ASCII representation of the ∃ symbol is *EX*.

1.5 nteraction an   nterfaces

Interaction with Isabelle can either occur at the shell level or through more advanced interfaces. To keep the tutorial independent of the interface, we have phrased the description of the interaction in a neutral language. For example, the phrase "to abandon a proof" means to type **oops** at the shell level, which is explained the first time the phrase is used. Other interfaces perform the same act by cursor movements and/or mouse clicks. Although shell-based interaction is quite feasible for the kind of proof scripts currently presented in this tutorial, the recommended interface for Isabelle/Isar is the Emacs-based **Proof General** [1, 2].

Some interfaces (including the shell level) offer special fonts with mathematical symbols. For those that do not, remember that ASCII-equivalents are shown in table A.1 in the appendix.

Finally, a word about semicolons. Commands may but need not be terminated by semicolons. At the shell level it is advisable to use semicolons to enforce that a command is executed immediately; otherwise Isabelle may wait for the next keyword before it knows that the command is complete.

1.6 Getting Starte

Assuming you have installed Isabelle, you start it by typing `isabelle -I`
`HOL` in a shell window.[1] This presents you with Isabelle's most basic ASCII
interface. In addition you need to open an editor window to create theory
files. While you are developing a theory, we recommend that you type each
command into the file first and then enter it into Isabelle by copy-and-paste,
thus ensuring that you have a complete record of your theory. As mentioned
above, Proof General offers a much superior interface. If you have installed
Proof General, you can start it by typing `Isabelle`.

---

[1] Simply executing `isabelle -I` starts the default logic, which usually is already
`HOL`. This is controlled by the `ISABELLE_LOGIC` setting, see *The Isabelle System
Manual* for more details.

2. Functional Programming in HOL

This chapter describes how to write functional programs in HOL and how to verify them. However, most of the constructs and proof procedures introduced are general and recur in any specification or verification task. We really should speak of functional *modelling* rather than functional *programming*: our primary aim is not to write programs but to design abstract models of systems. HOL is a specification language that goes well beyond what can be expressed as a program. However, for the time being we concentrate on the computable.

If you are a purist functional programmer, please note that all functions in HOL must be total: they must terminate for all inputs. Lazy data structures are not directly available.

2.1 An Introductory Theory

Functional programming needs datatypes and functions. Both of them can be defined in a theory with a syntax reminiscent of languages like ML or Haskell. As an example consider the theory in figure 2.1. We will now examine it line by line.

theory *ToyList* = *PreList*:

HOL already has a predefined theory of lists called *List* — *ToyList* is merely a small fragment of it chosen as an example. In contrast to what is recommended in Sect. 1.2, *ToyList* is not based on *Main* but on *PreList*, a theory that contains pretty much everything but lists, thus avoiding ambiguities caused by defining lists twice.

datatype *'a list* = *Nil*   ("*[]* ")
                        | *Cons 'a* "*'a list*"   (**infixr** "*#*" 65)

The datatype *list* introduces two constructors *Nil* and *Cons*, the empty list and the operator that adds an element to the front of a list. For example, the term *Cons True (Cons False Nil)* is a value of type *bool list*, namely the list with the elements *True* and *False*. Because this notation quickly becomes unwieldy, the datatype declaration is annotated with an alternative syntax: instead of *Nil* and *Cons x xs* we can write *[]* and *x # xs*. In fact,

```
theory ToyList = PreList:

datatype 'a list = Nil                          ("[]")
                 | Cons 'a "'a list"            (infixr "#" 65)

consts app :: "'a list => 'a list => 'a list"   (infixr "@" 65)
       rev :: "'a list => 'a list"

primrec
"[] @ ys      = ys"
"(x # xs) @ ys = x # (xs @ ys)"

primrec
"rev []       = []"
"rev (x # xs)  = (rev xs) @ (x # [])"
```

Fig. 2.1. A Theory of Lists

this alternative syntax is the familiar one. Thus the list *Cons True (Cons False Nil)* becomes *True # False # []*. The annotation **infixr** means that # associates to the right: the term *x # y # z* is read as *x # (y # z)* and not as *(x # y) # z*. The *65* is the priority of the infix *#*.

! Syntax annotations are can be powerful, but they are difficult to master and
• are never necessary. You could drop them from theory *ToyList* and go back to the identifiers *Nil* and *Cons*. Novices should avoid using syntax annotations in their own theories.

Next, two functions *app* and *rev* are declared:

consts *app* :: *"'a list ⇒ 'a list ⇒ 'a list"*   (**infixr** *"@" 65*)
       rev :: *"'a list ⇒ 'a list"*

In contrast to many functional programming languages, Isabelle insists on explicit declarations of all functions (keyword **consts**). Apart from the declaration-before-use restriction, the order of items in a theory file is unconstrained. Function *app* is annotated with concrete syntax too. Instead of the prefix syntax *app xs ys* the infix *xs @ ys* becomes the preferred form. Both functions are defined recursively:

primrec
"[] @ ys   = ys"
"(x # xs) @ ys = x # (xs @ ys)"

primrec
"rev []   = []"
"rev (x # xs) = (rev xs) @ (x # [])"

The equations for *app* and *rev* hardly need comments: *app* appends two lists and *rev* reverses a list. The keyword **primrec** indicates that the recursion is of a particularly primitive kind where each recursive call peels off a datatype constructor from one of the arguments. Thus the recursion always terminates, i.e. the function is **total**.

The termination requirement is absolutely essential in HOL, a logic of total functions. If we were to drop it, inconsistencies would quickly arise: the "definition" $f(n) = f(n) + 1$ immediately leads to $0 = 1$ by subtracting $f(n)$ on both sides.

!
• As we have indicated, the requirement for total functions is an essential characteristic of HOL. It is only because of totality that reasoning in HOL is comparatively easy. More generally, the philosophy in HOL is to refrain from asserting arbitrary axioms (such as function definitions whose totality has not been proved) because they quickly lead to inconsistencies. Instead, fixed constructs for introducing types and functions are offered (such as **datatype** and **primrec**) which are guaranteed to preserve consistency.

A remark about syntax. The textual definition of a theory follows a fixed syntax with keywords like **datatype** and **end**. Embedded in this syntax are the types and formulae of HOL, whose syntax is extensible (see Sect. 4.1), e.g. by new user-defined infix operators. To distinguish the two levels, everything HOL-specific (terms and types) should be enclosed in " ... ". To lessen this burden, quotation marks around a single identifier can be dropped, unless the identifier happens to be a keyword, as in

```
consts "end" :: "'a list ⇒ 'a"
```

When Isabelle prints a syntax error message, it refers to the HOL syntax as the **inner syntax** and the enclosing theory language as the **outer syntax**.

2.2 An Introductory Proof

Assuming you have input the declarations and definitions of ToyList presented so far, we are ready to prove a few simple theorems. This will illustrate not just the basic proof commands but also the typical proof process.

Main Goal. Our goal is to show that reversing a list twice produces the original list.

```
theorem rev_rev [simp]: "rev(rev xs) = xs"
```

This **theorem** command does several things:

- It establishes a new theorem to be proved, namely `rev (rev xs) = xs`.
- It gives that theorem the name `rev_rev`, for later reference.
- It tells Isabelle (via the bracketed attribute `simp`) to take the eventual theorem as a simplification rule: future proofs involving simplification will replace occurrences of `rev (rev xs)` by `xs`.

The name and the simplification attribute are optional. Isabelle's response is to print the initial proof state consisting of some header information (like how many subgoals there are) followed by

```
rev (rev xs) = xs
 1. rev (rev xs) = xs
```

For compactness reasons we omit the header in this tutorial. Until we have finished a proof, the proof state proper always looks like this:

G
 1. G_1
 $\vdots$
 n. G_n

where G is the overall goal that we are trying to prove, and the numbered lines contain the subgoals $G_1, \ldots, G_n$ that we need to prove to establish G. Initially there is only one subgoal, which is identical with the overall goal. Normally G is constant and only serves as a reminder. Hence we rarely show it in this tutorial.

Let us now get back to `rev (rev xs) = xs`. Properties of recursively defined functions are best established by induction. In this case there is nothing obvious except induction on `xs`:

apply (`induct_tac xs`)

This tells Isabelle to perform induction on variable `xs`. The suffix `tac` stands for **tactic**, a synonym for "theorem proving function". By default, induction acts on the first subgoal. The new proof state contains two subgoals, namely the base case (`Nil`) and the induction step (`Cons`):

```
 1. rev (rev []) = []
 2. ⋀a list.
       rev (rev list) = list ⟹ rev (rev (a # list)) = a # list
```

The induction step is an example of the general format of a subgoal:

i. $\bigwedge x_1 \ldots x_n$. *assumptions* $\implies$ *conclusion*

The prefix of bound variables $\bigwedge x_1 \ldots x_n$ can be ignored most of the time, or simply treated as a list of variables local to this subgoal. Their deeper significance is explained in Chapter 5. The *assumptions* are the local assumptions for this subgoal and *conclusion* is the actual proposition to be proved. Typical proof steps that add new assumptions are induction and case distinction. In our example the only assumption is the induction hypothesis `rev (rev list) = list`, where `list` is a variable name chosen by Isabelle. If there are multiple assumptions, they are enclosed in the bracket pair ⟦ and ⟧ and separated by semicolons.

Let us try to solve both goals automatically:

apply (`auto`)

This command tells Isabelle to apply a proof strategy called `auto` to all sub-goals. Essentially, `auto` tries to simplify the subgoals. In our case, subgoal 1 is solved completely (thanks to the equation `rev [] = []`) and disappears; the simplified version of subgoal 2 becomes the new subgoal 1:

```
1. ⋀a list.
     rev (rev list) = list ⟹ rev (rev list @ a # []) = a # list
```

In order to simplify this subgoal further, a lemma suggests itself.

First Lemma. After abandoning the above proof attempt (at the shell level type **oops**) we start a new proof:

lemma `rev_app [simp]: "rev(xs @ ys) = (rev ys) @ (rev xs)"`

The keywords **theorem** and **lemma** are interchangeable and merely indicate the importance we attach to a proposition. Therefore we use the words *theorem* and *lemma* pretty much interchangeably, too.

There are two variables that we could induct on: `xs` and `ys`. Because `@` is defined by recursion on the first argument, `xs` is the correct one:

apply`(induct_tac xs)`

This time not even the base case is solved automatically:

apply`(auto)`

```
1. rev ys = rev ys @ []
```

Again, we need to abandon this proof attempt and prove another simple lemma first. In the future the step of abandoning an incomplete proof before embarking on the proof of a lemma usually remains implicit.

Second Lemma. We again try the canonical proof procedure:

lemma `app_Nil2 [simp]: "xs @ [] = xs"`
apply`(induct_tac xs)`
apply`(auto)`

It works, yielding the desired message `No subgoals!`:

```
xs @ [] = xs
No subgoals!
```

We still need to confirm that the proof is now finished:

done

As a result of that final **done**, Isabelle associates the lemma just proved with its name. In this tutorial, we sometimes omit to show that final **done** if it is obvious from the context that the proof is finished.

Notice that in lemma `app_Nil2`, as printed out after the final **done**, the free variable `xs` has been replaced by the unknown `?xs`, just as explained in Sect. 1.4.

Going back to the proof of the first lemma

lemma `rev_app [simp]: "rev(xs @ ys) = (rev ys) @ (rev xs)"`
apply(`induct_tac xs`)
apply(`auto`)

we find that this time `auto` solves the base case, but the induction step merely simplifies to

```
1. ⋀a list.
     rev (list @ ys) = rev ys @ rev list ⟹
     (rev ys @ rev list) @ a # [] = rev ys @ rev list @ a # []
```

Now we need to remember that `@` associates to the right, and that `#` and `@` have the same priority (namely the `65` in their **infixr** annotation). Thus the conclusion really is

```
    (rev ys @ rev list) @ (a # []) = rev ys @ (rev list @ (a # []))
```

and the missing lemma is associativity of `@`.

Third Lemma. Abandoning the previous attempt, the canonical proof procedure succeeds without further ado.

lemma `app_assoc [simp]: "(xs @ ys) @ zs = xs @ (ys @ zs)"`
apply(`induct_tac xs`)
apply(`auto`)
done

Now we can prove the first lemma:

lemma `rev_app [simp]: "rev(xs @ ys) = (rev ys) @ (rev xs)"`
apply(`induct_tac xs`)
apply(`auto`)
done

Finally, we prove our main theorem:

theorem `rev_rev [simp]: "rev(rev xs) = xs"`
apply(`induct_tac xs`)
apply(`auto`)
done

The final **end** tells Isabelle to close the current theory because we are finished with its development:

end

The complete proof script is shown in Fig. 2.2. The concatenation of Figs. 2.1 and 2.2 constitutes the complete theory `ToyList` and should reside in file `ToyList.thy`.

```
lemma app_Nil2 [simp]: "xs @ [] = xs"
apply(induct_tac xs)
apply(auto)
done

lemma app_assoc [simp]: "(xs @ ys) @ zs = xs @ (ys @ zs)"
apply(induct_tac xs)
apply(auto)
done

lemma rev_app [simp]: "rev(xs @ ys) = (rev ys) @ (rev xs)"
apply(induct_tac xs)
apply(auto)
done

theorem rev_rev [simp]: "rev(rev xs) = xs"
apply(induct_tac xs)
apply(auto)
done

end
```

Fig. 2.2. Proofs about Lists

Review This is the end of our toy proof. It should have familiarized you
with

- the standard theorem proving procedure: state a goal (lemma or theorem);
  proceed with proof until a separate lemma is required; prove that lemma;
  come back to the original goal.
- a specific procedure that works well for functional programs: induction
  followed by all-out simplification via auto.
- a basic repertoire of proof commands.

! It is tempting to think that all lemmas should have the simp attribute just
• because this was the case in the example above. However, in that example all
lemmas were equations, and the right-hand side was simpler than the left-hand
side — an ideal situation for simplification purposes. Unless this is clearly the case,
novices should refrain from awarding a lemma the simp attribute, which has a
global effect. Instead, lemmas can be applied locally where they are needed, which
is discussed in the following chapter.

2.3 Some Helpful Commands

This section discusses a few basic commands for manipulating the proof state
and can be skipped by casual readers.

There are two kinds of commands used during a proof: the actual proof
commands and auxiliary commands for examining the proof state and con-
trolling the display. Simple proof commands are of the form **apply**(*method*),

where *method* is typically `induct_tac` or `auto`. All such theorem proving operations are referred to as **methods**, and further ones are introduced throughout the tutorial. Unless stated otherwise, you may assume that a method attacks merely the first subgoal. An exception is `auto`, which tries to solve all subgoals.

The most useful auxiliary commands are as follows:

Undoing: **undo** undoes the effect of the last command; **undo** can be undone by **redo**. Both are only needed at the shell level and should not occur in the final theory.

Printing the current state: **pr** redisplays the current proof state, for example when it has scrolled past the top of the screen.

Limiting the number of subgoals: **pr** n tells Isabelle to print only the first n subgoals from now on and redisplays the current proof state. This is helpful when there are many subgoals.

Modifying the order of subgoals: **defer** moves the first subgoal to the end and **prefer** n moves subgoal n to the front.

Printing theorems: **thm** $name_1$ ... $name_n$ prints the named theorems.

Displaying types: We have already mentioned the flag `show_types` above. It can also be useful for detecting misspellings in formulae. For example, if `show_types` is set and the goal `rev(rev xs) = xs` is started, Isabelle prints the additional output

```
variables:
  xs :: 'a list
```

which tells us that Isabelle has correctly inferred that `xs` is a variable of list type. On the other hand, had we made a typo as in `rev(re xs) = xs`, the response

```
variables:
  re :: 'a list ⇒ 'a list
  xs :: 'a list
```

would have alerted us because of the unexpected variable `re`.

Reading terms and types: **term** *string* reads, type-checks and prints the given string as a term in the current context; the inferred type is output as well. **typ** *string* reads and prints the given string as a type in the current context.

(Re)loading theories: When you start your interaction you must open a named theory with the line **theory** T = ...   :. Isabelle automatically loads all the required parent theories from their respective files (which may take a moment, unless the theories are already loaded and the files have not been modified).

If you suddenly discover that you need to modify a parent theory of your current theory, you must first abandon your current theory (at the shell level type **kill**). After the parent theory has been modified, you go back to your original theory. When its first line **theory** T = ...   : is processed, the modified parent is reloaded automatically.

Further commands are found in the Isabelle/Isar Reference Manual [33].

We now examine Isabelle's functional programming constructs systematically, starting with inductive datatypes.

2.4 Datatypes

Inductive datatypes are part of almost every non-trivial application of HOL. First we take another look at an important example, the datatype of lists, before we turn to datatypes in general. The section closes with a case study.

2.4.1 Lists

Lists are one of the essential datatypes in computing. We expect that you are already familiar with their basic operations. Theory *ToyList* is only a small fragment of HOL's predefined theory *List*[1]. The latter contains many further operations. For example, the functions *hd* ("head") and *tl* ("tail") return the first element and the remainder of a list. (However, pattern-matching is usually preferable to *hd* and *tl*.) Also available are higher-order functions like *map* and *filter*. Theory *List* also contains more syntactic sugar: $[x_1, \ldots, x_n]$ abbreviates $x_1 \# \ldots \# x_n \# []$. In the rest of the tutorial we always use HOL's predefined lists by building on theory *Main*.

2.4.2 The General Format

The general HOL **datatype** definition is of the form

$$\textbf{datatype } (\alpha_1, \ldots, \alpha_n)\, t \;=\; C_1\, \tau_{11}\, \cdots\, \tau_{1k_1} \;\mid\; \cdots \;\mid\; C_m\, \tau_{m1}\, \cdots\, \tau_{mk_m}$$

where α_i are distinct type variables (the parameters), C_i are distinct constructor names and τ_{ij} are types; it is customary to capitalize the first letter in constructor names. There are a number of restrictions (such as that the type should not be empty) detailed elsewhere [22]. Isabelle notifies you if you violate them.

Laws about datatypes, such as $[] \neq x\#xs$ and $(x\#xs = y\#ys) = (x=y \wedge xs=ys)$, are used automatically during proofs by simplification. The same is true for the equations in primitive recursive function definitions.

Every[2] datatype t comes equipped with a *size* function from t into the natural numbers (see Sect. 2.5.1 below). For lists, *size* is just the length, i.e. *size [] = 0* and *size(x # xs) = size xs + 1*. In general, *size* returns

- zero for all constructors that do not have an argument of type t
- one plus the sum of the sizes of all arguments of type t, for all other constructors

---

[1] http://isabelle.in.tum.de/library/HOL/List.html
[2] Except for advanced datatypes where the recursion involves "$\Rightarrow$" as in Sect. 3.4.3.

Note that because *size* is defined on every datatype, it is overloaded; on lists *size* is also called *length*, which is not overloaded. Isabelle will always show *size* on lists as *length*.

2.4.3 Primitive Recursion

Functions on datatypes are usually defined by recursion. In fact, most of the time they are defined by what is called **primitive recursion**. The keyword **primrec** is followed by a list of equations

$$f \ x_1 \ \ldots \ (C \ y_1 \ \ldots \ y_k) \ \ldots \ x_n = r$$

such that C is a constructor of the datatype t and all recursive calls of f in r are of the form $f \ \ldots \ y_i \ \ldots$ for some i. Thus Isabelle immediately sees that f terminates because one (fixed!) argument becomes smaller with every recursive call. There must be at most one equation for each constructor. Their order is immaterial. A more general method for defining total recursive functions is introduced in Sect. 3.5.

Exercise 2.4.1 Define the datatype of binary trees:

datatype *'a tree = Tip | Node "'a tree" 'a "'a tree"*

Define a function *mirror* that mirrors a binary tree by swapping subtrees recursively. Prove

lemma *mirror_mirror: "mirror(mirror t) = t"*

Define a function *flatten* that flattens a tree into a list by traversing it in infix order. Prove

lemma *"flatten(mirror t) = rev(flatten t)"*

2.4.4 Case Expressions

HOL also features *case*-expressions for analyzing elements of a datatype. For example,

    case xs of [] ⇒ [] | y # ys ⇒ y

evaluates to *[]* if *xs* is *[]* and to *y* if *xs* is *y # ys*. (Since the result in both branches must be of the same type, it follows that *y* is of type *'a list* and hence that *xs* is of type *'a list list*.)

In general, if e is a term of the datatype t defined in Sect. 2.4.2 above, the corresponding *case*-expression analyzing e is

$$\text{\textit{case e of}} \quad C_1 \ x_{11} \ \ldots \ x_{1k_1} \ \Rightarrow \ e_1$$
$$\vdots$$
$$| \ \ C_m \ x_{m1} \ \ldots \ x_{mk_m} \ \Rightarrow \ e_m$$

! *All* constructors must be present, their order is fixed, and nested patterns are
• not supported. Violating these restrictions results in strange error messages.

Nested patterns can be simulated by nested *case*-expressions: instead of

```
case xs of [] => [] | [x] => x | x # (y # zs) => y
```

write

```
case xs of [] ⇒ []
| x # ys ⇒ case ys of [] ⇒ x | y # zs ⇒ y
```

Note that *case*-expressions may need to be enclosed in parentheses to
indicate their scope

2.4.5 Structural Induction and Case Distinction

Induction is invoked by *induct_tac*, as we have seen above; it works for any
datatype. In some cases, induction is overkill and a case distinction over all
constructors of the datatype suffices. This is performed by *case_tac*. Here is
a trivial example:

lemma "(case xs of [] ⇒ [] | y#ys ⇒ xs) = xs"
apply(case_tac xs)

results in the proof state

```
1. xs = [] ⟹ (case xs of [] ⇒ [] | y # ys ⇒ xs) = xs
2. ⋀a list.
      xs = a # list ⟹ (case xs of [] ⇒ [] | y # ys ⇒ xs) = xs
```

which is solved automatically:

apply(auto)

Note that we do not need to give a lemma a name if we do not intend
to refer to it explicitly in the future. Other basic laws about a datatype
are applied automatically during simplification, so no special methods are
provided for them.

! Induction is only allowed on free (or ⋀-bound) variables that should not occur
• among the assumptions of the subgoal; see Sect. 9.3.1 for details. Case distinction (*case_tac*) works for arbitrary terms, which need to be quoted if they are
non-atomic. However, apart from ⋀-bound variables, the terms must not contain
variables that are bound outside. For example, given the goal ∀xs. xs = [] ∨
(∃y ys. xs = y # ys), *case_tac xs* will not work as expected because Isabelle
interprets the xs as a new free variable distinct from the bound xs in the goal.

2.4.6 Case Study: Boolean Expressions

The aim of this case study is twofold: it shows how to model boolean expressions and some algorithms for manipulating them, and it demonstrates the
constructs introduced above.

Modelling Boolean Expressions. We want to represent boolean expressions built up from variables and constants by negation and conjunction. The following datatype serves exactly that purpose:

datatype `boolex = Const bool | Var nat | Neg boolex`
`                   | And boolex boolex`

The two constants are represented by `Const True` and `Const False`. Variables are represented by terms of the form `Var n`, where `n` is a natural number (type `nat`). For example, the formula $P_0 \wedge \neg P_1$ is represented by the term `And (Var 0) (Neg (Var 1))`.

The Value of a Boolean Expression. The value of a boolean expression depends on the value of its variables. Hence the function `value` takes an additional parameter, an *environment* of type `nat ⇒ bool`, which maps variables to their values:

consts `value :: "boolex ⇒ (nat ⇒ bool) ⇒ bool"`
primrec
`"value (Const b) env = b"`
`"value (Var x)   env = env x"`
`"value (Neg b)   env = (¬ value b env)"`
`"value (And b c) env = (value b env ∧ value c env)"`

If-Expressions. An alternative and often more efficient (because in a certain sense canonical) representation are so-called *If-expressions* built up from constants (`CIF`), variables (`VIF`) and conditionals (`IF`):

datatype `ifex = CIF bool | VIF nat | IF ifex ifex ifex`

The evaluation of If-expressions proceeds as for `boolex`:

consts `valif :: "ifex ⇒ (nat ⇒ bool) ⇒ bool"`
primrec
`"valif (CIF b)   env = b"`
`"valif (VIF x)   env = env x"`
`"valif (IF b t e) env = (if valif b env then valif t env`
`                                        else valif e env)"`

Converting Boolean and If-Expressions. The type `boolex` is close to the customary representation of logical formulae, whereas `ifex` is designed for efficiency. It is easy to translate from `boolex` into `ifex`:

consts `bool2if :: "boolex ⇒ ifex"`
primrec
`"bool2if (Const b) = CIF b"`
`"bool2if (Var x)   = VIF x"`
`"bool2if (Neg b)   = IF (bool2if b) (CIF False) (CIF True)"`
`"bool2if (And b c) = IF (bool2if b) (bool2if c) (CIF False)"`

At last, we have something we can verify: that *bool2if* preserves the value of its argument:

lemma *"valif (bool2if b) env = value b env"*

The proof is canonical:

apply(*induct_tac b*)
apply(*auto*)
done

In fact, all proofs in this case study look exactly like this. Hence we do not show them below.

More interesting is the transformation of If-expressions into a normal form where the first argument of *IF* cannot be another *IF* but must be a constant or variable. Such a normal form can be computed by repeatedly replacing a subterm of the form *IF (IF b x y) z u* by *IF b (IF x z u) (IF y z u)*, which has the same value. The following primitive recursive functions perform this task:

consts *normif* :: *"ifex ⇒ ifex ⇒ ifex ⇒ ifex"*
primrec
"normif (CIF b)   t e = IF (CIF b) t e"
"normif (VIF x)   t e = IF (VIF x) t e"
"normif (IF b t e) u f = normif b (normif t u f) (normif e u f)"

consts *norm* :: *"ifex ⇒ ifex"*
primrec
"norm (CIF b)   = CIF b"
"norm (VIF x)   = VIF x"
"norm (IF b t e) = normif b (norm t) (norm e)"

Their interplay is tricky; we leave it to you to develop an intuitive understanding. Fortunately, Isabelle can help us to verify that the transformation preserves the value of the expression:

theorem *"valif (norm b) env = valif b env"*

The proof is canonical, provided we first show the following simplification lemma, which also helps to understand what *normif* does:

lemma *[simp]*:
  "∀ t e. valif (normif b t e) env = valif (IF b t e) env"

Note that the lemma does not have a name, but is implicitly used in the proof of the theorem shown above because of the *[simp]* attribute.

But how can we be sure that *norm* really produces a normal form in the above sense? We define a function that tests If-expressions for normality:

consts *normal* :: *"ifex ⇒ bool"*
primrec

```
"normal(CIF b) = True"
"normal(VIF x) = True"
"normal(IF b t e) = (normal t ∧ normal e ∧
    (case b of CIF b ⇒ True | VIF x ⇒ True | IF x y z ⇒ False))"
```

Now we prove *normal* (*norm b*). Of course, this requires a lemma about normality of *normif*:

lemma *[simp]:* "∀t e. normal(normif b t e) = (normal t ∧ normal e)"

How do we come up with the required lemmas? Try to prove the main theorems without them and study carefully what auto leaves unproved. This can provide the clue. The necessity of universal quantification (∀t e) in the two lemmas is explained in Sect. 3.2

Exercise 2.4.2 We strengthen the definition of a *normal* If-expression as follows: the first argument of all *IF*s must be a variable. Adapt the above development to this changed requirement. (Hint: you may need to formulate some of the goals as implications (⟶) rather than equalities (=).)

2.5 Some Basic Types

This section introduces the types of natural numbers and ordered pairs. Also described is type *option*, which is useful for modelling exceptional cases.

2.5.1 Natural Numbers

The type *nat* of natural numbers is predefined to have the constructors *0* and *Suc*. It behaves as if it were declared like this:

datatype *nat* = *0* | *Suc nat*

In particular, there are *case*-expressions, for example

```
case n of 0 ⇒ 0 | Suc m ⇒ m
```

primitive recursion, for example

```
consts sum :: "nat ⇒ nat"
primrec "sum 0 = 0"
        "sum (Suc n) = Suc n + sum n"
```

and induction, for example

```
lemma "sum n + sum n = n*(Suc n)"
apply(induct_tac n)
```

apply(auto)
done

The arithmetic operations +, -, *, div, mod, min and max are predefined, as are the relations ≤ and <. As usual, m - n = 0 if m < n. There is even a least number operation LEAST. For example, (LEAST n. 0 < n) = Suc 0.

! The constants 0 and 1 and the operations +, -, *, min, max, ≤ and < are
• overloaded: they are available not just for natural numbers but for other types as well. For example, given the goal x + 0 = x, there is nothing to indicate that you are talking about natural numbers. Hence Isabelle can only infer that x is of some arbitrary type where 0 and + are declared. As a consequence, you will be unable to prove the goal. To alert you to such pitfalls, Isabelle flags numerals without a fixed type in its output: x + (0::'a) = x. (In the absence of a numeral, it may take you some time to realize what has happened if show_types is not set). In this particular example, you need to include an explicit type constraint, for example x+0 = (x::nat). If there is enough contextual information this may not be necessary: Suc x = x automatically implies x::nat because Suc is not overloaded.

For details on overloading see Sect. 8.4.1. Table A.2 in the appendix shows the most important overloaded operations.

! Constant 1::nat is defined to equal Suc 0. This definition (see Sect. 2.6.2) is
• unfolded automatically by some tactics (like auto, simp and arith) but not by others (especially the single step tactics in Chapter 5). If you need the full set of numerals, see Sect. 8.1.1. *Novices are advised to stick to 0 and Suc.*

Both auto and simp (a method introduced below, Sect. 3.1) prove simple arithmetic goals automatically:

lemma "⟦ ¬ m < n; m < n + (1::nat) ⟧ ⟹ m = n"

For efficiency's sake, this built-in prover ignores quantified formulae, logical connectives, and all arithmetic operations apart from addition. In consequence, auto cannot prove this slightly more complex goal:

lemma "¬ m < n ∧ m < n + (1::nat) ⟹ m = n"

The method arith is more general. It attempts to prove the first subgoal provided it is a quantifier-free **linear arithmetic** formula. Such formulas may involve the usual logical connectives (¬, ∧, ∨, ⟶), the relations =, ≤ and <, and the operations +, -, min and max. For example,

lemma "min i (max j (k*k)) = max (min (k*k) i) (min i (j::nat))"
apply(arith)

succeeds because k * k can be treated as atomic. In contrast,

lemma "n*n = n ⟹ n=0 ∨ n=1"

is not proved even by arith because the proof relies on properties of multiplication.

! The running time of `arith` is exponential in the number of occurrences of `-`,
• `min` and `max` because they are first eliminated by case distinctions.
   Even for linear arithmetic formulae, `arith` is incomplete. If divisibility plays
a role, it may fail to prove a valid formula, for example `m+m ≠ n+n+(1::nat)`.
Fortunately, such examples are rare.

2.5.2 Pairs

HOL also has ordered pairs: (a_1, a_2) is of type $\tau_1 \times \tau_2$ provided each a_i
is of type τ_i. The functions `fst` and `snd` extract the components of a pair:
`fst(x,y) = x` and `snd(x,y) = y`. Tuples are simulated by pairs nested to the
right: (a_1, a_2, a_3) stands for $(a_1, (a_2, a_3))$ and $\tau_1 \times \tau_2 \times \tau_3$ for $\tau_1 \times (\tau_2 \times \tau_3)$.
Therefore we have `fst(snd(`a_1, a_2, a_3`)) = `a_2.
   Remarks:

- There is also the type `unit`, which contains exactly one element denoted
  by `()`. This type can be viewed as a degenerate product with 0 components.
- Products, like type `nat`, are datatypes, which means in particular that
  `induct_tac` and `case_tac` are applicable to terms of product type. Both
  replace the term by a pair of variables.
- Tuples with more than two or three components become unwieldy; records
  are preferable.

For more information on pairs and records see Chapter 8.

2.5.3 Datatype `option`

Our final datatype is very simple but still eminently useful:

datatype `'a option = None | Some 'a`

Frequently one needs to add a distinguished element to some existing type.
For example, type `t option` can model the result of a computation that may
either terminate with an error (represented by `None`) or return some value
v (represented by `Some v`). Similarly, `nat` extended with ∞ can be modeled
by type `nat option`. In both cases one could define a new datatype with
customized constructors like `Error` and `Infinity`, but it is often simpler to
use `option`. For an application see Sect. 3.4.4.

2.6 Definitions

A definition is simply an abbreviation, i.e. a new name for an existing construction. In particular, definitions cannot be recursive. Isabelle offers definitions on the level of types and terms. Those on the type level are called **type
synonyms**; those on the term level are simply called definitions.

2.6.1 Type Synonyms

Type synonyms are similar to those found in ML. They are created by a
types command:

```
types number      = nat
      gate        = "bool ⇒ bool ⇒ bool"
      ('a,'b)alist = "('a × 'b)list"
```

Internally all synonyms are fully expanded. As a consequence Isabelle's output never contains synonyms. Their main purpose is to improve the readability of theories. Synonyms can be used just like any other type. Here, we
declare two constants of type *gate*:

```
consts nand :: gate
       xor  :: gate
```

2.6.2 Constant Definitions

The constants *nand* and *xor* above are non-recursive and can be defined
directly:

```
defs nand_def: "nand A B ≡ ¬(A ∧ B)"
     xor_def:  "xor A B  ≡ A ∧ ¬B ∨ ¬A ∧ B"
```

Here **defs** is a keyword and *nand_def* and *xor_def* are user-supplied names.
The symbol ≡ is a special form of equality that must be used in constant
definitions. Pattern-matching is not allowed: each definition must be of the
form $f\, x_1 \ldots x_n \equiv t$. Section 3.1.6 explains how definitions are used in proofs.

A **constdefs** command combines the effects of **consts** and **defs**. For
instance, we can introduce *nand* and *xor* by a single command:

```
constdefs nor :: gate
          "nor A B ≡ ¬(A ∨ B)"
          xor2 :: gate
          "xor2 A B ≡ (A ∨ B) ∧ (¬A ∨ ¬B)"
```

The default name of each definition is *f_def*, where *f* is the name of the
defined constant.

! A common mistake when writing definitions is to introduce extra free variables
on the right-hand side. Consider the following, flawed definition (where *dvd*
means "divides"):

```
"prime p ≡ 1 < p ∧ (m dvd p ⟶ m = 1 ∨ m = p)"
```

Isabelle rejects this "definition" because of the extra *m* on the right-hand side, which
would introduce an inconsistency (why?). The correct version is

```
"prime p ≡ 1 < p ∧ (∀m. m dvd p ⟶ m = 1 ∨ m = p)"
```

2.7 The Definitional Approach

As we pointed out at the beginning of the chapter, asserting arbitrary axioms such as $f(n) = f(n) + 1$ can easily lead to contradictions. In order to avoid this danger, we advocate the definitional rather than the axiomatic approach: introduce new concepts by definitions. However, Isabelle/HOL seems to support many richer definitional constructs, such as **primrec**. The point is that Isabelle reduces such constructs to first principles. For example, each **primrec** function definition is turned into a proper (nonrecursive!) definition from which the user-supplied recursion equations are automatically proved. This process is hidden from the user, who does not have to understand the details. Other commands described later, like **recdef** and **inductive**, work similarly. This strict adherence to the definitional approach reduces the risk of soundness errors.

3. More Functional Programming

The purpose of this chapter is to deepen your understanding of the concepts encountered so far and to introduce advanced forms of datatypes and recursive functions. The first two sections give a structured presentation of theorem proving by simplification (Sect. 3.1) and discuss important heuristics for induction (Sect. 3.2). You can skip them if you are not planning to perform proofs yourself. We then present a case study: a compiler for expressions (Sect. 3.3). Advanced datatypes, including those involving function spaces, are covered in Sect. 3.4; it closes with another case study, search trees ("tries"). Finally we introduce **recdef**, a general form of recursive function definition that goes well beyond **primrec** (Sect. 3.5).

3.1 Simplification

So far we have proved our theorems by `auto`, which simplifies all subgoals. In fact, `auto` can do much more than that. To go beyond toy examples, you need to understand the ingredients of `auto`. This section covers the method that `auto` always applies first, simplification.

Simplification is one of the central theorem proving tools in Isabelle and many other systems. The tool itself is called the **simplifier**. This section introduces the many features of the simplifier and is required reading if you intend to perform proofs. Later on, Sect. 9.1 explains some more advanced features and a little bit of how the simplifier works. The serious student should read that section as well, in particular to understand why the simplifier did something unexpected.

3.1.1 What Is Simplification?

In its most basic form, simplification means repeated application of equations from left to right. For example, taking the rules for @ and applying them to the term `[0,1] @ []` results in a sequence of simplification steps:

```
(0#1#[]) @ []   ↝   0#((1#[]) @ [])   ↝   0#(1#([] @ []))   ↝   0#1#[]
```

This is also known as **term rewriting** and the equations are referred to as **rewrite rules**. "Rewriting" is more honest than "simplification" because the terms do not necessarily become simpler in the process.

T. Nipkow, L.C. Paulson, and M. Wenzel: Isabelle/HOL, LNCS 2283, pp. 27-51, 2002.
© Springer-Verlag Berlin Heidelberg 2002

The simplifier proves arithmetic goals as described in Sect. 2.5.1 above. Arithmetic expressions are simplified using built-in procedures that go beyond mere rewrite rules. New simplification procedures can be coded and installed, but they are definitely not a matter for this tutorial.

3.1.2 Simplification Rules

To facilitate simplification, the attribute *[simp]* declares theorems to be simplification rules, which the simplifier will use automatically. In addition, **datatype** and **primrec** declarations (and a few others) implicitly declare some simplification rules. Explicit definitions are *not* declared as simplification rules automatically!

Nearly any theorem can become a simplification rule. The simplifier will try to transform it into an equation. For example, the theorem ¬ *P* is turned into *P = False*. The details are explained in Sect. 9.1.2.

The simplification attribute of theorems can be turned on and off:

> **declare** *theorem-name* [simp]
> **declare** *theorem-name* [simp del]

Only equations that really simplify, like *rev (rev xs) = xs* and *xs @ [] = xs*, should be declared as default simplification rules. More specific ones should only be used selectively and should not be made default. Distributivity laws, for example, alter the structure of terms and can produce an exponential blow-up instead of simplification. A default simplification rule may need to be disabled in certain proofs. Frequent changes in the simplification status of a theorem may indicate an unwise use of defaults.

> **!** Simplification can run forever, for example if both $f(x) = g(x)$ and $g(x) = f(x)$ are simplification rules. It is the user's responsibility not to include simplification rules that can lead to nontermination, either on their own or in combination with other simplification rules.

> **!** It is inadvisable to toggle the simplification attribute of a theorem from a parent theory A in a child theory B for good. The reason is that if some theory C is based both on B and (via a differnt path) on A, it is not defined what the simplification attribute of that theorem will be in C: it could be either.

3.1.3 The simp Method

The general format of the simplification method is

> *simp list of modifiers*

where the list of *modifiers* fine tunes the behaviour and may be empty. Specific modifiers are discussed below. Most if not all of the proofs seen so far could have been performed with *simp* instead of *auto*, except that *simp* attacks only the first subgoal and may thus need to be repeated — use *simp_all* to simplify all subgoals. If nothing changes, *simp* fails.

3.1.4 Adding and Deleting Simplification Rules

If a certain theorem is merely needed in a few proofs by simplification, we do not need to make it a global simplification rule. Instead we can modify the set of simplification rules used in a simplification step by adding rules to it and/or deleting rules from it. The two modifiers for this are

   add: *list of theorem names*
   del: *list of theorem names*

Or you can use a specific list of theorems and omit all others:

   only: *list of theorem names*

In this example, we invoke the simplifier, adding two distributive laws:

    apply(simp add: mod_mult_distrib add_mult_distrib)

3.1.5 Assumptions

By default, assumptions are part of the simplification process: they are used as simplification rules and are simplified themselves. For example:

lemma "⟦ xs @ zs = ys @ xs; [] @ xs = [] @ [] ⟧ ⟹ ys = zs"
apply *simp*
done

The second assumption simplifies to xs = [], which in turn simplifies the first assumption to zs = ys, thus reducing the conclusion to ys = ys and hence to *True*.

In some cases, using the assumptions can lead to nontermination:

lemma "∀x. f x = g (f (g x)) ⟹ f [] = f [] @ []"

An unmodified application of *simp* loops. The culprit is the simplification rule f x = g (f (g x)), which is extracted from the assumption. (Isabelle notices certain simple forms of nontermination but not this one.) The problem can be circumvented by telling the simplifier to ignore the assumptions:

apply(simp (no_asm))
done

Three modifiers influence the treatment of assumptions:

(no_asm) means that assumptions are completely ignored.
(no_asm_simp) means that the assumptions are not simplified but are used in the simplification of the conclusion.

(no_asm_use) means that the assumptions are simplified but are not used in the simplification of each other or the conclusion.

Both *(no_asm_simp)* and *(no_asm_use)* run forever on the problematic subgoal above. Only one of the modifiers is allowed, and it must precede all other modifiers.

! Assumptions are simplified in a left-to-right fashion. If an assumption can help
• in simplifying one to the left of it, this may get overlooked. In such cases you have to rotate the assumptions explicitly: **apply**(*rotate_tac n*) causes a cyclic shift by n positions from right to left, if n is positive, and from left to right, if n is negative. Beware that such rotations make proofs quite brittle.

3.1.6 Rewriting with Definitions

Constant definitions (Sect. 2.6.2) can be used as simplification rules, but by default they are not: the simplifier does not expand them automatically. Definitions are intended for introducing abstract concepts and not merely as abbreviations. Of course, we need to expand the definition initially, but once we have proved enough abstract properties of the new constant, we can forget its original definition. This style makes proofs more robust: if the definition has to be changed, only the proofs of the abstract properties will be affected.

For example, given

constdefs *xor* :: *"bool* ⇒ *bool* ⇒ *bool"*
         "xor A B ≡ *(A* ∧ *¬B)* ∨ *(¬A* ∧ *B)"*

we may want to prove

lemma *"xor A (¬A)"*

Typically, we begin by unfolding some definitions:

apply(*simp only: xor_def*)

In this particular case, the resulting goal

   1. A ∧ ¬ ¬ *A* ∨ ¬ *A* ∧ ¬ *A*

can be proved by simplification. Thus we could have proved the lemma outright by

apply(*simp add: xor_def*)

Of course we can also unfold definitions in the middle of a proof.

! If you have defined $f\,x\,y \equiv t$ then you can only unfold occurrences of f with at
• least two arguments. This may be helpful for unfolding f selectively, but it may also get in the way. Defining $f \equiv \lambda x\,y.\,t$ allows to unfold all occurrences of f.

There is also the special method *unfold* which merely unfolds one or several definitions, as in **apply**(*unfold xor_def*). This is can be useful in situations where *simp* does too much. Warning: *unfold* acts on all subgoals!

3.1.7 Simplifying `let`-Expressions

Proving a goal containing `let`-expressions almost invariably requires the `let`-constructs to be expanded at some point. Since `let ... = ... in ...` is just syntactic sugar for the predefined constant `Let`, expanding `let`-constructs means rewriting with `Let_def`:

lemma `"(let xs = [] in xs@ys@xs) = ys"`
apply`(simp add: Let_def)`
done

If, in a particular context, there is no danger of a combinatorial explosion of nested `let`s, you could even simplify with `Let_def` by default:

declare `Let_def [simp]`

3.1.8 Conditional Simplification Rules

So far all examples of rewrite rules were equations. The simplifier also accepts *conditional* equations, for example

lemma `hd_Cons_tl[simp]: "xs ≠ [] ⟹ hd xs # tl xs = xs"`
apply`(case_tac xs, simp, simp)`
done

Note the use of "," to string together a sequence of methods. Assuming that the simplification rule `(rev xs = []) = (xs = [])` is present as well, the lemma below is proved by plain simplification:

lemma `"xs ≠ [] ⟹ hd(rev xs) # tl(rev xs) = rev xs"`

The conditional equation `hd_Cons_tl` above can simplify `hd (rev xs) # tl (rev xs)` to `rev xs` because the corresponding precondition `rev xs ≠ []` simplifies to `xs ≠ []`, which is exactly the local assumption of the subgoal.

3.1.9 Automatic Case Splits

Goals containing `if`-expressions are usually proved by case distinction on the boolean condition. Here is an example:

lemma `"∀xs. if xs = [] then rev xs = [] else rev xs ≠ []"`

The goal can be split by a special method, `split`:

apply`(split split_if)`

1. `∀xs. (xs = [] ⟶ rev xs = []) ∧ (xs ≠ [] ⟶ rev xs ≠ [])`

where `split_if` is a theorem that expresses splitting of `if`s. Because splitting the `if`s is usually the right proof strategy, the simplifier does it automatically. Try **apply**`(simp)` on the initial goal above.

This splitting idea generalizes from *if* to *case*. Let us simplify a case analysis over lists:

lemma "(case xs of [] ⇒ zs | y#ys ⇒ y#(ys@zs)) = xs@zs"
apply(split list.split)

1. (xs = [] ⟶ zs = xs @ zs) ∧
   (∀a list. xs = a # list ⟶ a # list @ zs = xs @ zs)

The simplifier does not split *case*-expressions, as it does *if*-expressions, because with recursive datatypes it could lead to nontermination. Instead, the simplifier has a modifier *split* for adding splitting rules explicitly. The lemma above can be proved in one step by

apply(simp split: list.split)

whereas **apply**(simp) alone will not succeed.

Every datatype *t* comes with a theorem *t*.split which can be declared to be a **split rule** either locally as above, or by giving it the *split* attribute globally:

declare list.split [split]

The *split* attribute can be removed with the *del* modifier, either locally

apply(simp split del: split_if)

or globally:

declare list.split [split del]

Polished proofs typically perform splitting within *simp* rather than invoking the *split* method. However, if a goal contains several *if* and *case* expressions, the *split* method can be helpful in selectively exploring the effects of splitting.

The split rules shown above are intended to affect only the subgoal's conclusion. If you want to split an *if* or *case*-expression in the assumptions, you have to apply *split_if_asm* or *t*.split_asm:

lemma "if xs = [] then ys ≠ [] else ys = [] ⟹ xs @ ys ≠ []"
apply(split split_if_asm)

Unlike splitting the conclusion, this step creates two separate subgoals, which here can be solved by *simp_all*:

1. ⟦xs = []; ys ≠ []⟧ ⟹ xs @ ys ≠ []
2. ⟦xs ≠ []; ys = []⟧ ⟹ xs @ ys ≠ []

If you need to split both in the assumptions and the conclusion, use *t*.splits which subsumes *t*.split and *t*.split_asm. Analogously, there is *if_splits*.

! The simplifier merely simplifies the condition of an *if* but not the *then* or
● *else* parts. The latter are simplified only after the condition reduces to *True*
or *False*, or after splitting. The same is true for *case*-expressions: only the selector
is simplified at first, until either the expression reduces to one of the cases or it is
split.

3.1.10 Tracing

Using the simplifier effectively may take a bit of experimentation. Set the
trace_simp flag to get a better idea of what is going on:

ML *"set trace_simp"*
lemma *"rev [a] = []"*
apply(*simp*)

produces the trace

```
Applying instance of rewrite rule:
rev (?x1 # ?xs1) == rev ?xs1 @ [?x1]
Rewriting:
rev [a] == rev [] @ [a]
Applying instance of rewrite rule:
rev [] == []
Rewriting:
rev [] == []
Applying instance of rewrite rule:
[] @ ?y == ?y
Rewriting:
[] @ [a] == [a]
Applying instance of rewrite rule:
?x3 # ?t3 = ?t3 == False
Rewriting:
[a] = [] == False
```

The trace lists each rule being applied, both in its general form and the
instance being used. For conditional rules, the trace lists the rule it is trying
to rewrite and gives the result of attempting to prove each of the rule's
conditions. Many other hints about the simplifier's actions will appear.

In more complicated cases, the trace can be quite lengthy. Invocations of
the simplifier are often nested, for instance when solving conditions of rewrite
rules. Thus it is advisable to reset it:

ML *"reset trace_simp"*

3.2 Induction Heuristics

The purpose of this section is to illustrate some simple heuristics for inductive
proofs. The first one we have already mentioned in our initial example:

Theorems about recursive functions are proved by induction.

In case the function has more than one argument

> *Do induction on argument number i if the function is defined by recursion in argument number i.*

When we look at the proof of *(xs@ys) @ zs = xs @ (ys@zs)* in Sect. 2.2 we find

– @ is recursive in the first argument
– *xs* occurs only as the first argument of @
– both *ys* and *zs* occur at least once as the second argument of @

Hence it is natural to perform induction on *xs*.

The key heuristic, and the main point of this section, is to *generalize the goal before induction*. The reason is simple: if the goal is too specific, the induction hypothesis is too weak to allow the induction step to go through. Let us illustrate the idea with an example.

Function *rev* has quadratic worst-case running time because it calls function @ for each element of the list and @ is linear in its first argument. A linear time version of *rev* reqires an extra argument where the result is accumulated gradually, using only #:

```
consts itrev :: "'a list ⇒ 'a list ⇒ 'a list"
primrec
"itrev []      ys = ys"
"itrev (x#xs) ys = itrev xs (x#ys)"
```

The behaviour of *itrev* is simple: it reverses its first argument by stacking its elements onto the second argument, and returning that second argument when the first one becomes empty. Note that *itrev* is tail-recursive: it can be compiled into a loop.

Naturally, we would like to show that *itrev* does indeed reverse its first argument provided the second one is empty:

```
lemma "itrev xs [] = rev xs"
```

There is no choice as to the induction variable, and we immediately simplify:

```
apply(induct_tac xs, simp_all)
```

Unfortunately, this attempt does not prove the induction step:

```
1. ⋀a list.
     itrev list [] = rev list ⟹ itrev list [a] = rev list @ [a]
```

The induction hypothesis is too weak. The fixed argument, *[]*, prevents it from rewriting the conclusion. This example suggests a heuristic:

> *Generalize goals for induction by replacing constants by variables.*

Of course one cannot do this naïvely: *itrev xs ys = rev xs* is just not true. The correct generalization is

```
lemma "itrev xs ys = rev xs @ ys"
```

If *ys* is replaced by *[]*, the right-hand side simplifies to *rev xs*, as required.

In this instance it was easy to guess the right generalization. Other situations can require a good deal of creativity.

Although we now have two variables, only *xs* is suitable for induction, and we repeat our proof attempt. Unfortunately, we are still not there:

```
1. ⋀a list.
      itrev list ys = rev list @ ys ⟹
      itrev list (a # ys) = rev list @ a # ys
```

The induction hypothesis is still too weak, but this time it takes no intuition to generalize: the problem is that *ys* is fixed throughout the subgoal, but the induction hypothesis needs to be applied with *a # ys* instead of *ys*. Hence we prove the theorem for all *ys* instead of a fixed one:

lemma "∀ ys. itrev xs ys = rev xs @ ys"

This time induction on *xs* followed by simplification succeeds. This leads to another heuristic for generalization:

> *Generalize goals for induction by universally quantifying all free variables* (except the induction variable itself!).

This prevents trivial failures like the one above and does not affect the validity of the goal. However, this heuristic should not be applied blindly. It is not always required, and the additional quantifiers can complicate matters in some cases, The variables that should be quantified are typically those that change in recursive calls.

A final point worth mentioning is the orientation of the equation we just proved: the more complex notion (*itrev*) is on the left-hand side, the simpler one (*rev*) on the right-hand side. This constitutes another, albeit weak heuristic that is not restricted to induction:

> *The right-hand side of an equation should (in some sense) be simpler than the left-hand side.*

This heuristic is tricky to apply because it is not obvious that *rev xs @ ys* is simpler than *itrev xs ys*. But see what happens if you try to prove *rev xs @ ys = itrev xs ys*!

If you have tried these heuristics and still find your induction does not go through, and no obvious lemma suggests itself, you may need to generalize your proposition even further. This requires insight into the problem at hand and is beyond simple rules of thumb. Additionally, you can read Sect. 9.3 to learn about some advanced techniques for inductive proofs.

Exercise 3.2.1 In Exercise 2.4.1 we defined a function *flatten* from trees to lists. The straightforward version of *flatten* is based on *@* and is thus, like *rev*, quadratic. A linear time version of *flatten* again reqires an extra argument, the accumulator:

consts flatten2 :: "'a tree => 'a list => 'a list"

Define `flatten2` and prove

lemma `"flatten2 t [] = flatten t"`

3.3 Case Study: Compiling Expressions

The task is to develop a compiler from a generic type of expressions (built from variables, constants and binary operations) to a stack machine. This generic type of expressions is a generalization of the boolean expressions in Sect. 2.4.6. This time we do not commit ourselves to a particular type of variables or values but make them type parameters. Neither is there a fixed set of binary operations: instead the expression contains the appropriate function itself.

types `'v binop = "'v ⇒ 'v ⇒ 'v"`
datatype `('a,'v)expr = Cex 'v`
`                | Vex 'a`
`                | Bex "'v binop"  "('a,'v)expr"  "('a,'v)expr"`

The three constructors represent constants, variables and the application of a binary operation to two subexpressions.

The value of an expression with respect to an environment that maps variables to values is easily defined:

consts `value :: "('a,'v)expr ⇒ ('a ⇒ 'v) ⇒ 'v"`
primrec
`"value (Cex v) env = v"`
`"value (Vex a) env = env a"`
`"value (Bex f e1 e2) env = f (value e1 env) (value e2 env)"`

The stack machine has three instructions: load a constant value onto the stack, load the contents of an address onto the stack, and apply a binary operation to the two topmost elements of the stack, replacing them by the result. As for `expr`, addresses and values are type parameters:

datatype `('a,'v) instr = Const 'v`
`                | Load 'a`
`                | Apply "'v binop"`

The execution of the stack machine is modelled by a function `exec` that takes a list of instructions, a store (modelled as a function from addresses to values, just like the environment for evaluating expressions), and a stack (modelled as a list) of values, and returns the stack at the end of the execution — the store remains unchanged:

consts `exec :: "('a,'v)instr list ⇒ ('a⇒'v) ⇒ 'v list ⇒ 'v list"`
primrec
`"exec [] s vs = vs"`

```
"exec (i#is) s vs = (case i of
    Const v  ⇒ exec is s (v#vs)
  | Load a   ⇒ exec is s ((s a)#vs)
  | Apply f  ⇒ exec is s ((f (hd vs) (hd(tl vs)))#(tl(tl vs))))"
```

Recall that *hd* and *tl* return the first element and the remainder of a list. Because all functions are total, *hd* is defined even for the empty list, although we do not know what the result is. Thus our model of the machine always terminates properly, although the definition above does not tell us much about the result in situations where *Apply* was executed with fewer than two elements on the stack.

The compiler is a function from expressions to a list of instructions. Its definition is obvious:

consts *comp* :: *"('a,'v)expr ⇒ ('a,'v)instr list"*
primrec
```
"comp (Cex v)     = [Const v]"
"comp (Vex a)     = [Load a]"
"comp (Bex f e1 e2) = (comp e2) @ (comp e1) @ [Apply f]"
```

Now we have to prove the correctness of the compiler, i.e. that the execution of a compiled expression results in the value of the expression:

theorem *"exec (comp e) s [] = [value e s]"*

This theorem needs to be generalized:

theorem *"∀vs. exec (comp e) s vs = (value e s) # vs"*

It will be proved by induction on *e* followed by simplification. First, we must prove a lemma about executing the concatenation of two instruction sequences:

lemma *exec_app[simp]*:
    "∀vs. exec (xs@ys) s vs = exec ys s (exec xs s vs)"

This requires induction on *xs* and ordinary simplification for the base cases. In the induction step, simplification leaves us with a formula that contains two *case*-expressions over instructions. Thus we add automatic case splitting, which finishes the proof:

apply(*induct_tac xs, simp, simp split: instr.split*)

Note that because both *simp_all* and *auto* perform simplification, they can be modified in the same way as *simp*. Thus the proof can be rewritten as

apply(*induct_tac xs, simp_all split: instr.split*)

Although this is more compact, it is less clear for the reader of the proof.

We could now go back and prove *exec (comp e) s [] = [value e s]* merely by simplification with the generalized version we just proved. However, this is unnecessary because the generalized version fully subsumes its instance.

3.4 Advanced Datatypes

This section presents advanced forms of datatypes: mutual and nested recursion. A series of examples will culminate in a treatment of the trie data structure.

3.4.1 Mutual Recursion

Sometimes it is necessary to define two datatypes that depend on each other. This is called **mutual recursion**. As an example consider a language of arithmetic and boolean expressions where

- arithmetic expressions contain boolean expressions because there are conditional expressions like "if $m < n$ then $n - m$ else $m - n$", and
- boolean expressions contain arithmetic expressions because of comparisons like "$m < n$".

In Isabelle this becomes

```
datatype 'a aexp = IF    "'a bexp" "'a aexp" "'a aexp"
                 | Sum   "'a aexp" "'a aexp"
                 | Diff  "'a aexp" "'a aexp"
                 | Var 'a
                 | Num nat
and      'a bexp = Less  "'a aexp" "'a aexp"
                 | And   "'a bexp" "'a bexp"
                 | Neg   "'a bexp"
```

Type `aexp` is similar to `expr` in Sect. 3.3, except that we have added an `IF` constructor, fixed the values to be of type `nat` and declared the two binary operations `Sum` and `Diff`. Boolean expressions can be arithmetic comparisons, conjunctions and negations. The semantics is given by two evaluation functions:

```
consts  evala :: "'a aexp ⇒ ('a ⇒ nat) ⇒ nat"
        evalb :: "'a bexp ⇒ ('a ⇒ nat) ⇒ bool"
```

Both take an expression and an environment (a mapping from variables 'a to values `nat`) and return its arithmetic/boolean value. Since the datatypes are mutually recursive, so are functions that operate on them. Hence they need to be defined in a single **primrec** section:

```
primrec
  "evala (IF b a1 a2) env =
     (if evalb b env then evala a1 env else evala a2 env)"
  "evala (Sum a1 a2) env = evala a1 env + evala a2 env"
  "evala (Diff a1 a2) env = evala a1 env - evala a2 env"
```

```
"evala (Var v) env = env v"
"evala (Num n) env = n"


"evalb (Less a1 a2) env = (evala a1 env < evala a2 env)"
"evalb (And b1 b2) env = (evalb b1 env ∧ evalb b2 env)"
"evalb (Neg b) env = (¬ evalb b env)"
```

In the same fashion we also define two functions that perform substitution:

consts *substa* :: *"('a* ⇒ *'b aexp)* ⇒ *'a aexp* ⇒ *'b aexp"*
         substb :: *"('a* ⇒ *'b aexp)* ⇒ *'a bexp* ⇒ *'b bexp"*

The first argument is a function mapping variables to expressions, the substitution. It is applied to all variables in the second argument. As a result, the type of variables in the expression may change from *'a* to *'b*. Note that there are only arithmetic and no boolean variables.

primrec
```
"substa s (IF b a1 a2) =
   IF (substb s b) (substa s a1) (substa s a2)"
"substa s (Sum a1 a2) = Sum (substa s a1) (substa s a2)"
"substa s (Diff a1 a2) = Diff (substa s a1) (substa s a2)"
"substa s (Var v) = s v"
"substa s (Num n) = Num n"

"substb s (Less a1 a2) = Less (substa s a1) (substa s a2)"
"substb s (And b1 b2) = And (substb s b1) (substb s b2)"
"substb s (Neg b) = Neg (substb s b)"
```

Now we can prove a fundamental theorem about the interaction between evaluation and substitution: applying a substitution s to an expression a and evaluating the result in an environment *env* yields the same result as evaluation a in the environment that maps every variable x to the value of $s(x)$ under *env*. If you try to prove this separately for arithmetic or boolean expressions (by induction), you find that you always need the other theorem in the induction step. Therefore you need to state and prove both theorems simultaneously:

lemma *"evala (substa s a) env = evala a (λx. evala (s x) env)* ∧
        evalb (substb s b) env = evalb b (λx. evala (s x) env)"
apply(*induct_tac a* **and** *b*)

The resulting 8 goals (one for each constructor) are proved in one fell swoop:

apply *simp_all*

In general, given n mutually recursive datatypes $\tau_1, \ldots, \tau_n$, an inductive proof expects a goal of the form

$$P_1(x_1) \ \wedge \cdots \wedge P_n(x_n)$$

where each variable x_i is of type τ_i. Induction is started by

apply (induct_tac x_1 **and** ...   **and** x_n)

Exercise 3.4.1 Define a function norma of type 'a aexp $\Rightarrow$ 'a aexp that replaces IFs with complex boolean conditions by nested IFs; it should eliminate the constructors And and Neg, leaving only Less. Prove that norma preserves the value of an expression and that the result of norma is really normal, i.e. no more Ands and Negs occur in it. (*Hint:* proceed as in Sect. 2.4.6 and read the discussion of type annotations following lemma subst_id below).

3.4.2 Nested Recursion

So far, all datatypes had the property that on the right-hand side of their definition they occurred only at the top-level: directly below a constructor. Now we consider *nested recursion*, where the recursive datatype occurs nested in some other datatype (but not inside itself!). Consider the following model of terms where function symbols can be applied to a list of arguments:

datatype ('v,'f)"term" = Var 'v | App 'f "('v,'f)term list"

Note that we need to quote term on the left to avoid confusion with the Isabelle command **term**. Parameter 'v is the type of variables and 'f the type of function symbols. A mathematical term like $f(x, g(y))$ becomes App f [Var x, App g [Var y]], where f, g, x, y are suitable values, e.g. numbers or strings.

What complicates the definition of term is the nested occurrence of term inside list on the right-hand side. In principle, nested recursion can be eliminated in favour of mutual recursion by unfolding the offending datatypes, here list. The result for term would be something like

datatype ('v,'f)"term" = Var 'v | App 'f "('v,'f)term_list"
and ('v,'f)term_list = Nil | Cons "('v,'f)term" "('v,'f)term_list"

Although we do not recommend this unfolding to the user, it shows how to simulate nested recursion by mutual recursion. Now we return to the initial definition of term using nested recursion.

Let us define a substitution function on terms. Because terms involve term lists, we need to define two substitution functions simultaneously:

consts
subst :: "('v$\Rightarrow$('v,'f)term) $\Rightarrow$ ('v,'f)term $\Rightarrow$ ('v,'f)term"
substs:: "('v$\Rightarrow$('v,'f)term) $\Rightarrow$ ('v,'f)term list $\Rightarrow$ ('v,'f)term list"

primrec
  "subst s (Var x) = s x"
  subst_App:
  "subst s (App f ts) = App f (substs s ts)"

```
"substs s [] = []"
"substs s (t # ts) = subst s t # substs s ts"
```

Individual equations in a **primrec** definition may be named as shown for
subst_App. The significance of this device will become apparent below.

Similarly, when proving a statement about terms inductively, we need
to prove a related statement about term lists simultaneously. For example,
the fact that the identity substitution does not change a term needs to be
strengthened and proved as follows:

lemma *subst_id:* "subst Var t = (t ::('v,'f)term) ∧
                substs Var ts = (ts::('v,'f)term list)"
apply(induct_tac t **and** ts, simp_all)
done

Note that *Var* is the identity substitution because by definition it leaves variables unchanged: *subst Var (Var x) = Var x*. Note also that the type annotations are necessary because otherwise there is nothing in the goal to enforce
that both halves of the goal talk about the same type parameters ('v,'f).
As a result, induction would fail because the two halves of the goal would be
unrelated.

Exercise 3.4.2 The fact that substitution distributes over composition can
be expressed roughly as follows:

> subst (f ∘ g) t = subst f (subst g t)

Correct this statement (you will find that it does not type-check), strengthen
it, and prove it. (Note: ∘ is function composition; its definition is found in
theorem *o_def*).

Exercise 3.4.3 Define a function *trev* of type ('v, 'f) term ⇒ ('v, 'f)
term that recursively reverses the order of arguments of all function symbols
in a term. Prove that *trev (trev t) = t*.

The experienced functional programmer may feel that our definition of
subst is too complicated in that *substs* is unnecessary. The *App*-case can be
defined directly as

> subst s (App f ts) = App f (map (subst s) ts)

where *map* is the standard list function such that *map f [x1,...,xn] = [f
x1,...,f xn]*. This is true, but Isabelle insists on the conjunctive format.
Fortunately, we can easily *prove* that the suggested equation holds:

lemma [simp]: "subst s (App f ts) = App f (map (subst s) ts)"
apply(induct_tac ts, simp_all)
done

What is more, we can now disable the old defining equation as a simplification rule:

declare *subst_App [simp del]*

The advantage is that now we have replaced *substs* by *map*, we can profit from the large number of pre-proved lemmas about *map*. Unfortunately inductive proofs about type *term* are still awkward because they expect a conjunction. One could derive a new induction principle as well (see Sect. 9.3.3), but simpler is to stop using **primrec** and to define functions with **recdef** instead. Simple uses of **recdef** are described in Sect. 3.5 below, and later (Sect. 9.2.2) we shall see how **recdef** can handle nested recursion.

Of course, you may also combine mutual and nested recursion of datatypes. For example, constructor *Sum* in Sect. 3.4.1 could take a list of expressions as its argument: *Sum "'a aexp list"*.

3.4.3 The Limits of Nested Recursion

How far can we push nested recursion? By the unfolding argument above, we can reduce nested to mutual recursion provided the nested recursion only involves previously defined datatypes. This does not include functions:

datatype *t = C "t ⇒ bool"*

This declaration is a real can of worms. In HOL it must be ruled out because it requires a type *t* such that *t* and its power set *t ⇒ bool* have the same cardinality — an impossibility. For the same reason it is not possible to allow recursion involving the type *t set*, which is isomorphic to *t ⇒ bool*.

Fortunately, a limited form of recursion involving function spaces is permitted: the recursive type may occur on the right of a function arrow, but never on the left. Hence the above can of worms is ruled out but the following example of a potentially infinitely branching tree is accepted:

datatype *('a,'i)bigtree = Tip | Br 'a "'i ⇒ ('a,'i)bigtree"*

Parameter *'a* is the type of values stored in the *Br*anches of the tree, whereas *'i* is the index type over which the tree branches. If *'i* is instantiated to *bool*, the result is a binary tree; if it is instantiated to *nat*, we have an infinitely branching tree because each node has as many subtrees as there are natural numbers. How can we possibly write down such a tree? Using functional notation! For example, the term

    Br 0 (λi. Br i (λn. Tip))

of type *(nat, nat) bigtree* is the tree whose root is labeled with 0 and whose ith subtree is labeled with i and has merely *Tip*s as further subtrees.

Function *map_bt* applies a function to all labels in a *bigtree*:

consts *map_bt* :: *"('a ⇒ 'b) ⇒ ('a,'i)bigtree ⇒ ('b,'i)bigtree"*
primrec

```
"map_bt f Tip      = Tip"
"map_bt f (Br a F) = Br (f a) (λi. map_bt f (F i))"
```

This is a valid **primrec** definition because the recursive calls of `map_bt` involve only subtrees obtained from `F`: the left-hand side. Thus termination is assured. The seasoned functional programmer might try expressing `λi.` `map_bt f (F i)` as `map_bt f o F`, which Isabelle however will reject. Applying `map_bt` to only one of its arguments makes the termination proof less obvious.

The following lemma has a simple proof by induction:

lemma `"map_bt (g o f) T = map_bt g (map_bt f T)"`
apply`(induct_tac T, simp_all)`
done

Because of the function type, the the proof state after induction looks unusual. Notice the quantified induction hypothesis:

```
1. map_bt (g o f) Tip = map_bt g (map_bt f Tip)
2. ⋀a F. (⋀x. map_bt (g o f) (F x) = map_bt g (map_bt f (F x))) ⟹
         map_bt (g o f) (Br a F) = map_bt g (map_bt f (Br a F))
```

If you need nested recursion on the left of a function arrow, there are alternatives to pure HOL. In the Logic for Computable Functions (LCF), types like

datatype `lam = C "lam → lam"`

do indeed make sense [25]. Note the different arrow, → instead of ⇒, expressing the type of *continuous* functions. There is even a version of LCF on top of HOL, called HOLCF [18].

3.4.4 Case Study: Tries

Tries are a classic search tree data structure [15] for fast indexing with strings. Figure 3.1 gives a graphical example of a trie containing the words "all", "an", "ape", "can", "car" and "cat". When searching a string in a trie, the letters of the string are examined sequentially. Each letter determines which subtrie to search next. In this case study we model tries as a datatype, define a lookup and an update function, and prove that they behave as expected.

Proper tries associate some value with each string. Since the information is stored only in the final node associated with the string, many nodes do not carry any value. This distinction is modeled with the help of the predefined datatype `option` (see Sect. 2.5.3).

To minimize running time, each node of a trie should contain an array that maps letters to subtries. We have chosen a representation where the subtries are held in an association list, i.e. a list of (letter,trie) pairs. Abstracting over the alphabet `'a` and the values `'v` we define a trie as follows:

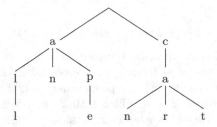

Fig. 3.1. A Sample Trie

```
datatype ('a,'v)trie = Trie  "'v option"  "('a * ('a,'v)trie)list"
```

The first component is the optional value, the second component the association list of subtries. This is an example of nested recursion involving products, which is fine because products are datatypes as well. We define two selector functions:

```
consts value :: "('a,'v)trie ⇒ 'v option"
       alist :: "('a,'v)trie ⇒ ('a * ('a,'v)trie)list"
primrec "value(Trie ov al) = ov"
primrec "alist(Trie ov al) = al"
```

Association lists come with a generic lookup function. Its result involves type *option* because a lookup can fail:

```
consts    assoc :: "('key * 'val)list ⇒ 'key ⇒ 'val option"
primrec "assoc [] x = None"
        "assoc (p#ps) x =
            (let (a,b) = p in if a=x then Some b else assoc ps x)"
```

Now we can define the lookup function for tries. It descends into the trie examining the letters of the search string one by one. As recursion on lists is simpler than on tries, let us express this as primitive recursion on the search string argument:

```
consts    lookup :: "('a,'v)trie ⇒ 'a list ⇒ 'v option"
primrec "lookup t [] = value t"
        "lookup t (a#as) = (case assoc (alist t) a of
                              None ⇒ None
                            | Some at ⇒ lookup at as)"
```

As a first simple property we prove that looking up a string in the empty trie *Trie None []* always returns *None*. The proof merely distinguishes the two cases whether the search string is empty or not:

```
lemma [simp]: "lookup (Trie None []) as = None"
apply(case_tac as, simp_all)
done
```

Things begin to get interesting with the definition of an update function that adds a new (string, value) pair to a trie, overwriting the old value associated with that string:

```
consts update :: "('a,'v)trie ⇒ 'a list ⇒ 'v ⇒ ('a,'v)trie"
primrec
  "update t []      v = Trie (Some v) (alist t)"
  "update t (a#as) v =
     (let tt = (case assoc (alist t) a of
                     None ⇒ Trie None [] | Some at ⇒ at)
      in Trie (value t) ((a,update tt as v) # alist t))"
```

The base case is obvious. In the recursive case the subtrie `tt` associated with the first letter `a` is extracted, recursively updated, and then placed in front of the association list. The old subtrie associated with `a` is still in the association list but no longer accessible via `assoc`. Clearly, there is room here for optimizations!

Before we start on any proofs about `update` we tell the simplifier to expand all `let`s and to split all `case`-constructs over options:

```
declare Let_def[simp] option.split[split]
```

The reason becomes clear when looking (probably after a failed proof attempt) at the body of `update`: it contains both `let` and a case distinction over type `option`.

Our main goal is to prove the correct interaction of `update` and `lookup`:

```
theorem "∀t v bs. lookup (update t as v) bs =
                  (if as=bs then Some v else lookup t bs)"
```

Our plan is to induct on `as`; hence the remaining variables are quantified. From the definitions it is clear that induction on either `as` or `bs` is required. The choice of `as` is guided by the intuition that simplification of `lookup` might be easier if `update` has already been simplified, which can only happen if `as` is instantiated. The start of the proof is conventional:

```
apply(induct_tac as, auto)
```

Unfortunately, this time we are left with three intimidating looking subgoals:

```
1. ... ⟹ lookup ...  bs = lookup t bs
2. ... ⟹ lookup ...  bs = lookup t bs
3. ... ⟹ lookup ...  bs = lookup t bs
```

Clearly, if we want to make headway we have to instantiate `bs` as well now. It turns out that instead of induction, case distinction suffices:

```
apply(case_tac[!] bs, auto)
done
```

All methods ending in `tac` take an optional first argument that specifies the range of subgoals they are applied to, where `[!]` means all subgoals, i.e. `[1-3]` in our case. Individual subgoal numbers, e.g. `[2]` are also allowed.

This proof may look surprisingly straightforward. However, note that this comes at a cost: the proof script is unreadable because the intermediate proof states are invisible, and we rely on the (possibly brittle) magic of `auto` (`simp_all` will not do — try it) to split the subgoals of the induction up in such a way that case distinction on `bs` makes sense and solves the proof.

Exercise 3.4.4 Modify `update` (and its type) such that it allows both insertion and deletion of entries with a single function. Prove the corresponding version of the main theorem above. Optimize your function such that it shrinks tries after deletion if possible.

Exercise 3.4.5 Write an improved version of `update` that does not suffer from the space leak (pointed out above) caused by not deleting overwritten entries from the association list. Prove the main theorem for your improved `update`.

Exercise 3.4.6 Conceptually, each node contains a mapping from letters to optional subtries. Above we have implemented this by means of an association list. Replay the development replacing (`'a` × (`'a`, `'v`) `trie`) `list` with `'a` ⇒ (`'a`, `'v`) `trie option`.

3.5 Total Recursive Functions

Although many total functions have a natural primitive recursive definition, this is not always the case. Arbitrary total recursive functions can be defined by means of **recdef**: you can use full pattern-matching, recursion need not involve datatypes, and termination is proved by showing that the arguments of all recursive calls are smaller in a suitable (user supplied) sense. In this section we restrict ourselves to measure functions; more advanced termination proofs are discussed in Sect. 9.2.1.

3.5.1 Defining Recursive Functions

Here is a simple example, the Fibonacci function:

```
consts fib :: "nat ⇒ nat"
recdef fib "measure(λn. n)"
  "fib 0 = 0"
  "fib (Suc 0) = 1"
  "fib (Suc(Suc x)) = fib x + fib (Suc x)"
```

The definition of `fib` is accompanied by a **measure function** $\lambda n.\ n$ which maps the argument of `fib` to a natural number. The requirement is that in each equation the measure of the argument on the left-hand side is strictly greater than the measure of the argument of each recursive call. In the case of *fib* this is obviously true because the measure function is the identity and *Suc (Suc x)* is strictly greater than both *x* and *Suc x*.

Slightly more interesting is the insertion of a fixed element between any two elements of a list:

```
consts sep :: "'a × 'a list ⇒ 'a list"
recdef sep "measure (λ(a,xs). length xs)"
  "sep(a, [])    = []"
  "sep(a, [x])   = [x]"
  "sep(a, x#y#zs) = x # a # sep(a,y#zs)"
```

This time the measure is the length of the list, which decreases with the recursive call; the first component of the argument tuple is irrelevant. The details of tupled λ-abstractions $\lambda(x_1, \ldots, x_n)$ are explained in Sect. 8.2, but for now your intuition is all you need.

Pattern matching need not be exhaustive:

```
consts last :: "'a list ⇒ 'a"
recdef last "measure (λxs. length xs)"
  "last [x]      = x"
  "last (x#y#zs) = last (y#zs)"
```

Overlapping patterns are disambiguated by taking the order of equations into account, just as in functional programming:

```
consts sep1 :: "'a × 'a list ⇒ 'a list"
recdef sep1 "measure (λ(a,xs). length xs)"
  "sep1(a, x#y#zs) = x # a # sep1(a,y#zs)"
  "sep1(a, xs)     = xs"
```

To guarantee that the second equation can only be applied if the first one does not match, Isabelle internally replaces the second equation by the two possibilities that are left: *sep1 (a, []) = []* and *sep1 (a, [x]) = [x]*. Thus the functions *sep* and *sep1* are identical.

! **recdef** only takes the first argument of a (curried) recursive function into account. This means both the termination measure and pattern matching can only use that first argument. In general, you will therefore have to combine several arguments into a tuple. In case only one argument is relevant for termination, you can also rearrange the order of arguments as in the following definition:

```
consts sep2 :: "'a list ⇒ 'a ⇒ 'a list"
recdef sep2 "measure length"
  "sep2 (x#y#zs) = (λa. x # a # sep2 (y#zs) a)"
  "sep2 xs       = (λa. xs)"
```

Because of its pattern-matching syntax, **recdef** is also useful for the definition of non-recursive functions, where the termination measure degenerates to the empty set *{}*:

```
consts swap12 :: "'a list ⇒ 'a list"
recdef swap12 "{}"
  "swap12 (x#y#zs) = y#x#zs"
  "swap12 zs      = zs"
```

3.5.2 Proving Termination

When a function f is defined via **recdef**, Isabelle tries to prove its termination with the help of the user-supplied measure. Each of the examples above is simple enough that Isabelle can automatically prove that the argument's measure decreases in each recursive call. As a result, f.simps will contain the defining equations (or variants derived from them) as theorems. For example, look (via **thm**) at sep.simps and sep1.simps to see that they define the same function. What is more, those equations are automatically declared as simplification rules.

Isabelle may fail to prove the termination condition for some recursive call. Let us try to define Quicksort:

```
consts qs :: "nat list ⇒ nat list"
recdef qs "measure length"
  "qs [] = []"
  "qs(x#xs) = qs(filter (λy. y≤x) xs) @ [x] @ qs(filter (λy. x<y) xs)"
```

where filter is predefined and filter P xs is the list of elements of xs satisfying P. This definition of qs fails, and Isabelle prints an error message showing you what it was unable to prove:

```
    length (filter ... xs) < Suc (length xs)
```

We can either prove this as a separate lemma, or try to figure out which existing lemmas may help. We opt for the second alternative. The theory of lists contains the simplification rule length (filter P xs) ≤ length xs, which is already close to what we need, except that we still need to turn < Suc into ≤ for the simplification rule to apply. Lemma less_Suc_eq_le does just that: $(m < Suc\ n) = (m \leq n)$.

Now we retry the above definition but supply the lemma(s) just found (or proved). Because **recdef**'s termination prover involves simplification, we include in our second attempt a hint: the recdef_simp attribute says to use less_Suc_eq_le as a simplification rule.

```
recdef qs "measure length"
  "qs [] = []"
  "qs(x#xs) = qs(filter (λy. y≤x) xs) @ [x] @ qs(filter (λy. x<y) xs)"
(hints recdef_simp: less_Suc_eq_le)
```

This time everything works fine. Now qs.simps contains precisely the stated recursion equations for qs and they have become simplification rules. Thus we can automatically prove results such as this one:

theorem *"qs[2,3,0] = qs[3,0,2]"*
apply(*simp*)
done

More exciting theorems require induction, which is discussed below.

If the termination proof requires a lemma that is of general use, you can turn it permanently into a simplification rule, in which case the above **hint** is not necessary. But in the case of *less_Suc_eq_le* this would be of dubious value.

3.5.3 Simplification and Recursive Functions

Once we have proved all the termination conditions, the **recdef** recursion equations become simplification rules, just as with **primrec**. In most cases this works fine, but there is a subtle problem that must be mentioned: simplification may not terminate because of automatic splitting of *if*. Let us look at an example:

consts *gcd* :: *"nat×nat ⇒ nat"*
recdef *gcd "measure (λ(m,n).n)"*
  "gcd (m, n) = (if n=0 then m else gcd(n, m mod n))"

According to the measure function, the second argument should decrease with each recursive call. The resulting termination condition

$$n \neq 0 \implies m \bmod n < n$$

is proved automatically because it is already present as a lemma in HOL. Thus the recursion equation becomes a simplification rule. Of course the equation is nonterminating if we are allowed to unfold the recursive call inside the *else* branch, which is why programming languages and our simplifier don't do that. Unfortunately the simplifier does something else that leads to the same problem: it splits each *if*-expression unless its condition simplifies to *True* or *False*. For example, simplification reduces

$$gcd (m, n) = k$$

in one step to

$$(if\ n = 0\ then\ m\ else\ gcd\ (n,\ m\ mod\ n)) = k$$

where the condition cannot be reduced further, and splitting leads to

$$(n = 0 \longrightarrow m = k) \wedge (n \neq 0 \longrightarrow gcd\ (n,\ m\ mod\ n) = k)$$

Since the recursive call *gcd (n, m mod n)* is no longer protected by an *if*, it is unfolded again, which leads to an infinite chain of simplification steps. Fortunately, this problem can be avoided in many different ways.

The most radical solution is to disable the offending theorem *split_if*, as shown in Sect. 3.1.9. However, we do not recommend this approach: you will often have to invoke the rule explicitly when *if* is involved.

If possible, the definition should be given by pattern matching on the left rather than *if* on the right. In the case of *gcd* the following alternative definition suggests itself:

```
consts gcd1 :: "nat × nat ⇒ nat"
recdef gcd1 "measure (λ(m,n).n)"
  "gcd1 (m, 0) = m"
  "gcd1 (m, n) = gcd1(n, m mod n)"
```

The order of equations is important: it hides the side condition $n \neq 0$. Unfortunately, in general the case distinction may not be expressible by pattern matching.

A simple alternative is to replace *if* by *case*, which is also available for *bool* and is not split automatically:

```
consts gcd2 :: "nat × nat ⇒ nat"
recdef gcd2 "measure (λ(m,n).n)"
  "gcd2(m,n) = (case n=0 of True ⇒ m | False ⇒ gcd2(n,m mod n))"
```

This is probably the neatest solution next to pattern matching, and it is always available.

A final alternative is to replace the offending simplification rules by derived conditional ones. For *gcd* it means we have to prove these lemmas:

```
lemma [simp]: "gcd (m, 0) = m"
apply(simp)
done
```

```
lemma [simp]: "n ≠ 0 ⟹ gcd(m, n) = gcd(n, m mod n)"
apply(simp)
done
```

Simplification terminates for these proofs because the condition of the *if* simplifies to *True* or *False*. Now we can disable the original simplification rule:

```
declare gcd.simps [simp del]
```

3.5.4 Induction and Recursive Functions

Assuming we have defined our function such that Isabelle could prove termination and that the recursion equations (or some suitable derived equations) are simplification rules, we might like to prove something about our function. Since the function is recursive, the natural proof principle is again induction. But this time the structural form of induction that comes with datatypes is unlikely to work well — otherwise we could have defined the function by **primrec**. Therefore **recdef** automatically proves a suitable induction rule

f.induct that follows the recursion pattern of the particular function f. We call this **recursion induction**. Roughly speaking, it requires you to prove for each **recdef** equation that the property you are trying to establish holds for the left-hand side provided it holds for all recursive calls on the right-hand side. Here is a simple example involving the predefined map functional on lists:

lemma "map f (sep(x,xs)) = sep(f x, map f xs)"

Note that map f xs is the result of applying f to all elements of xs. We prove this lemma by recursion induction over sep:

apply(induct_tac x xs rule: sep.induct)

The resulting proof state has three subgoals corresponding to the three clauses for sep:

1. ⋀a. map f (sep (a, [])) = sep (f a, map f [])
2. ⋀a x. map f (sep (a, [x])) = sep (f a, map f [x])
3. ⋀a x y zs.
         map f (sep (a, y # zs)) = sep (f a, map f (y # zs)) ⟹
         map f (sep (a, x # y # zs)) = sep (f a, map f (x # y # zs))

The rest is pure simplification:

apply simp_all
done

Try proving the above lemma by structural induction, and you find that you need an additional case distinction. What is worse, the names of variables are invented by Isabelle and have nothing to do with the names in the definition of sep.

In general, the format of invoking recursion induction is

   apply(induct_tac $x_1 \ldots x_n$ rule: f.induct)

where $x_1 \ldots x_n$ is a list of free variables in the subgoal and f the name of a function that takes an n-tuple. Usually the subgoal will contain the term $f(x_1, \ldots, x_n)$ but this need not be the case. The induction rules do not mention f at all. Here is sep.induct:

⟦ ⋀a. P a [];
   ⋀a x. P a [x];
   ⋀a x y zs. P a (y # zs) ⟹ P a (x # y # zs)⟧
⟹ P u v

It merely says that in order to prove a property P of u and v you need to prove it for the three cases where v is the empty list, the singleton list, and the list with at least two elements. The final case has an induction hypothesis: you may assume that P holds for the tail of that list.

4. Presenting Theories

By now the reader should have become sufficiently acquainted with elementary theory development in Isabelle/HOL. The following interlude describes how to present theories in a typographically pleasing manner. Isabelle provides a rich infrastructure for concrete syntax of the underlying λ-calculus language (see Sect. 4.1), as well as document preparation of theory texts based on existing PDF-LATEX technology (see Sect. 4.2).

As pointed out by Leibniz more than 300 years ago, *notions* are in principle more important than *notations*, but suggestive textual representation of ideas is vital to reduce the mental effort to comprehend and apply them.

4.1 Concrete Syntax

The core concept of Isabelle's framework for concrete syntax is that of **mixfix annotations**. Associated with any kind of constant declaration, mixfixes affect both the grammar productions for the parser and output templates for the pretty printer.

In full generality, parser and pretty printer configuration is a subtle affair [23]. Your syntax specifications need to interact properly with the existing setup of Isabelle/Pure and Isabelle/HOL. To avoid creating ambiguities with existing elements, it is particularly important to give new syntactic constructs the right precedence.

Subsequently we introduce a few simple syntax declaration forms that already cover many common situations fairly well.

4.1.1 Infix Annotations

Syntax annotations may be included wherever constants are declared, such as **consts** and **constdefs** — and also **datatype**, which declares constructor operations. Type-constructors may be annotated as well, although this is less frequently encountered in practice (the infix type × comes to mind).

Infix declarations provide a useful special case of mixfixes. The following example of the exclusive-or operation on boolean values illustrates typical infix declarations.

T. Nipkow, L.C. Paulson, and M. Wenzel: Isabelle/HOL, LNCS 2283, pp. 53-64, 2002.
© Springer-Verlag Berlin Heidelberg 2002

constdefs

   xor :: *"bool* ⇒ *bool* ⇒ *bool"*   (**infixl** *"[+]"* *60*)
   "A [+] B ≡ *(A* ∧ ¬ *B)* ∨ *(*¬ *A* ∧ *B)"*

Now *xor A B* and *A [+] B* refer to the same expression internally. Any curried function with at least two arguments may be given infix syntax. For partial applications with fewer than two operands, there is a notation using the prefix *op*. For instance, *xor* without arguments is represented as *op [+]*; together with ordinary function application, this turns *xor A* into *op [+] A*.

The keyword **infixl** seen above specifies an infix operator that is nested to the *left*: in iterated applications the more complex expression appears on the left-hand side, and *A [+] B [+] C* stands for *(A [+] B) [+] C*. Similarly, **infixr** means nesting to the *right*, reading *A [+] B [+] C* as *A [+] (B [+] C)*. A *non-oriented* declaration via **infix** would render *A [+] B [+] C* illegal, but demand explicit parentheses to indicate the intended grouping.

The string *"[+]"* in our annotation refers to the concrete syntax to represent the operator (a literal token), while the number *60* determines the precedence of the construct: the syntactic priorities of the arguments and result. Isabelle/HOL already uses up many popular combinations of ASCII symbols for its own use, including both + and ++. Longer character combinations are more likely to be still available for user extensions, such as our *[+]*.

Operator precedences have a range of 0–1000. Very low or high priorities are reserved for the meta-logic. HOL syntax mainly uses the range of 10–100: the equality infix = is centered at 50; logical connectives (like ∨ and ∧) are below 50; algebraic ones (like + and *) are above 50. User syntax should strive to coexist with common HOL forms, or use the mostly unused range 100–900.

4.1.2 Mathematical Symbols

Concrete syntax based on ASCII characters has inherent limitations. Mathematical notation demands a larger repertoire of glyphs. Several standards of extended character sets have been proposed over decades, but none has become universally available so far. Isabelle has its own notion of **symbols** as the smallest entities of source text, without referring to internal encodings. There are three kinds of such "generalized characters":

1. 7-bit ASCII characters
2. named symbols: \<*ident*>
3. named control symbols: \<^*ident*>

Here *ident* may be any identifier according to the usual Isabelle conventions. This results in an infinite store of symbols, whose interpretation is left to further front-end tools. For example, the user-interface of Proof General

+ X-Symbol and the Isabelle document processor (see Sect. 4.2) display the
`\<forall>` symbol as ∀.

A list of standard Isabelle symbols is given in [35, appendix A]. You
may introduce your own interpretation of further symbols by configuring the
appropriate front-end tool accordingly, e.g. by defining certain LATEX macros
(see also Sect. 4.2.4). There are also a few predefined control symbols, such
as `\<^sub>` and `\<^sup>` for sub- and superscript of the subsequent printable
symbol, respectively. For example, `A\<^sup>\<star>` is output as A^*.

Replacing our definition of *xor* by the following specifies a Isabelle symbol
for the new operator:

```
constdefs
  xor :: "bool ⇒ bool ⇒ bool"    (infixl "⊕" 60)
  "A ⊕ B ≡ (A ∧ ¬ B) ∨ (¬ A ∧ B)"
```

The X-Symbol package within Proof General provides several input methods
to enter ⊕ in the text. If all fails one may just type a named entity `\<oplus>`
by hand; the corresponding symbol will be displayed after further input.

More flexible is to provide alternative syntax forms through the **print
mode** concept [23]. By convention, the mode of "*xsymbols*" is enabled whenever Proof General's X-Symbol mode or LATEX output is active. Now consider
the following hybrid declaration of *xor*:

```
constdefs
  xor :: "bool ⇒ bool ⇒ bool"    (infixl "[+]" 60)
  "A [+] B ≡ (A ∧ ¬ B) ∨ (¬ A ∧ B)"

syntax (xsymbols)
  xor :: "bool ⇒ bool ⇒ bool"    (infixl "⊕" 60)
```

The **syntax** command introduced here acts like **consts**, but without
declaring a logical constant. The print mode specification of **syntax**, here
(*xsymbols*), is optional. Also note that its type merely serves for syntactic
purposes, and is *not* checked for consistency with the real constant.

We may now write *A [+] B* or *A ⊕ B* in input, while output uses the nicer
syntax of *xsymbols* whenever that print mode is active. Such an arrangement is particularly useful for interactive development, where users may type
ASCII text and see mathematical symbols displayed during proofs.

4.1.3 Prefix Annotations

Prefix syntax annotations are another form of mixfixes [23], without any
template arguments or priorities — just some literal syntax. The following
example associates common symbols with the constructors of a datatype.

datatype *currency* =
   Euro nat   *("€")*
  | *Pounds nat* *("£")*
  | *Yen nat*   *("¥")*
  | *Dollar nat* *("$")*

Here the mixfix annotations on the rightmost column happen to consist of a single Isabelle symbol each: \<euro>, \<pounds>, \<yen>, and $. Recall that a constructor like *Euro* actually is a function *nat* $\Rightarrow$ *currency*. The expression *Euro 10* will be printed as € 10; only the head of the application is subject to our concrete syntax. This rather simple form already achieves conformance with notational standards of the European Commission.

Prefix syntax works the same way for **consts** or **constdefs**.

4.1.4 Syntax Translations

Mixfix syntax annotations merely decorate particular constant application forms with concrete syntax, for instance replacing *xor A B* by *A ⊕ B*. Occasionally, the relationship between some piece of notation and its internal form is more complicated. Here we need **syntax translations**.

Using the **syntax**, command we introduce uninterpreted notational elements. Then **translations** relate input forms to complex logical expressions. This provides a simple mechanism for syntactic macros; even heavier transformations may be written in ML [23].

A typical use of syntax translations is to introduce relational notation for membership in a set of pair, replacing *(x, y)* $\in$ *sim* by *x* $\approx$ *y*.

consts
  sim :: *"('a × 'a) set"*

syntax
  "_sim" :: *"'a* $\Rightarrow$ *'a* $\Rightarrow$ *bool"*   (**infix** *"≈"* 50)
translations
  "x $\approx$ *y"* $\rightleftharpoons$ *"(x, y)* $\in$ *sim"*

Here the name of the dummy constant *_sim* does not matter, as long as it is not used elsewhere. Prefixing an underscore is a common convention. The **translations** declaration already uses concrete syntax on the left-hand side; internally we relate a raw application *_sim x y* with *(x, y)* $\in$ *sim*.

Another common application of syntax translations is to provide variant versions of fundamental relational expressions, such as $\neq$ for negated equalities. The following declaration stems from Isabelle/HOL itself:

syntax *"_not_equal"* :: *"'a* $\Rightarrow$ *'a* $\Rightarrow$ *bool"*   (**infixl** *"≠"* 50)
translations *"x* $\neq$ *y"* $\rightleftharpoons$ *"¬ (x = y)"*

Normally one would introduce derived concepts like this within the logic, using **consts** + **defs** instead of **syntax** + **translations**. The present formulation has the virtue that expressions are immediately replaced by the "definition" upon parsing; the effect is reversed upon printing.

This sort of translation is appropriate when the defined concept is a trivial variation on an existing one. On the other hand, syntax translations do not scale up well to large hierarchies of concepts. Translations do not replace definitions!

4.2 Document Preparation

Isabelle/Isar is centered around the concept of **formal proof documents**. The outcome of a formal development effort is meant to be a human-readable record, presented as browsable PDF file or printed on paper. The overall document structure follows traditional mathematical articles, with sections, intermediate explanations, definitions, theorems and proofs.

The Isabelle document preparation system essentially acts as a front-end to LATEX. After checking specifications and proofs formally, the theory sources are turned into typesetting instructions in a schematic manner. This lets you write authentic reports on theory developments with little effort: many technical consistency checks are handled by the system.

Here is an example to illustrate the idea of Isabelle document preparation.

The following datatype definition of $'a$ *bintree* models binary trees with nodes being decorated by elements of type $'a$.

```
datatype 'a bintree =
    Leaf | Branch 'a  "'a bintree"  "'a bintree"
```

The datatype induction rule generated here is of the form

```
⟦P Leaf;
    ⋀a bintree1 bintree2.
        ⟦P bintree1; P bintree2⟧ ⟹ P (Branch a bintree1 bintree2)⟧
⟹ P bintree
```

The above document output has been produced as follows:

```
text {*
    The following datatype definition of @{text "'a bintree"}
    models binary trees with nodes being decorated by elements
    of type @{typ 'a}.
*}

datatype 'a bintree =
    Leaf | Branch 'a  "'a bintree"  "'a bintree"
```

```
text {*
  \noindent The datatype induction rule generated here is
  of the form @{thm [display] bintree.induct [no_vars]}
*}
```

Here we have augmented the theory by formal comments (using **text** blocks), the informal parts may again refer to formal entities by means of "antiquotations" (such as @{text "'a bintree"} or @{typ 'a}), see also Sect. 4.2.3.

4.2.1 Isabelle Sessions

In contrast to the highly interactive mode of Isabelle/Isar theory development, the document preparation stage essentially works in batch-mode. An Isabelle **session** consists of a collection of source files that may contribute to an output document. Each session is derived from a single parent, usually an object-logic image like HOL. This results in an overall tree structure, which is reflected by the output location in the file system (usually rooted at ~/isabelle/browser_info).

The easiest way to manage Isabelle sessions is via isatool mkdir (generates an initial session source setup) and isatool make (run sessions controlled by IsaMakefile). For example, a new session MySession derived from HOL may be produced as follows:

```
isatool mkdir HOL MySession
isatool make
```

The isatool make job also informs about the file-system location of the ultimate results. The above dry run should be able to produce some document.pdf (with dummy title, empty table of contents etc.). Any failure at this stage usually indicates technical problems of the LATEX installation.[1]

The detailed arrangement of the session sources is as follows.

– Directory MySession holds the required theory files T_1.thy, ..., T_n.thy.
– File MySession/ROOT.ML holds appropriate ML commands for loading all wanted theories, usually just "use_thy" T_i";" for any T_i in leaf position of the dependency graph.
– Directory MySession/document contains everything required for the LATEX stage; only root.tex needs to be provided initially.
  The latter file holds appropriate LATEX code to commence a document (\documentclass etc.), and to include the generated files T_i.tex for each theory. Isabelle will generate a file session.tex holding LATEX commands to include all generated theory output files in topologically sorted order, so \input{session} in the body of root.tex does the job in most situations.

---

[1] Especially make sure that pdflatex is present; if in doubt one may fall back on DVI output by changing usedir options in IsaMakefile [35].

- IsaMakefile holds appropriate dependencies and invocations of Isabelle tools to control the batch job. In fact, several sessions may be managed by the same IsaMakefile. See the *Isabelle System Manual* [35] for further details, especially on isatool usedir and isatool make.

One may now start to populate the directory MySession, and the file MySession/ROOT.ML accordingly. The file MySession/document/root.tex should also be adapted at some point; the default version is mostly self-explanatory. Note that \isabellestyle enables fine-tuning of the general appearance of characters and mathematical symbols (see also Sect. 4.2.4).

Especially observe the included LaTeX packages isabelle (mandatory), isabellesym (required for mathematical symbols), and the final pdfsetup (provides sane defaults for hyperref, including URL markup). All three are distributed with Isabelle. Further packages may be required in particular applications, say for unusual mathematical symbols.

Any additional files for the LaTeX stage go into the MySession/document directory as well. In particular, adding a file named root.bib causes an automatic run of bibtex to process a bibliographic database; see also isatool document [35].

Any failure of the document preparation phase in an Isabelle batch session leaves the generated sources in their target location, identified by the accompanying error message. This lets you trace LaTeX problems with the generated files at hand.

4.2.2 Structure Markup

The large-scale structure of Isabelle documents follows existing LaTeX conventions, with chapters, sections, subsubsections etc. The Isar language includes separate **markup commands**, which do not affect the formal meaning of a theory (or proof), but result in corresponding LaTeX elements.

There are separate markup commands depending on the textual context: in header position (just before **theory**), within the theory body, or within a proof. The header needs to be treated specially here, since ordinary theory and proof commands may only occur *after* the initial **theory** specification.

header	theory	proof	default meaning
	chapter		\chapter
header	**section**	**sect**	\section
	subsection	**subsect**	\subsection
	subsubsection	**subsubsect**	\subsubsection

From the Isabelle perspective, each markup command takes a single *text* argument (delimited by " ... " or {* ... *}). After stripping any surrounding white space, the argument is passed to a LaTeX macro \isamarkupXYZ for command **XYZ**. These macros are defined in `isabelle.sty` according to the meaning given in the rightmost column above.

The following source fragment illustrates structure markup of a theory. Note that LaTeX labels may be included inside of section headings as well.

```
header {* Some properties of Foo Bar elements *}

theory Foo_Bar = Main:

subsection {* Basic definitions *}

consts
  foo :: ...
  bar :: ...

defs ...

subsection {* Derived rules *}

lemma fooI: ...
lemma fooE: ...

subsection {* Main theorem \label{sec:main-theorem} *}

theorem main: ...

end
```

You may occasionally want to change the meaning of markup commands, say via `\renewcommand` in `root.tex`. For example, `\isamarkupheader` is a good candidate for some tuning. We could move it up in the hierarchy to become `\chapter`.

```
\renewcommand{\isamarkupheader}[1]{\chapter{#1}}
```

Now we must change the document class given in `root.tex` to something that supports chapters. A suitable command is `\documentclass{report}`.

The LaTeX macro `\isabellecontext` is maintained to hold the name of the current theory context. This is particularly useful for document headings:

```
\renewcommand{\isamarkupheader}[1]
{\chapter{#1}\markright{THEORY~\isabellecontext}}
```

Make sure to include something like `\pagestyle{headings}` in `root.tex`; the document should have more than two pages to show the effect.

4.2.3 Formal Comments and Antiquotations

Isabelle **source comments**, which are of the form (* ... *), essentially act like white space and do not really contribute to the content. They mainly serve technical purposes to mark certain oddities in the raw input text. In contrast, **formal comments** are portions of text that are associated with formal Isabelle/Isar commands (**marginal comments**), or as standalone paragraphs within a theory or proof context (**text blocks**).

Marginal comments are part of each command's concrete syntax [23]; the common form is "*-- text*" where *text* is delimited by "*...*" or {* ... *} as before. Multiple marginal comments may be given at the same time. Here is a simple example:

lemma *"A --> A"*
    — a triviality of propositional logic
    — (should not really bother)
by *(rule impI)* — implicit assumption step involved here

The above output has been produced as follows:

```
lemma "A --> A"
    -- "a triviality of propositional logic"
    -- "(should not really bother)"
    by (rule impI) -- "implicit assumption step involved here"
```

From the LATEX viewpoint, "--" acts like a markup command, associated with the macro \isamarkupcmt (taking a single argument).

Text blocks are introduced by the commands **text** and **txt**, for theory and proof contexts, respectively. Each takes again a single *text* argument, which is interpreted as a free-form paragraph in LATEX (surrounded by some additional vertical space). This behavior may be changed by redefining the LATEX environments of isamarkuptext or isamarkuptxt, respectively (via \renewenvironment) The text style of the body is determined by \isastyletext and \isastyletxt; the default setup uses a smaller font within proofs. This may be changed as follows:

```
\renewcommand{\isastyletxt}{\isastyletext}
```

The *text* part of Isabelle markup commands essentially inserts *quoted material* into a formal text, mainly for instruction of the reader. An **antiquotation** is again a formal object embedded into such an informal portion. The interpretation of antiquotations is limited to some well-formedness checks, with the result being pretty printed to the resulting document. Quoted text blocks together with antiquotations provide an attractive means of referring to formal entities, with good confidence in getting the technical details right (especially syntax and types).

The general syntax of antiquotations is as follows: @{*name arguments*}, or @{*name* [*options*] *arguments*} for a comma-separated list of options consisting of a *name* or *name=value* each. The syntax of *arguments* depends on the kind of antiquotation, it generally follows the same conventions for types, terms, or theorems as in the formal part of a theory.

This sentence demonstrates quotations and antiquotations: $\lambda x\ y.\ x$ is a well-typed term.

The output above was produced as follows:

```
text {*
  This sentence demonstrates quotations and antiquotations:
  @{term "%x y. x"} is a well-typed term.
*}
```

The notational change from the ASCII character % to the symbol λ reveals that Isabelle printed this term, after parsing and type-checking. Document preparation enables symbolic output by default.

The next example includes an option to modify Isabelle's `show_types` flag. The antiquotation `@{term [show_types] "%x y. x"}` produces the output $\lambda(x::'a)\ y::'b.\ x$. Type inference has figured out the most general typings in the present theory context. Terms may acquire different typings due to constraints imposed by their environment; within a proof, for example, variables are given the same types as they have in the main goal statement.

Several further kinds of antiquotations and options are available [35]. Here are a few commonly used combinations:

`@{typ `τ`}`	print type τ
`@{term `t`}`	print term t
`@{prop `ϕ`}`	print proposition ϕ
`@{prop [display] `ϕ`}`	print large proposition ϕ (with linebreaks)
`@{prop [source] `ϕ`}`	check proposition ϕ, print its input
`@{thm `a`}`	print fact a
`@{thm `a` [no_vars]}`	print fact a, fixing schematic variables
`@{thm [source] `a`}`	check availability of fact a, print its name
`@{text `s`}`	print uninterpreted text s

Note that `no_vars` given above is *not* an antiquotation option, but an attribute of the theorem argument given here. This might be useful with a diagnostic command like **thm**, too.

The `@{text `s`}` antiquotation is particularly interesting. Embedding uninterpreted text within an informal body might appear useless at first sight. Here the key virtue is that the string s is processed as Isabelle output, interpreting Isabelle symbols appropriately.

For example, `@{text "\<forall>\<exists>"}` produces $\forall\exists$, according to the standard interpretation of these symbol (cf. Sect. 4.2.4). Thus we achieve consistent mathematical notation in both the formal and informal parts of the document very easily, independently of the term language of Isabelle. Manual LaTeX code would leave more control over the typesetting, but is also slightly more tedious.

4.2.4 Interpretation of Symbols

As has been pointed out before (Sect. 4.1.2), Isabelle symbols are the smallest syntactic entities — a straightforward generalization of ASCII characters. While Isabelle does not impose any interpretation of the infinite collection of named symbols, LaTeX documents use canonical glyphs for certain standard symbols [35, appendix A].

The LaTeX code produced from Isabelle text follows a simple scheme. You can tune the final appearance by redefining certain macros, say in `root.tex` of the document.

1. 7-bit ASCII characters: letters `A` ... `Z` and `a` ... `z` are output directly, digits are passed as an argument to the `\isadigit` macro, other characters are replaced by specifically named macros of the form `\isacharXYZ`.
2. Named symbols: `\<XYZ>` is turned into `{\isasymXYZ}`; note the additional braces.
3. Named control symbols: `\<^XYZ>` is turned into `\isactrlXYZ`; subsequent symbols may act as arguments if the control macro is defined accordingly.

You may occasionally wish to give new LaTeX interpretations of named symbols. This merely requires an appropriate definition of `\isasymXYZ`, for `\<XYZ>` (see `isabelle.sty` for working examples). Control symbols are slightly more difficult to get right, though.

The `\isabellestyle` macro provides a high-level interface to tune the general appearance of individual symbols. For example, `\isabellestyle{it}` uses the italics text style to mimic the general appearance of the LaTeX math mode; double quotes are not printed at all. The resulting quality of typesetting is quite good, so this should be the default style for work that gets distributed to a broader audience.

4.2.5 Suppressing Output

By default, Isabelle's document system generates a LaTeX file for each theory that gets loaded while running the session. The generated `session.tex` will include all of these in order of appearance, which in turn gets included by the standard `root.tex`. Certainly one may change the order or suppress unwanted theories by ignoring `session.tex` and load individual files directly in `root.tex`. On the other hand, such an arrangement requires additional maintenance whenever the collection of theories changes.

Alternatively, one may tune the theory loading process in `ROOT.ML` itself: traversal of the theory dependency graph may be fine-tuned by adding `use_thy` invocations, although topological sorting still has to be observed. Moreover, the ML operator `no_document` temporarily disables document generation while executing a theory loader command. Its usage is like this:

```
no_document use_thy "T";
```

Theory output may be suppressed more selectively. Research articles and slides usually do not include the formal content in full. Delimiting **ignored material** by the special source comments (*<*) and (*>*) tells the document preparation system to suppress these parts; the formal checking of the theory is unchanged, of course.

In this example, we hide a theory's **theory** and **end** brackets:

```
(*<*)
theory T = Main:
(*>*)
    ⋮
(*<*)
end
(*>*)
```

Text may be suppressed in a fine-grained manner. We may even hide vital parts of a proof, pretending that things have been simpler than they really were. For example, this "fully automatic" proof is actually a fake:

lemma "x ≠ (0::int) ⟹ 0 < x * x"
  by (auto)

Here the real source of the proof has been as follows:

```
by (auto(*<*)simp add: int_less_le(*>*))
```

Suppressing portions of printed text demands care. You should not misrepresent the underlying theory development. It is easy to invalidate the visible text by hiding references to questionable axioms.

Authentic reports of Isabelle/Isar theories, say as part of a library, should suppress nothing. Other users may need the full information for their own derivative work. If a particular formalization appears inadequate for general public coverage, it is often more appropriate to think of a better way in the first place.

Some technical subtleties of the (*<*) (*>*) elements need to be kept in mind, too — the system performs few sanity checks here. Arguments of markup commands and formal comments must not be hidden, otherwise presentation fails. Open and close parentheses need to be inserted carefully; it is easy to hide the wrong parts, especially after rearranging the theory text.

Part II

Logic and Sets

5. The Rules of the Game

This chapter outlines the concepts and techniques that underlie reasoning in Isabelle. Until now, we have proved everything using only induction and simplification, but any serious verification project require more elaborate forms of inference. The chapter also introduces the fundamentals of predicate logic. The first examples in this chapter will consist of detailed, low-level proof steps. Later, we shall see how to automate such reasoning using the methods *blast*, *auto* and others. Backward or goal-directed proof is our usual style, but the chapter also introduces forward reasoning, where one theorem is transformed to yield another.

5.1 Natural Deduction

In Isabelle, proofs are constructed using inference rules. The most familiar inference rule is probably *modus ponens*:

$$\frac{P \to Q \quad P}{Q}$$

This rule says that from $P \to Q$ and P we may infer Q.

Natural deduction is an attempt to formalize logic in a way that mirrors human reasoning patterns. For each logical symbol (say, $\wedge$), there are two kinds of rules: **introduction** and **elimination** rules. The introduction rules allow us to infer this symbol (say, to infer conjunctions). The elimination rules allow us to deduce consequences from this symbol. Ideally each rule should mention one symbol only. For predicate logic this can be done, but when users define their own concepts they typically have to refer to other symbols as well. It is best not to be dogmatic.

Natural deduction generally deserves its name. It is easy to use. Each proof step consists of identifying the outermost symbol of a formula and applying the corresponding rule. It creates new subgoals in an obvious way from parts of the chosen formula. Expanding the definitions of constants can blow up the goal enormously. Deriving natural deduction rules for such constants lets us reason in terms of their key properties, which might otherwise be obscured by the technicalities of its definition. Natural deduction rules also

T. Nipkow, L.C. Paulson, and M. Wenzel: Isabelle/HOL, LNCS 2283, pp. 67-104, 2002.

lend themselves to automation. Isabelle's **classical reasoner** accepts any suitable collection of natural deduction rules and uses them to search for proofs automatically. Isabelle is designed around natural deduction and many of its tools use the terminology of introduction and elimination rules.

5.2 Introduction Rules

An introduction rule tells us when we can infer a formula containing a specific logical symbol. For example, the conjunction introduction rule says that if we have P and if we have Q then we have $P \wedge Q$. In a mathematics text, it is typically shown like this:

$$\frac{P \quad Q}{P \wedge Q}$$

The rule introduces the conjunction symbol ($\wedge$) in its conclusion. In Isabelle proofs we mainly reason backwards. When we apply this rule, the subgoal already has the form of a conjunction; the proof step makes this conjunction symbol disappear.

In Isabelle notation, the rule looks like this:

⟦?P; ?Q⟧ ⟹ ?P ∧ ?Q   (conjI)

Carefully examine the syntax. The premises appear to the left of the arrow and the conclusion to the right. The premises (if more than one) are grouped using the fat brackets. The question marks indicate **schematic variables** (also called **unknowns**): they may be replaced by arbitrary formulas. If we use the rule backwards, Isabelle tries to unify the current subgoal with the conclusion of the rule, which has the form *?P ∧ ?Q*. (Unification is discussed below, Sect. 5.8.) If successful, it yields new subgoals given by the formulas assigned to *?P* and *?Q*.

The following trivial proof illustrates how rules work. It also introduces a style of indentation. If a command adds a new subgoal, then the next command's indentation is increased by one space; if it proves a subgoal, then the indentation is reduced. This provides the reader with hints about the subgoal structure.

```
lemma conj_rule: "⟦P; Q⟧ ⟹ P ∧ (Q ∧ P)"
apply (rule conjI)
 apply assumption
apply (rule conjI)
 apply assumption
apply assumption
```

At the start, Isabelle presents us with the assumptions (*P* and *Q*) and with the goal to be proved, *P ∧ (Q ∧ P)*. We are working backwards, so when we apply conjunction introduction, the rule removes the outermost occurrence of the ∧ symbol. To apply a rule to a subgoal, we apply the proof method *rule* — here with *conjI*, the conjunction introduction rule.

    1. [P; Q] ⟹ P
    2. [P; Q] ⟹ Q ∧ P

Isabelle leaves two new subgoals: the two halves of the original conjunction. The first is simply P, which is trivial, since P is among the assumptions. We can apply the `assumption` method, which proves a subgoal by finding a matching assumption.

    1. [P; Q] ⟹ Q ∧ P

We are left with the subgoal of proving Q ∧ P from the assumptions P and Q. We apply `rule conjI` again.

    1. [P; Q] ⟹ Q
    2. [P; Q] ⟹ P

We are left with two new subgoals, Q and P, each of which can be proved using the `assumption` method.

5.3 Elimination Rules

Elimination rules work in the opposite direction from introduction rules. In the case of conjunction, there are two such rules. From $P \wedge Q$ we infer P. also, from $P \wedge Q$ we infer Q:

$$\frac{P \wedge Q}{P} \qquad \frac{P \wedge Q}{Q}$$

Now consider disjunction. There are two introduction rules, which resemble inverted forms of the conjunction elimination rules:

$$\frac{P}{P \vee Q} \qquad \frac{Q}{P \vee Q}$$

What is the disjunction elimination rule? The situation is rather different from conjunction. From $P \vee Q$ we cannot conclude that P is true and we cannot conclude that Q is true; there are no direct elimination rules of the sort that we have seen for conjunction. Instead, there is an elimination rule that works indirectly. If we are trying to prove something else, say R, and we know that $P \vee Q$ holds, then we have to consider two cases. We can assume that P is true and prove R and then assume that Q is true and prove R a second time. Here we see a fundamental concept used in natural deduction: that of the **assumptions**. We have to prove R twice, under different assumptions. The assumptions are local to these subproofs and are visible nowhere else.

In a logic text, the disjunction elimination rule might be shown like this:

$$\frac{P \vee Q \quad \overset{[P]}{\overset{\vdots}{R}} \quad \overset{[Q]}{\overset{\vdots}{R}}}{R}$$

The assumptions $[P]$ and $[Q]$ are bracketed to emphasize that they are local to their subproofs. In Isabelle notation, the already-familiar $\Longrightarrow$ syntax serves the same purpose:

$$\llbracket ?P \lor ?Q;\ ?P \Longrightarrow ?R;\ ?Q \Longrightarrow ?R \rrbracket \Longrightarrow ?R \qquad\qquad (disjE)$$

When we use this sort of elimination rule backwards, it produces a case split. (We have seen this before, in proofs by induction.) The following proof illustrates the use of disjunction elimination.

```
lemma disj_swap: "P ∨ Q ⟹ Q ∨ P"
apply (erule disjE)
 apply (rule disjI2)
 apply assumption
apply (rule disjI1)
apply assumption
```

We assume $P \lor Q$ and must prove $Q \lor P$. Our first step uses the disjunction elimination rule, $disjE$. We invoke it using $erule$, a method designed to work with elimination rules. It looks for an assumption that matches the rule's first premise. It deletes the matching assumption, regards the first premise as proved and returns subgoals corresponding to the remaining premises. When we apply $erule$ to $disjE$, only two subgoals result. This is better than applying it using $rule$ to get three subgoals, then proving the first by assumption: the other subgoals would have the redundant assumption $P \lor Q$. Most of the time, $erule$ is the best way to use elimination rules, since it replaces an assumption by its subformulas; only rarely does the original assumption remain useful.

```
1. P ⟹ Q ∨ P
2. Q ⟹ Q ∨ P
```

These are the two subgoals returned by $erule$. The first assumes P and the second assumes Q. Tackling the first subgoal, we need to show $Q \lor P$. The second introduction rule ($disjI2$) can reduce this to P, which matches the assumption. So, we apply the $rule$ method with $disjI2$ ...

```
1. P ⟹ P
2. Q ⟹ Q ∨ P
```

... and finish off with the $assumption$ method. We are left with the other subgoal, which assumes Q.

```
1. Q ⟹ Q ∨ P
```

Its proof is similar, using the introduction rule $disjI1$.

The result of this proof is a new inference rule $disj\_swap$, which is neither an introduction nor an elimination rule, but which might be useful. We can use it to replace any goal of the form $Q \lor P$ by a one of the form $P \lor Q$.

5.4 Destruction Rules: Some Examples

Now let us examine the analogous proof for conjunction.

```
lemma conj_swap: "P ∧ Q ⟹ Q ∧ P"
apply (rule conjI)
 apply (drule conjunct2)
 apply assumption
apply (drule conjunct1)
apply assumption
```

Recall that the conjunction elimination rules — whose Isabelle names are `conjunct1` and `conjunct2` — simply return the first or second half of a conjunction. Rules of this sort (where the conclusion is a subformula of a premise) are called **destruction** rules because they take apart and destroy a premise.[1]

The first proof step applies conjunction introduction, leaving two subgoals:

```
1. P ∧ Q ⟹ Q
2. P ∧ Q ⟹ P
```

To invoke the elimination rule, we apply a new method, `drule`. Think of the `d` as standing for **destruction** (or **direct**, if you prefer). Applying the second conjunction rule using `drule` replaces the assumption $P \wedge Q$ by Q.

```
1. Q ⟹ Q
2. P ∧ Q ⟹ P
```

The resulting subgoal can be proved by applying `assumption`. The other subgoal is similarly proved, using the `conjunct1` rule and the `assumption` method.

Choosing among the methods `rule`, `erule` and `drule` is up to you. Isabelle does not attempt to work out whether a rule is an introduction rule or an elimination rule. The method determines how the rule will be interpreted. Many rules can be used in more than one way. For example, `disj_swap` can be applied to assumptions as well as to goals; it replaces any assumption of the form $P \vee Q$ by a one of the form $Q \vee P$.

Destruction rules are simpler in form than indirect rules such as `disjE`, but they can be inconvenient. Each of the conjunction rules discards half of the formula, when usually we want to take both parts of the conjunction as new assumptions. The easiest way to do so is by using an alternative conjunction elimination rule that resembles `disjE`. It is seldom, if ever, seen in logic books. In Isabelle syntax it looks like this:

$$\llbracket ?P \wedge ?Q; \; \llbracket ?P; \; ?Q \rrbracket \Longrightarrow ?R \rrbracket \Longrightarrow ?R \qquad\qquad (conjE)$$

Exercise 5.4.1 Use the rule `conjE` to shorten the proof above.

---

[1] This Isabelle terminology has no counterpart in standard logic texts, although the distinction between the two forms of elimination rule is well known. Girard [9, page 74], for example, writes "The elimination rules [for $\vee$ and $\exists$] are very bad. What is catastrophic about them is the parasitic presence of a formula [R] which has no structural link with the formula which is eliminated."

5.5 Implication

At the start of this chapter, we saw the rule *modus ponens*. It is, in fact, a destruction rule. The matching introduction rule looks like this in Isabelle:

$$(?P \Longrightarrow ?Q) \Longrightarrow ?P \longrightarrow ?Q \qquad\qquad (\text{impI})$$

And this is *modus ponens*:

$$[\![?P \longrightarrow ?Q;\ ?P]\!] \Longrightarrow ?Q \qquad\qquad (\text{mp})$$

Here is a proof using the implication rules. This lemma performs a sort of uncurrying, replacing the two antecedents of a nested implication by a conjunction. The proof illustrates how assumptions work. At each proof step, the subgoals inherit the previous assumptions, perhaps with additions or deletions. Rules such as `impI` and `disjE` add assumptions, while applying `erule` or `drule` deletes the matching assumption.

```
lemma imp_uncurry: "P ⟶ (Q ⟶ R) ⟹ P ∧ Q ⟶ R"
apply (rule impI)
apply (erule conjE)
apply (drule mp)
 apply assumption
apply (drule mp)
  apply assumption
 apply assumption
```

First, we state the lemma and apply implication introduction (`rule impI`), which moves the conjunction to the assumptions.

1. $[\![P \longrightarrow Q \longrightarrow R;\ P \wedge Q]\!] \Longrightarrow R$

Next, we apply conjunction elimination (`erule conjE`), which splits this conjunction into two parts.

1. $[\![P \longrightarrow Q \longrightarrow R;\ P;\ Q]\!] \Longrightarrow R$

Now, we work on the assumption $P \longrightarrow (Q \longrightarrow R)$, where the parentheses have been inserted for clarity. The nested implication requires two applications of *modus ponens*: `drule mp`. The first use yields the implication $Q \longrightarrow R$, but first we must prove the extra subgoal P, which we do by assumption.

1. $[\![P;\ Q]\!] \Longrightarrow P$
2. $[\![P;\ Q;\ Q \longrightarrow R]\!] \Longrightarrow R$

Repeating these steps for $Q \longrightarrow R$ yields the conclusion we seek, namely R.

1. $[\![P;\ Q;\ Q \longrightarrow R]\!] \Longrightarrow R$

The symbols $\Longrightarrow$ and $\longrightarrow$ both stand for implication, but they differ in many respects. Isabelle uses $\Longrightarrow$ to express inference rules; the symbol is built-in and Isabelle's inference mechanisms treat it specially. On the other hand, $\longrightarrow$ is just one of the many connectives available in higher-order logic. We reason about it using inference rules such as `impI` and `mp`, just as we reason about the other connectives. You will have to use $\longrightarrow$ in any context that requires a formula of higher-order logic. Use $\Longrightarrow$ to separate a theorem's preconditions from its conclusion.

The **by** command is useful for proofs like these that use `assumption` heavily. It executes an **apply** command, then tries to prove all remaining subgoals using `assumption`. Since (if successful) it ends the proof, it also replaces the **done** symbol. For example, the proof above can be shortened:

```
lemma imp_uncurry: "P ⟶ (Q ⟶ R) ⟹ P ∧ Q ⟶ R"
apply (rule impI)
apply (erule conjE)
apply (drule mp)
 apply assumption
by (drule mp)
```

We could use **by** to replace the final **apply** and **done** in any proof, but typically we use it to eliminate calls to `assumption`. It is also a nice way of expressing a one-line proof.

5.6 Negation

Negation causes surprising complexity in proofs. Its natural deduction rules are straightforward, but additional rules seem necessary in order to handle negated assumptions gracefully. This section also illustrates the `intro` method: a convenient way of applying introduction rules.

Negation introduction deduces $\neg P$ if assuming P leads to a contradiction. Negation elimination deduces any formula in the presence of $\neg P$ together with P:

$$(?P \Longrightarrow \mathtt{False}) \Longrightarrow \neg\ ?P \qquad\qquad (\mathit{notI})$$
$$[\![\neg\ ?P;\ ?P]\!] \Longrightarrow ?R \qquad\qquad (\mathit{notE})$$

Classical logic allows us to assume $\neg P$ when attempting to prove P:

$$(\neg\ ?P \Longrightarrow ?P) \Longrightarrow ?P \qquad\qquad (\mathit{classical})$$

The implications $P \to Q$ and $\neg Q \to \neg P$ are logically equivalent, and each is called the **contrapositive** of the other. Four further rules support reasoning about contrapositives. They differ in the placement of the negation symbols:

$$[\![?Q;\ \neg\ ?P \Longrightarrow \neg\ ?Q]\!] \Longrightarrow ?P \qquad\qquad (\mathit{contrapos\_pp})$$
$$[\![?Q;\ ?P \Longrightarrow \neg\ ?Q]\!] \Longrightarrow \neg\ ?P \qquad\qquad (\mathit{contrapos\_pn})$$
$$[\![\neg\ ?Q;\ \neg\ ?P \Longrightarrow ?Q]\!] \Longrightarrow ?P \qquad\qquad (\mathit{contrapos\_np})$$
$$[\![\neg\ ?Q;\ ?P \Longrightarrow ?Q]\!] \Longrightarrow \neg\ ?P \qquad\qquad (\mathit{contrapos\_nn})$$

These rules are typically applied using the `erule` method, where their effect is to form a contrapositive from an assumption and the goal's conclusion.

The most important of these is `contrapos_np`. It is useful for applying introduction rules to negated assumptions. For instance, the assumption

$\neg(P \to Q)$ is equivalent to the conclusion $P \to Q$ and we might want to use conjunction introduction on it. Before we can do so, we must move that assumption so that it becomes the conclusion. The following proof demonstrates this technique:

```
lemma "[¬(P⟶Q); ¬(R⟶Q)] ⟹ R"
apply (erule_tac Q = "R⟶Q" in contrapos_np)
apply (intro impI)
by (erule notE)
```

There are two negated assumptions and we need to exchange the conclusion with the second one. The method `erule contrapos_np` would select the first assumption, which we do not want. So we specify the desired assumption explicitly using a new method, `erule_tac`. This is the resulting subgoal:

```
1. [¬ (P ⟶ Q); ¬ R] ⟹ R ⟶ Q
```

The former conclusion, namely `R`, now appears negated among the assumptions, while the negated formula `R ⟶ Q` becomes the new conclusion.

We can now apply introduction rules. We use the `intro` method, which repeatedly applies the given introduction rules. Here its effect is equivalent to `rule impI`.

```
1. [¬ (P ⟶ Q); ¬ R; R] ⟹ Q
```

We can see a contradiction in the form of assumptions ¬ `R` and `R`, which suggests using negation elimination. If applied on its own, `notE` will select the first negated assumption, which is useless. Instead, we invoke the rule using the `by` command. Now when Isabelle selects the first assumption, it tries to prove `P ⟶ Q` and fails; it then backtracks, finds the assumption ¬ `R` and finally proves `R` by assumption. That concludes the proof.

The following example may be skipped on a first reading. It involves a peculiar but important rule, a form of disjunction introduction:

$$(\neg\ ?Q \implies ?P) \implies ?P \lor ?Q \qquad\qquad (disjCI)$$

This rule combines the effects of `disjI1` and `disjI2`. Its great advantage is that we can remove the disjunction symbol without deciding which disjunction to prove. This treatment of disjunction is standard in sequent and tableau calculi.

```
lemma "(P ∨ Q) ∧ R ⟹ P ∨ (Q ∧ R)"
apply (intro disjCI conjI)
apply (elim conjE disjE)
 apply assumption
by (erule contrapos_np, rule conjI)
```

The first proof step uses `intro` to apply the introduction rules `disjCI` and `conjI`. The resulting subgoal has the negative assumption ¬(`Q` ∧ `R`).

```
1. [(P ∨ Q) ∧ R; ¬ (Q ∧ R)] ⟹ P
```

Next we apply the `elim` method, which repeatedly applies elimination rules; here, the elimination rules given in the command. One of the subgoals is trivial (**apply** `assumption`), leaving us with one other:

1. $[\![\neg (Q \wedge R);\ R;\ Q]\!] \Longrightarrow P$

Now we must move the formula $Q \wedge R$ to be the conclusion. The combination

    (`erule contrapos_np, rule conjI`)

is robust: the `conjI` forces the `erule` to select a conjunction. The two subgoals are the ones we would expect from applying conjunction introduction to $Q \wedge R$:

1. $[\![R;\ Q;\ \neg P]\!] \Longrightarrow Q$
2. $[\![R;\ Q;\ \neg P]\!] \Longrightarrow R$

They are proved by assumption, which is implicit in the **by** command.

5.7 Interlude: The Basic Methods for Rules

We have seen examples of many tactics that operate on individual rules. It may be helpful to review how they work given an arbitrary rule such as this:

$$\frac{P_1 \ \ldots \ P_n}{Q}$$

Below, we refer to P_1 as the **major premise**. This concept applies only to elimination and destruction rules. These rules act upon an instance of their major premise, typically to replace it by subformulas of itself.

Suppose that the rule above is called `R`. Here are the basic rule methods, most of which we have already seen:

– Method `rule R` unifies Q with the current subgoal, replacing it by n new subgoals: instances of $P_1, \ldots, P_n$. This is backward reasoning and is appropriate for introduction rules.
– Method `erule R` unifies Q with the current subgoal and simultaneously unifies P_1 with some assumption. The subgoal is replaced by the $n-1$ new subgoals of proving instances of $P_2, \ldots, P_n$, with the matching assumption deleted. It is appropriate for elimination rules. The method (`rule R, assumption`) is similar, but it does not delete an assumption.
– Method `drule R` unifies P_1 with some assumption, which it then deletes. The subgoal is replaced by the $n-1$ new subgoals of proving $P_2, \ldots, P_n$; an nth subgoal is like the original one but has an additional assumption: an instance of Q. It is appropriate for destruction rules.
– Method `frule R` is like `drule R` except that the matching assumption is not deleted. (See Sect. 5.9.5 below.)

Other methods apply a rule while constraining some of its variables. The typical form is

　　　`rule_tac` v_1 = t_1 **and** ... **and** v_k = t_k **in** `R`

This method behaves like `rule R`, while instantiating the variables $v_1, \ldots, v_k$ as specified. We similarly have `erule_tac`, `drule_tac` and `frule_tac`. These methods also let us specify which subgoal to operate on. By default it is the first subgoal, as with nearly all methods, but we can specify that rule `R` should be applied to subgoal number i:

　　　`rule_tac [i] R`

5.8 Unification and Substitution

As we have seen, Isabelle rules involve schematic variables, which begin with a question mark and act as placeholders for terms. **Unification** refers to the process of making two terms identical, possibly by replacing their schematic variables by terms. The simplest case is when the two terms are already the same. Next simplest is **pattern-matching**, which replaces variables in only one of the terms. The `rule` method typically matches the rule's conclusion against the current subgoal. In the most complex case, variables in both terms are replaced; the `rule` method can do this if the goal itself contains schematic variables. Other occurrences of the variables in the rule or proof state are updated at the same time.

Schematic variables in goals represent unknown terms. Given a goal such as $\exists x.\, P$, they let us proceed with a proof. They can be filled in later, sometimes in stages and often automatically.

Unification is well known to Prolog programmers. Isabelle uses **higher-order** unification, which works in the typed λ-calculus. The general case is undecidable, but for our purposes, the differences from ordinary unification are straightforward. It handles bound variables correctly, avoiding capture. The two terms $\lambda x.\ ?P$ and $\lambda x.\ t\ x$ are not unifiable; replacing `?P` by `t x` is forbidden because the free occurrence of x would become bound. The two terms $\lambda x.\ f(x,z)$ and $\lambda y.\ f(y,z)$ are trivially unifiable because they differ only by a bound variable renaming.

! **•** Higher-order unification sometimes must invent λ-terms to replace function variables, which can lead to a combinatorial explosion. However, Isabelle proofs tend to involve easy cases where there are few possibilities for the λ-term being constructed. In the easiest case, the function variable is applied only to bound variables, as when we try to unify $\lambda x\ y.\ f(?h\ x\ y)$ and $\lambda x\ y.\ f(x+y+a)$. The only solution is to replace `?h` by $\lambda x\ y.\ x+y+a$. Such cases admit at most one unifier, like ordinary unification. A harder case is unifying `?h a` with `a+b`; it admits two solutions for `?h`, namely $\lambda x.\ a+b$ and $\lambda x.\ x+b$. Unifying `?h a` with `a+a+b` admits four solutions; their number is exponential in the number of occurrences of `a` in the second term.

5.8.1 Substitution and the *subst* Method

Isabelle also uses function variables to express **substitution**. A typical substitution rule allows us to replace one term by another if we know that two terms are equal.

$$\frac{s = t \quad P[s/x]}{P[t/x]}$$

The rule uses a notation for substitution: $P[t/x]$ is the result of replacing x by t in P. The rule only substitutes in the positions designated by x. For example, it can derive symmetry of equality from reflexivity. Using $x = s$ for P replaces just the first s in $s = s$ by t:

$$\frac{s = t \quad \overline{s = s}}{t = s}$$

The Isabelle version of the substitution rule looks like this:

⟦?t = ?s; ?P ?s⟧ ⟹ ?P ?t   (ssubst)

Crucially, ?P is a function variable. It can be replaced by a λ-term with one bound variable, whose occurrences identify the places in which s will be replaced by t. The proof above requires the term λx. x=s.

The *simp* method replaces equals by equals, but the substitution rule gives us more control. The *subst* method is the easiest way to use the substitution rule. Suppose a proof has reached this point:

1. ⟦P x y z; Suc x < y⟧ ⟹ f z = x * y

Now we wish to apply a commutative law:

?m * ?n = ?n * ?m   (mult_commute)

Isabelle rejects our first attempt:

apply (simp add: mult_commute)

The simplifier notices the danger of looping and refuses to apply the rule.[2] The *subst* method applies mult_commute exactly once.

apply (subst mult_commute)
1. ⟦P x y z; Suc x < y⟧ ⟹ f z = y * x

As we wanted, x * y has become y * x.

The *subst* method is convenient, but to see how it works, let us examine an explicit use of the rule *ssubst*. Consider this proof:

lemma "⟦x = f x; odd(f x)⟧ ⟹ odd x"
by (erule ssubst)

---

[2] More precisely, it only applies such a rule if the new term is smaller under a specified ordering; here, x * y is already smaller than y * x.

The simplifier might loop, replacing x by f x and then by $f(f$ $x)$ and so forth. (Here *simp* can see the danger and would re-orient the equality, but in more complicated cases it can be fooled.) When we apply substitution, Isabelle replaces every x in the subgoal by f x just once: it cannot loop. The resulting subgoal is trivial by assumption, so the **by** command proves it implicitly.

We are using the *erule* method it in a novel way. Hitherto, the conclusion of the rule was just a variable such as *?R*, but it may be any term. The conclusion is unified with the subgoal just as it would be with the *rule* method. At the same time *erule* looks for an assumption that matches the rule's first premise, as usual. With *ssubst* the effect is to find, use and delete an equality assumption.

5.8.2 Unification and Its Pitfalls

Higher-order unification can be tricky. Here is an example, which you may want to skip on your first reading:

lemma "⟦x = f x; triple (f x) (f x) x⟧ $\Longrightarrow$ triple x x x"
apply (erule ssubst)
back
back
back
back
apply assumption
done

By default, Isabelle tries to substitute for all the occurrences. Applying *erule ssubst* yields this subgoal:

1. triple (f x) (f x) x $\Longrightarrow$ triple (f x) (f x) (f x)

The substitution should have been done in the first two occurrences of x only. Isabelle has gone too far. The **back** command allows us to reject this possibility and demand a new one:

1. triple (f x) (f x) x $\Longrightarrow$ triple x (f x) (f x)

Now Isabelle has left the first occurrence of x alone. That is promising but it is not the desired combination. So we use **back** again:

1. triple (f x) (f x) x $\Longrightarrow$ triple (f x) x (f x)

This also is wrong, so we use **back** again:

1. triple (f x) (f x) x $\Longrightarrow$ triple x x (f x)

And this one is wrong too. Looking carefully at the series of alternatives, we see a binary countdown with reversed bits: 111, 011, 101, 001. Invoke **back** again:

1. triple (f x) (f x) x $\Longrightarrow$ triple (f x) (f x) x

At last, we have the right combination! This goal follows by assumption.

This example shows that unification can do strange things with function variables. We were forced to select the right unifier using the **back** command. That is all right during exploration, but **back** should never appear in the final version of a proof. You can eliminate the need for **back** by giving Isabelle less freedom when you apply a rule.

One way to constrain the inference is by joining two methods in a **apply** command. Isabelle applies the first method and then the second. If the second method fails then Isabelle automatically backtracks. This process continues until the first method produces an output that the second method can use. We get a one-line proof of our example:

lemma "⟦x = f x; triple (f x) (f x) x⟧ ⟹ triple x x x"
apply (erule ssubst, assumption)
done

The **by** command works too, since it backtracks when proving subgoals by assumption:

lemma "⟦x = f x; triple (f x) (f x) x⟧ ⟹ triple x x x"
by (erule ssubst)

The most general way to constrain unification is by instantiating variables in the rule. The method `rule_tac` is similar to `rule`, but it makes some of the rule's variables denote specified terms. Also available are `drule_tac` and `erule_tac`. Here we need `erule_tac` since above we used `erule`.

lemma "⟦x = f x; triple (f x) (f x) x⟧ ⟹ triple x x x"
by (erule_tac P = "λu. triple u u x" in ssubst)

To specify a desired substitution requires instantiating the variable `?P` with a λ-expression. The bound variable occurrences in λu. P u u x indicate that the first two arguments have to be substituted, leaving the third unchanged. With this instantiation, backtracking is neither necessary nor possible.

An alternative to `rule_tac` is to use `rule` with a theorem modified using `of`, described in Sect. 5.14 below. But `rule_tac`, unlike `of`, can express instantiations that refer to ⋀-bound variables in the current subgoal.

5.9 Quantifiers

Quantifiers require formalizing syntactic substitution and the notion of arbitrary value. Consider the universal quantifier. In a logic book, its introduction rule looks like this:

$$\frac{P}{\forall x.\,P}$$

Typically, a proviso written in English says that x must not occur in the assumptions. This proviso guarantees that x can be regarded as arbitrary, since it has not been assumed to satisfy any special conditions. Isabelle's under-lying formalism, called the **meta-logic**, eliminates the need for English. It provides its own universal quantifier ($\bigwedge$) to express the notion of an arbitrary value. We have already seen another symbol of the meta-logic, namely $\Longrightarrow$, which expresses inference rules and the treatment of assumptions. The only other symbol in the meta-logic is $\equiv$, which can be used to define constants.

5.9.1 The Universal Introduction Rule

Returning to the universal quantifier, we find that having a similar quantifier as part of the meta-logic makes the introduction rule trivial to express:

$(\bigwedge x.\ ?P\ x) \implies \forall x.\ ?P\ x$ (allI)

The following trivial proof demonstrates how the universal introduction rule works.

lemma "$\forall x.\ P\ x \longrightarrow P\ x$"
apply (rule allI)
by (rule impI)

The first step invokes the rule by applying the method rule allI.

1. $\bigwedge x.\ P\ x \longrightarrow P\ x$

Note that the resulting proof state has a bound variable, namely x. The rule has replaced the universal quantifier of higher-order logic by Isabelle's meta-level quantifier. Our goal is to prove $P\ x \longrightarrow P\ x$ for arbitrary x; it is an implication, so we apply the corresponding introduction rule (impI).

1. $\bigwedge x.\ P\ x \implies P\ x$

This last subgoal is implicitly proved by assumption.

5.9.2 The Universal Elimination Rule

Now consider universal elimination. In a logic text, the rule looks like this:

$$\frac{\forall x.\ P}{P[t/x]}$$

The conclusion is P with t substituted for the variable x. Isabelle expresses substitution using a function variable:

$\forall x.\ ?P\ x \implies ?P\ ?x$ (spec)

This destruction rule takes a universally quantified formula and removes the quantifier, replacing the bound variable x by the schematic variable ?x. Recall that a schematic variable starts with a question mark and acts as a placeholder: it can be replaced by any term.

The universal elimination rule is also available in the standard elimination format. Like conjE, it never appears in logic books:

⟦∀x. ?P x; ?P ?x ⟹ ?R⟧ ⟹ ?R   (allE)

The methods *drule spec* and *erule allE* do precisely the same inference.

To see how ∀-elimination works, let us derive a rule about reducing the scope of a universal quantifier. In mathematical notation we write

$$\frac{\forall x.\, P \to Q}{P \to \forall x.\, Q}$$

with the proviso "x not free in P." Isabelle's treatment of substitution makes the proviso unnecessary. The conclusion is expressed as $P \longrightarrow (\forall x.\ Q\ x)$. No substitution for the variable P can introduce a dependence upon x: that would be a bound variable capture. Let us walk through the proof.

lemma "$(\forall x.\ P \longrightarrow Q\ x) \Longrightarrow P \longrightarrow (\forall x.\ Q\ x)$"

First we apply implies introduction (*impI*), which moves the P from the conclusion to the assumptions. Then we apply universal introduction (*allI*).

apply *(rule impI, rule allI)*
  1. ⋀x. ⟦∀x. P ⟶ Q x; P⟧ ⟹ Q x

As before, it replaces the HOL quantifier by a meta-level quantifier, producing a subgoal that binds the variable x. The leading bound variables (here x) and the assumptions (here ∀x. P ⟶ Q x and P) form the **context** for the conclusion, here Q x. Subgoals inherit the context, although assumptions can be added or deleted (as we saw earlier), while rules such as *allI* add bound variables.

Now, to reason from the universally quantified assumption, we apply the elimination rule using the *drule* method. This rule is called *spec* because it specializes a universal formula to a particular term.

apply *(drule spec)*
  1. ⋀x. ⟦P; P ⟶ Q (?x2 x)⟧ ⟹ Q x

Observe how the context has changed. The quantified formula is gone, replaced by a new assumption derived from its body. We have removed the quantifier and replaced the bound variable by the curious term *?x2 x*. This term is a placeholder: it may become any term that can be built from x. (Formally, *?x2* is an unknown of function type, applied to the argument x.) This new assumption is an implication, so we can use *modus ponens* on it, which concludes the proof.

by *(drule mp)*

Let us take a closer look at this last step. *Modus ponens* yields two subgoals: one where we prove the antecedent (in this case P) and one where we may assume the consequent. Both of these subgoals are proved by the *assumption* method, which is implicit in the **by** command. Replacing the **by** command by **apply** *(drule mp, assumption)* would have left one last subgoal:

  1. ⋀x. ⟦P; Q (?x2 x)⟧ ⟹ Q x

The consequent is Q applied to that placeholder. It may be replaced by any term built from x, and here it should simply be x. The assumption need not be identical to the conclusion, provided the two formulas are unifiable.

5.9.3 The Existential Quantifier

The concepts just presented also apply to the existential quantifier, whose introduction rule looks like this in Isabelle:

`?P ?x ⟹ ∃x. ?P x`   (exI)

If we can exhibit some x such that $P(x)$ is true, then $\exists x.P(x)$ is also true. It is a dual of the universal elimination rule, and logic texts present it using the same notation for substitution.

The existential elimination rule looks like this in a logic text:

$$\frac{\exists x.\, P \quad \begin{array}{c}[P]\\ \vdots\\ Q\end{array}}{Q}$$

It looks like this in Isabelle:

`⟦∃x. ?P x; ⋀x. ?P x ⟹ ?Q⟧ ⟹ ?Q`   (exE)

Given an existentially quantified theorem and some formula Q to prove, it creates a new assumption by removing the quantifier. As with the universal introduction rule, the textbook version imposes a proviso on the quantified variable, which Isabelle expresses using its meta-logic. It is enough to have a universal quantifier in the meta-logic; we do not need an existential quantifier to be built in as well.

Exercise 5.9.1 Prove the lemma

$$\exists x.\, P \wedge Q(x) \Longrightarrow P \wedge (\exists x.\, Q(x)).$$

Hint: the proof is similar to the one just above for the universal quantifier.

5.9.4 Renaming an Assumption: `rename_tac`

When you apply a rule such as `allI`, the quantified variable becomes a new bound variable of the new subgoal. Isabelle tries to avoid changing its name, but sometimes it has to choose a new name in order to avoid a clash. The result may not be ideal:

```
lemma "x < y ⟹ ∀x y. P x (f y)"
apply (intro allI)
 1. ⋀xa ya. x < y ⟹ P xa (f ya)
```

The names x and y were already in use, so the new bound variables are called xa and ya. You can rename them by invoking `rename_tac`:

apply *(rename_tac v w)*
 1. $\bigwedge$*v w. x < y* $\Longrightarrow$ *P v (f w)*

Recall that `rule_tac` instantiates a theorem with specified terms. These terms may involve the goal's bound variables, but beware of referring to variables like xa. A future change to your theories could change the set of names produced at top level, so that xa changes to xb or reverts to x. It is safer to rename automatically-generated variables before mentioning them.

If the subgoal has more bound variables than there are names given to `rename_tac`, the rightmost ones are renamed.

5.9.5 Reusing an Assumption: `frule`

Note that `drule spec` removes the universal quantifier and — as usual with elimination rules — discards the original formula. Sometimes, a universal formula has to be kept so that it can be used again. Then we use a new method: `frule`. It acts like `drule` but copies rather than replaces the selected assumption. The f is for *forward*.

In this example, going from P a to $P(h(h \ a))$ requires two uses of the quantified assumption, one for each h in $h(h \ a)$.

lemma *"*$[\![\forall x.\ P \ x \longrightarrow P \ (h \ x); \ \ P \ a]\!] \Longrightarrow P(h \ (h \ a))$*"*

Examine the subgoal left by `frule`:

apply *(frule spec)*
 1. $[\![\forall x.\ P \ x \longrightarrow P \ (h \ x); \ P \ a; \ P \ ?x \longrightarrow P \ (h \ ?x)]\!] \Longrightarrow P \ (h \ (h \ a))$

It is what `drule` would have left except that the quantified assumption is still present. Next we apply `mp` to the implication and the assumption P a:

apply *(drule mp, assumption)*
 1. $[\![\forall x.\ P \ x \longrightarrow P \ (h \ x); \ P \ a; \ P \ (h \ a)]\!] \Longrightarrow P \ (h \ (h \ a))$

We have created the assumption $P(h \ a)$, which is progress. To continue the proof, we apply `spec` again. We shall not need it again, so we can use `drule`.

apply *(drule spec)*
 1. $[\![P \ a; \ P \ (h \ a); \ P \ ?x2 \longrightarrow P \ (h \ ?x2)]\!] \Longrightarrow P \ (h \ (h \ a))$

The new assumption bridges the gap between $P(h \ a)$ and $P(h(h \ a))$.

by *(drule mp)*

A final remark. Replacing this **by** command with

apply *(drule mp, assumption)*

would not work: it would add a second copy of $P(h \ a)$ instead of the desired assumption, $P(h(h \ a))$. The **by** command forces Isabelle to backtrack until it finds the correct one. Alternatively, we could have used the **apply** command and bundled the `drule mp` with *two* calls of `assumption`. Or, of course, we could have given the entire proof to `auto`.

5.9.6 Instantiating a Quantifier Explicitly

We can prove a theorem of the form $\exists x.\, P\, x$ by exhibiting a suitable term t such that $P\, t$ is true. Dually, we can use an assumption of the form $\forall x.\, P\, x$ to generate a new assumption $P\, t$ for a suitable term t. In many cases, Isabelle makes the correct choice automatically, constructing the term by unification. In other cases, the required term is not obvious and we must specify it ourselves. Suitable methods are `rule_tac`, `drule_tac` and `erule_tac`.

We have seen (just above, Sect. 5.9.5) a proof of this lemma:

lemma "$[\![\forall x.\ P\ x \longrightarrow P\ (h\ x);\ P\ a]\!] \implies P(h\ (h\ a))$"

We had reached this subgoal:

1. $[\![\forall x.\ P\ x \longrightarrow P\ (h\ x);\ P\ a;\ P\ (h\ a)]\!] \implies P\ (h\ (h\ a))$

The proof requires instantiating the quantified assumption with the term $h\ a$.

apply *(drule_tac x = "h a" in spec)*
1. $[\![P\ a;\ P\ (h\ a);\ P\ (h\ a) \longrightarrow P\ (h\ (h\ a))]\!] \implies P\ (h\ (h\ a))$

We have forced the desired instantiation.

Existential formulas can be instantiated too. The next example uses the **divides** relation of number theory:

$?m\ dvd\ ?n \equiv \exists k.\ ?n = ?m * k$ (dvd_def)

Let us prove that multiplication of natural numbers is monotone with respect to the divides relation:

lemma *mult_dvd_mono:* "$[\![i\ dvd\ m;\ j\ dvd\ n]\!] \implies i*j\ dvd\ (m*n\ ::\ nat)$"
apply *(simp add: dvd_def)*

Unfolding the definition of divides has left this subgoal:

1. $[\![\exists k.\ m = i * k;\ \exists k.\ n = j * k]\!] \implies \exists k.\ m * n = i * j * k$

Next, we eliminate the two existential quantifiers in the assumptions:

apply *(erule exE)*
1. $\bigwedge k.\ [\![\exists k.\ n = j * k;\ m = i * k]\!] \implies \exists k.\ m * n = i * j * k$
apply *(erule exE)*
1. $\bigwedge k\ ka.\ [\![m = i * k;\ n = j * ka]\!] \implies \exists k.\ m * n = i * j * k$

The term needed to instantiate the remaining quantifier is $k*ka$. But ka is an automatically-generated name. As noted above, references to such variable names makes a proof less resilient to future changes. So, first we rename the most recent variable to l:

apply *(rename_tac l)*
1. $\bigwedge k\ l.\ [\![m = i * k;\ n = j * l]\!] \implies \exists k.\ m * n = i * j * k$

We instantiate the quantifier with $k*l$:

apply *(rule_tac x="k*l" in exI)*
1. $\bigwedge k\ ka.\ [\![m = i * k;\ n = j * ka]\!] \implies m * n = i * j * (k * ka)$

The rest is automatic, by arithmetic.

apply *simp*
done

5.10 Description Operators

HOL provides two description operators. A **definite description** formalizes the word "the," as in "the greatest divisior of n." It returns an arbitrary value unless the formula has a unique solution. An **indefinite description** formalizes the word "some," as in "some member of S." It differs from a definite description in not requiring the solution to be unique: it uses the axiom of choice to pick any solution.

!
• Description operators can be hard to reason about. Novices should try to avoid them. Fortunately, descriptions are seldom required.

5.10.1 Definite Descriptions

A definite description is traditionally written $\iota x.P(x)$. It denotes the x such that $P(x)$ is true, provided there exists a unique such x; otherwise, it returns an arbitrary value of the expected type. Isabelle uses THE for the Greek letter ι.

We reason using this rule, where a is the unique solution:

$$[\![P\ a;\ \textstyle\bigwedge x.\ P\ x \implies x = a]\!] \implies (THE\ x.\ P\ x) = a \qquad (the\_equality)$$

For instance, we can define the cardinality of a finite set A to be that n such that A is in one-to-one correspondence with $\{1, \dots, n\}$. We can then prove that the cardinality of the empty set is zero (since $n = 0$ satisfies the description) and proceed to prove other facts.

A more challenging example illustrates how Isabelle/HOL defines the least number operator, which denotes the least x satisfying P:

$$(LEAST\ x.\ P\ x) = (THE\ x.\ P\ x\ \wedge\ (\forall y.\ P\ y\ \longrightarrow\ x \leq y))$$

Let us prove the analogue of the_equality for LEAST.

theorem *Least_equality:*
    "$[\![P\ (k::nat);\ \ \forall x.\ P\ x\ \longrightarrow\ k \leq x]\!] \implies (LEAST\ x.\ P\ x) = k$"
apply *(simp add: Least_def)*

1. $[\![P\ k;\ \forall x.\ P\ x\ \longrightarrow\ k \leq x]\!]$
    $\implies (THE\ x.\ P\ x\ \wedge\ (\forall y.\ P\ y\ \longrightarrow\ x \leq y)) = k$

The first step has merely unfolded the definition.

apply *(rule the_equality)*

1. $[\![P\ k;\ \forall x.\ P\ x\ \longrightarrow\ k \leq x]\!] \Longrightarrow P\ k\ \wedge\ (\forall y.\ P\ y\ \longrightarrow\ k \leq y)$
2. $\bigwedge x.\ [\![P\ k;\ \forall x.\ P\ x\ \longrightarrow\ k \leq x;\ P\ x\ \wedge\ (\forall y.\ P\ y\ \longrightarrow\ x \leq y)]\!]$
   $\Longrightarrow x = k$

As always with *the_equality*, we must show existence and uniqueness of the claimed solution, *k*. Existence, the first subgoal, is trivial. Uniqueness, the second subgoal, follows by antisymmetry:

$$[\![x \leq y;\ y \leq x]\!] \Longrightarrow x = y \qquad\qquad (order\_antisym)$$

The assumptions imply both $k \leq x$ and $x \leq k$. One call to **auto** does it all:

by *(auto intro: order_antisym)*

5.10.2 Indefinite Descriptions

An indefinite description is traditionally written $\varepsilon x.P(x)$ and is known as Hilbert's ε-operator. It denotes some x such that $P(x)$ is true, provided one exists. Isabelle uses *SOME* for the Greek letter ε.

Here is the definition of *inv*, which expresses inverses of functions:

$$inv\ f\ \equiv\ \lambda y.\ SOME\ x.\ f\ x = y \qquad\qquad (inv\_def)$$

Using *SOME* rather than *THE* makes *inv f* behave well even if *f* is not injective. As it happens, most useful theorems about *inv* do assume the function to be injective.

The inverse of *f*, when applied to *y*, returns some *x* such that *f x = y*. For example, we can prove *inv Suc* really is the inverse of the *Suc* function

lemma *"inv Suc (Suc n) = n"*
by *(simp add: inv_def)*

The proof is a one-liner: the subgoal simplifies to a degenerate application of *SOME*, which is then erased. In detail, the left-hand side simplifies to *SOME x. Suc x = Suc n*, then to *SOME x. x = n* and finally to *n*.

We know nothing about what *inv Suc* returns when applied to zero. The proof above still treats *SOME* as a definite description, since it only reasons about situations in which the value is described uniquely. Indeed, *SOME* satisfies this rule:

$$[\![P\ a;\ \bigwedge x.\ P\ x \Longrightarrow x = a]\!] \Longrightarrow (SOME\ x.\ P\ x) = a \qquad (some\_equality)$$

To go further is tricky and requires rules such as these:

$$P\ x \Longrightarrow P\ (SOME\ x.\ P\ x) \qquad\qquad\qquad\qquad (someI)$$
$$[\![P\ a;\ \bigwedge x.\ P\ x \Longrightarrow Q\ x]\!] \Longrightarrow Q\ (SOME\ x.\ P\ x) \qquad\qquad (someI2)$$

Rule *someI* is basic: if anything satisfies *P* then so does *SOME x. P x*. The repetition of *P* in the conclusion makes it difficult to apply in a backward proof, so the derived rule *someI2* is also provided.

For example, let us prove the axiom of choice:

theorem `axiom_of_choice:` `"(∀x. ∃y. P x y) ⟹ ∃f. ∀x. P x (f x)"`
apply `(rule exI, rule allI)`

1. ⋀x. ∀x. ∃y. P x y ⟹ P x (?f x)

We have applied the introduction rules; now it is time to apply the elimination rules.

apply `(drule spec, erule exE)`

1. ⋀x y. P (?x2 x) y ⟹ P x (?f x)

The rule *someI* automatically instantiates f to λx. SOME y. P x y, which is the choice function. It also instantiates ?x2 x to x.

by `(rule someI)`

Historical Note. The original purpose of Hilbert's ε-operator was to express an existential destruction rule:

$$\frac{\exists x.\, P}{P[(\varepsilon x.P)/\,x]}$$

This rule is seldom used for that purpose — it can cause exponential blow-up — but it is occasionally used as an introduction rule for ε-operator. Its name in HOL is *someI_ex*.

5.11 Some Proofs That Fail

Most of the examples in this tutorial involve proving theorems. But not every conjecture is true, and it can be instructive to see how proofs fail. Here we attempt to prove a distributive law involving the existential quantifier and conjunction.

lemma `"(∃x. P x) ∧ (∃x. Q x) ⟹ ∃x. P x ∧ Q x"`

The first steps are routine. We apply conjunction elimination to break the assumption into two existentially quantified assumptions. Applying existential elimination removes one of the quantifiers.

apply `(erule conjE)`
apply `(erule exE)`
1. ⋀x. ⟦∃x. Q x; P x⟧ ⟹ ∃x. P x ∧ Q x

When we remove the other quantifier, we get a different bound variable in the subgoal. (The name xa is generated automatically.)

apply `(erule exE)`
1. ⋀x xa. ⟦P x; Q xa⟧ ⟹ ∃x. P x ∧ Q x

The proviso of the existential elimination rule has forced the variables to differ: we can hardly expect two arbitrary values to be equal! There is no way to prove this subgoal. Removing the conclusion's existential quantifier yields two identical placeholders, which can become any term involving the variables x and xa. We need one to become x and the other to become xa, but Isabelle requires all instances of a placeholder to be identical.

apply *(rule exI)*
apply *(rule conjI)*
1. $\bigwedge x\ xa.\ [\![P\ x;\ Q\ xa]\!] \implies P\ (?x3\ x\ xa)$
2. $\bigwedge x\ xa.\ [\![P\ x;\ Q\ xa]\!] \implies Q\ (?x3\ x\ xa)$

We can prove either subgoal using the `assumption` method. If we prove the first one, the placeholder changes into x.

 apply *assumption*
 1. $\bigwedge x\ xa.\ [\![P\ x;\ Q\ xa]\!] \implies Q\ x$

We are left with a subgoal that cannot be proved. Applying the `assumption` method results in an error message:

*** *empty result sequence -- proof command failed*

When interacting with Isabelle via the shell interface, you can abandon a proof using the **oops** command.

   Here is another abortive proof, illustrating the interaction between bound variables and unknowns. If R is a reflexive relation, is there an x such that $R\,x\,y$ holds for all y? Let us see what happens when we attempt to prove it.

lemma *"*$\forall y.\ R\ y\ y \implies \exists x.\ \forall y.\ R\ x\ y$*"*

First, we remove the existential quantifier. The new proof state has an unknown, namely $?x$.

apply *(rule exI)*
 1. $\forall y.\ R\ y\ y \implies \forall y.\ R\ ?x\ y$

It looks like we can just apply `assumption`, but it fails. Isabelle refuses to substitute y, a bound variable, for $?x$; that would be a bound variable capture. We can still try to finish the proof in some other way. We remove the universal quantifier from the conclusion, moving the bound variable y into the subgoal. But note that it is still bound!

apply *(rule allI)*
 1. $\bigwedge y.\ \forall y.\ R\ y\ y \implies R\ ?x\ y$

Finally, we try to apply our reflexivity assumption. We obtain a new assumption whose identical placeholders may be replaced by any term involving y.

apply *(drule spec)*
 1. $\bigwedge y.\ R\ (?z2\ y)\ (?z2\ y) \implies R\ ?x\ y$

This subgoal can only be proved by putting y for all the placeholders, making the assumption and conclusion become $R\ y\ y$. Isabelle can replace ?z2 y by y; this involves instantiating ?z2 to the identity function. But, just as two steps earlier, Isabelle refuses to substitute y for ?x. This example is typical of how Isabelle enforces sound quantifier reasoning.

5.12 Proving Theorems Using the `blast` Method

It is hard to prove many theorems using the methods described above. A proof may be hundreds of steps long. You may need to search among different ways of proving certain subgoals. Often a choice that proves one subgoal renders another impossible to prove. There are further complications that we have not discussed, concerning negation and disjunction. Isabelle's **classical reasoner** is a family of tools that perform such proofs automatically. The most important of these is the `blast` method.

In this section, we shall first see how to use the classical reasoner in its default mode and then how to insert additional rules, enabling it to work in new problem domains.

We begin with examples from pure predicate logic. The following example is known as Andrew's challenge. Peter Andrews designed it to be hard to prove by automatic means. It is particularly hard for a resolution prover, where converting the nested biconditionals to clause form produces a combinatorial explosion [30]. However, the `blast` method proves it in a fraction of a second.

lemma "$((\exists x.\ \forall y.\ p(x)=p(y)) = ((\exists x.\ q(x))=(\forall y.\ p(y)))) = ((\exists x.\ \forall y.\ q(x)=q(y)) = ((\exists x.\ p(x))=(\forall y.\ q(y))))$"
by `blast`

The next example is a logic problem composed by Lewis Carroll. The `blast` method finds it trivial. Moreover, it turns out that not all of the assumptions are necessary. We can experiment with variations of this formula and see which ones can be proved.

lemma "$(\forall x.\ honest(x)\ \wedge\ industrious(x)\ \longrightarrow\ healthy(x))\ \wedge$
    $\neg\ (\exists x.\ grocer(x)\ \wedge\ healthy(x))\ \wedge$
    $(\forall x.\ industrious(x)\ \wedge\ grocer(x)\ \longrightarrow\ honest(x))\ \wedge$
    $(\forall x.\ cyclist(x)\ \longrightarrow\ industrious(x))\ \wedge$
    $(\forall x.\ \neg healthy(x)\ \wedge\ cyclist(x)\ \longrightarrow\ \neg honest(x))$
    $\longrightarrow\ (\forall x.\ grocer(x)\ \longrightarrow\ \neg cyclist(x))$"
by `blast`

The `blast` method is also effective for set theory, which is described in the next chapter. The formula below may look horrible, but the `blast` method proves it in milliseconds.

lemma "$(\bigcup i{\in}I.\ A(i))\ \cap\ (\bigcup j{\in}J.\ B(j)) = (\bigcup i{\in}I.\ \bigcup j{\in}J.\ A(i)\ \cap\ B(j))$"
by `blast`

Few subgoals are couched purely in predicate logic and set theory. We can extend the scope of the classical reasoner by giving it new rules. Extending it effectively requires understanding the notions of introduction, elimination and destruction rules. Moreover, there is a distinction between safe and unsafe rules. A **safe** rule is one that can be applied backwards without losing information; an **unsafe** rule loses information, perhaps transforming the subgoal into one that cannot be proved. The safe/unsafe distinction affects the proof search: if a proof attempt fails, the classical reasoner backtracks to the most recent unsafe rule application and makes another choice.

An important special case avoids all these complications. A logical equivalence, which in higher-order logic is an equality between formulas, can be given to the classical reasoner and simplifier by using the attribute `iff`. You should do so if the right hand side of the equivalence is simpler than the left-hand side.

For example, here is a simple fact about list concatenation. The result of appending two lists is empty if and only if both of the lists are themselves empty. Obviously, applying this equivalence will result in a simpler goal. When stating this lemma, we include the `iff` attribute. Once we have proved the lemma, Isabelle will make it known to the classical reasoner (and to the simplifier).

```
lemma [iff]: "(xs@ys = []) = (xs=[] ∧ ys=[])"
apply (induct_tac xs)
apply (simp_all)
done
```

This fact about multiplication is also appropriate for the `iff` attribute:

```
(?m * ?n = 0) = (?m = 0 ∨ ?n = 0)
```

A product is zero if and only if one of the factors is zero. The reasoning involves a disjunction. Proving new rules for disjunctive reasoning is hard, but translating to an actual disjunction works: the classical reasoner handles disjunction properly.

In more detail, this is how the `iff` attribute works. It converts the equivalence $P = Q$ to a pair of rules: the introduction rule $Q \implies P$ and the destruction rule $P \implies Q$. It gives both to the classical reasoner as safe rules, ensuring that all occurrences of P in a subgoal are replaced by Q. The simplifier performs the same replacement, since `iff` gives $P = Q$ to the simplifier.

Classical reasoning is different from simplification. Simplification is deterministic. It applies rewrite rules repeatedly, as long as possible, transforming a goal into another goal. Classical reasoning uses search and backtracking in order to prove a goal outright.

5.13 Other Classical Reasoning Methods

The `blast` method is our main workhorse for proving theorems automatically. Other components of the classical reasoner interact with the simplifier. Still others perform classical reasoning to a limited extent, giving the user fine control over the proof.

Of the latter methods, the most useful is `clarify`. It performs all obvious reasoning steps without splitting the goal into multiple parts. It does not apply unsafe rules that could render the goal unprovable. By performing the obvious steps, `clarify` lays bare the difficult parts of the problem, where human intervention is necessary.

For example, the following conjecture is false:

lemma "$(\forall x.\ P\ x) \land (\exists x.\ Q\ x) \longrightarrow (\forall x.\ P\ x \land Q\ x)$"
apply `clarify`

The `blast` method would simply fail, but `clarify` presents a subgoal that helps us see why we cannot continue the proof.

   1. $\bigwedge x\ xa.\ [\![\forall x.\ P\ x;\ Q\ xa]\!] \Longrightarrow P\ x \land Q\ x$

The proof must fail because the assumption $Q\ xa$ and conclusion $Q\ x$ refer to distinct bound variables. To reach this state, `clarify` applied the introduction rules for $\longrightarrow$ and $\forall$ and the elimination rule for $\land$. It did not apply the introduction rule for $\land$ because of its policy never to split goals.

Also available is `clarsimp`, a method that interleaves `clarify` and `simp`. Also there is `safe`, which like `clarify` performs obvious steps but even applies those that split goals.

The `force` method applies the classical reasoner and simplifier to one goal. Unless it can prove the goal, it fails. Contrast that with the `auto` method, which also combines classical reasoning with simplification. The latter's purpose is to prove all the easy subgoals and parts of subgoals. Unfortunately, it can produce large numbers of new subgoals; also, since it proves some subgoals and splits others, it obscures the structure of the proof tree. The `force` method does not have these drawbacks. Another difference: `force` tries harder than `auto` to prove its goal, so it can take much longer to terminate.

Older components of the classical reasoner have largely been superseded by `blast`, but they still have niche applications. Most important among these are `fast` and `best`. While `blast` searches for proofs using a built-in first-order reasoner, these earlier methods search for proofs using standard Isabelle inference. That makes them slower but enables them to work in the presence of the more unusual features of Isabelle rules, such as type classes and function unknowns. For example, recall the introduction rule for Hilbert's ε-operator:

`?P ?x` $\Longrightarrow$ `?P (SOME x. ?P x)`   (someI)

The repeated occurrence of the variable `?P` makes this rule tricky to apply. Consider this contrived example:

lemma "$[\![Q\ a;\ P\ a]\!]$
      $\Longrightarrow P\ (SOME\ x.\ P\ x \land Q\ x) \land Q\ (SOME\ x.\ P\ x \land Q\ x)$"
apply (`rule someI`)

We can apply rule *someI* explicitly. It yields the following subgoal:

1. $\llbracket Q\ a;\ P\ a \rrbracket \implies P\ ?x \wedge Q\ ?x$

The proof from this point is trivial. Could we have proved the theorem with a single command? Not using *blast*: it cannot perform the higher-order unification needed here. The *fast* method succeeds:

apply (*fast intro!: someI*)

The *best* method is similar to *fast* but it uses a best-first search instead of depth-first search. Accordingly, it is slower but is less susceptible to divergence. Transitivity rules usually cause *fast* to loop where *best* can often manage.

Here is a summary of the classical reasoning methods:

- *blast* works automatically and is the fastest
- *clarify* and *clarsimp* perform obvious steps without splitting the goal; *safe* even splits goals
- *force* uses classical reasoning and simplification to prove a goal; *auto* is similar but leaves what it cannot prove
- *fast* and *best* are legacy methods that work well with rules involving unusual features

A table illustrates the relationships among four of these methods.

	no split	split
no simp	clarify	safe
simp	clarsimp	auto

5.14 Forward Proof: Transforming Theorems

Forward proof means deriving new facts from old ones. It is the most fundamental type of proof. Backward proof, by working from goals to subgoals, can help us find a difficult proof. But it is not always the best way of presenting the proof so found. Forward proof is particularly good for reasoning from the general to the specific. For example, consider this distributive law for the greatest common divisor:

$$k \times \gcd(m, n) = \gcd(k \times m, k \times n)$$

Putting $m = 1$ we get (since $\gcd(1, n) = 1$ and $k \times 1 = k$)

$$k = \gcd(k, k \times n)$$

We have derived a new fact; if re-oriented, it might be useful for simplification. After re-orienting it and putting $n = 1$, we derive another useful law:

$$\gcd(k, k) = k$$

Substituting values for variables — instantiation — is a forward step. Re-orientation works by applying the symmetry of equality to an equation, so it too is a forward step.

5.14.1 Modifying a Theorem Using *of* and *THEN*

Let us reproduce our examples in Isabelle. Recall that in Sect. 3.5.3 we declared the recursive function *gcd*:

```
consts gcd :: "nat*nat ⇒ nat"
recdef gcd "measure ((λ(m,n).n))"
    "gcd (m,n) = (if n=0 then m else gcd(n, m mod n))"
```

From this definition, it is possible to prove the distributive law. That takes us to the starting point for our example.

```
?k * gcd (?m, ?n) = gcd (?k * ?m, ?k * ?n)          (gcd_mult_distrib2)
```

The first step in our derivation is to replace ?m by 1. We instantiate the theorem using *of*, which identifies variables in order of their appearance from left to right. In this case, the variables are ?k, ?m and ?n. So, the expression [of k 1] replaces ?k by k and ?m by 1.

```
lemmas gcd_mult_0 = gcd_mult_distrib2 [of k 1]
```

The keyword **lemmas** declares a new theorem, which can be derived from an existing one using attributes such as [of k 1]. The command *thm gcd_mult_0* displays the result:

```
    k * gcd (1, ?n) = gcd (k * 1, k * ?n)
```

Something is odd: k is an ordinary variable, while ?n is schematic. We did not specify an instantiation for ?n. In its present form, the theorem does not allow substitution for k. One solution is to avoid giving an instantiation for ?k: instead of a term we can put an underscore (_). For example,

```
    gcd_mult_distrib2 [of _ 1]
```

replaces ?m by 1 but leaves ?k unchanged.

The next step is to put the theorem gcd_mult_0 into a simplified form, performing the steps $gcd(1, n) = 1$ and $k \times 1 = k$. The *simplified* attribute takes a theorem and returns the result of simplifying it, with respect to the default simplification rules:

```
lemmas gcd_mult_1 = gcd_mult_0 [simplified]
```

Again, we display the resulting theorem:

```
    k = gcd (k, k * ?n)
```

To re-orient the equation requires the symmetry rule:

```
?s = ?t ⟹ ?t = ?s                                             (sym)
```

The following declaration gives our equation to `sym`:

   lemmas `gcd_mult = gcd_mult_1 [THEN sym]`

Here is the result:

   `gcd (k, k * ?n) = k`

`THEN sym` gives the current theorem to the rule `sym` and returns the resulting conclusion. The effect is to exchange the two operands of the equality. Typically `THEN` is used with destruction rules. Also useful is `THEN spec`, which removes the quantifier from a theorem of the form $\forall x.\, P$, and `THEN mp`, which converts the implication $P \to Q$ into the rule $\dfrac{P}{Q}$. Similar to `mp` are the following two rules, which extract the two directions of reasoning about a boolean equivalence:

$\llbracket ?Q = ?P;\ ?Q \rrbracket \implies ?P$ (iffD1)
$\llbracket ?P = ?Q;\ ?Q \rrbracket \implies ?P$ (iffD2)

Normally we would never name the intermediate theorems such as `gcd_mult_0` and `gcd_mult_1` but would combine the three forward steps:

lemmas `gcd_mult = gcd_mult_distrib2 [of k 1, simplified, THEN sym]`

The directives, or attributes, are processed from left to right. This declaration of `gcd_mult` is equivalent to the previous one.

   Such declarations can make the proof script hard to read. Better is to state the new lemma explicitly and to prove it using a single `rule` method whose operand is expressed using forward reasoning:

lemma `gcd_mult [simp]: "gcd(k, k*n) = k"`
by `(rule gcd_mult_distrib2 [of k 1, simplified, THEN sym])`

Compared with the previous proof of `gcd_mult`, this version shows the reader what has been proved. Also, the result will be processed in the normal way. In particular, Isabelle generalizes over all variables: the resulting theorem will have `?k` instead of `k`.

   At the start of this section, we also saw a proof of $\gcd(k, k) = k$. Here is the Isabelle version:

lemma `gcd_self [simp]: "gcd(k,k) = k"`
by `(rule gcd_mult [of k 1, simplified])`

! To give `of` a nonatomic term, enclose it in quotation marks, as in `[of "k*m"]`.
• The term must not contain unknowns: an attribute such as `[of "?k*m"]` will be rejected.

Exercise 5.14.1 In Sect. 5.8.1 the method `subst mult_commute` was applied. How can we achieve the same effect using `THEN` with the rule `ssubst`?

5.14.2 Modifying a Theorem Using *OF*

Recall that *of* generates an instance of a rule by specifying values for its variables. Analogous is *OF*, which generates an instance of a rule by specifying facts for its premises.

We again need the divides relation of number theory, which as we recall is defined by

```
?m dvd ?n ≡ ∃k. ?n = ?m * k                                   (dvd_def)
```

Suppose, for example, that we have proved the following rule. It states that if k and n are relatively prime and if k divides $m \times n$ then k divides m.

```
[gcd(?k,?n)=1; ?k dvd ?m * ?n] ⟹ ?k dvd ?m      (relprime_dvd_mult)
```

We can use *OF* to create an instance of this rule. First, we prove an instance of its first premise:

```
lemma relprime_20_81: "gcd(20,81) = 1"
by (simp add: gcd.simps)
```

We have evaluated an application of the *gcd* function by simplification. Expression evaluation involving recursive functions is not guaranteed to terminate, and it can be slow; Isabelle performs arithmetic by rewriting symbolic bit strings. Here, however, the simplification takes less than one second. We can give this new lemma to *OF*. The expression

```
    relprime_dvd_mult [OF relprime_20_81]
```

yields the theorem

```
    20 dvd (?m * 81) ⟹ 20 dvd ?m
```

OF takes any number of operands. Consider the following facts about the divides relation:

```
[?k dvd ?m; ?k dvd ?n] ⟹ ?k dvd ?m + ?n                       (dvd_add)
?m dvd ?m                                                     (dvd_refl)
```

Let us supply *dvd_refl* for each of the premises of *dvd_add*:

```
    dvd_add [OF dvd_refl dvd_refl]
```

Here is the theorem that we have expressed:

```
    ?k dvd (?k + ?k)
```

As with *of*, we can use the _ symbol to leave some positions unspecified:

```
    dvd_add [OF _ dvd_refl]
```

The result is

```
    ?k dvd ?m ⟹ ?k dvd ?m + ?k
```

You may have noticed that *THEN* and *OF* are based on the same idea, namely to combine two rules. They differ in the order of the combination and thus in their effect. We use *THEN* typically with a destruction rule to extract a subformula of the current theorem. We use *OF* with a list of facts to generate an instance of the current theorem.

Here is a summary of some primitives for forward reasoning:

- *of* instantiates the variables of a rule to a list of terms
- *OF* applies a rule to a list of theorems
- *THEN* gives a theorem to a named rule and returns the conclusion
- *simplified* applies the simplifier to a theorem
- **lemmas** assigns a name to the theorem produced by the attributes above

5.15 Forward Reasoning in a Backward Proof

We have seen that the forward proof directives work well within a backward proof. There are many ways to achieve a forward style using our existing proof methods. We shall also meet some new methods that perform forward reasoning.

The methods *drule*, *frule*, *drule_tac*, etc., reason forward from a subgoal. We have seen them already, using rules such as *mp* and *spec* to operate on formulae. They can also operate on terms, using rules such as these:

$$x = y \implies f\ x = f\ y \qquad\qquad \text{(arg\_cong)}$$
$$i \leq j \implies i * k \leq j * k \qquad\qquad \text{(mult\_le\_mono1)}$$

For example, let us prove a fact about divisibility in the natural numbers:

lemma "2 ≤ u ⟹ u*m ≠ Suc(u*n)"
apply (intro notI)
  1. ⟦2 ≤ u; u * m = Suc (u * n)⟧ ⟹ False

The key step is to apply the function ... *mod u* to both sides of the equation u*m = Suc(u*n):

apply (drule_tac f="λx. x mod u" in arg_cong)
  1. ⟦2 ≤ u; u * m mod u = Suc (u * n) mod u⟧ ⟹ False

Simplification reduces the left side to 0 and the right side to 1, yielding the required contradiction.

apply (simp add: mod_Suc)
done

Our proof has used a fact about remainder:

Suc m mod n =
(if Suc (m mod n) = n then 0 else Suc (m mod n))   (mod_Suc)

5.15.1 The Method `insert`

The `insert` method inserts a given theorem as a new assumption of the current subgoal. This already is a forward step; moreover, we may (as always when using a theorem) apply `of`, `THEN` and other directives. The new assumption can then be used to help prove the subgoal.

For example, consider this theorem about the divides relation. The first proof step inserts the distributive law for `gcd`. We specify its variables as shown.

lemma `relprime_dvd_mult:`
        `"⟦gcd(k,n)=1; k dvd m*n⟧ ⟹ k dvd m"`
apply `(insert gcd_mult_distrib2 [of m k n])`

In the resulting subgoal, note how the equation has been inserted:

1. `⟦gcd (k, n) = 1; k dvd m * n; m * gcd (k, n) = gcd (m * k, m * n)⟧`
   `⟹ k dvd m`

The next proof step utilizes the assumption `gcd(k,n) = 1`:

apply`(simp)`
   1. `⟦gcd (k, n) = 1; k dvd (m * n);  m = gcd (m * k, m * n)⟧`
      `⟹ k dvd m`

Simplification has yielded an equation for `m`. The rest of the proof is omitted.

Here is another demonstration of `insert`. Division and remainder obey a well-known law:

`(?m div ?n) * ?n + ?m mod ?n = ?m`   (`mod_div_equality`)

We refer to this law explicitly in the following proof:

lemma `div_mult_self_is_m:`
        `"0<n ⟹ (m*n) div n = (m::nat)"`
apply `(insert mod_div_equality [of "m*n" n])`
apply `(simp)`
done

The first step inserts the law, specifying `m*n` and `n` for its variables. Notice that non-trivial expressions must be enclosed in quotation marks. Here is the resulting subgoal, with its new assumption:

1. `⟦0 < n;  (m * n) div n * n + (m * n) mod n = m * n⟧`
   `⟹ (m * n) div n = m`

Simplification reduces `(m * n) mod n` to zero. Then it cancels the factor `n` on both sides of the equation `(m * n) div n * n = m * n`, proving the theorem.

! Any unknowns in the theorem given to `insert` will be universally quantified in
• the new assumption.

5.15.2 The Method `subgoal_tac`

A related method is `subgoal_tac`, but instead of inserting a theorem as an assumption, it inserts an arbitrary formula. This formula must be proved later as a separate subgoal. The idea is to claim that the formula holds on the basis of the current assumptions, to use this claim to complete the proof, and finally to justify the claim. It gives the proof some structure. If you find yourself generating a complex assumption by a long series of forward steps, consider using `subgoal_tac` instead: you can state the formula you are aiming for, and perhaps prove it automatically.

Look at the following example.

```
lemma "⟦(z::int) < 37; 66 < 2*z; z*z ≠ 1225; Q(34); Q(36)⟧
        ⟹ Q(z)"
apply (subgoal_tac "z = 34 ∨ z = 36")
apply blast
apply (subgoal_tac "z ≠ 35")
apply arith
apply force
done
```

The first assumption tells us that z is no greater than 36. The second tells us that z is at least 34. The third assumption tells us that z cannot be 35, since $35 \times 35 = 1225$. So z is either 34 or 36, and since Q holds for both of those values, we have the conclusion.

The Isabelle proof closely follows this reasoning. The first step is to claim that z is either 34 or 36. The resulting proof state gives us two subgoals:

```
 1. ⟦z < 37; 66 < 2 * z; z * z ≠ 1225; Q 34; Q 36;
     z = 34 ∨ z = 36⟧
     ⟹ Q z
 2. ⟦z < 37; 66 < 2 * z; z * z ≠ 1225; Q 34; Q 36⟧
     ⟹ z = 34 ∨ z = 36
```

The first subgoal is trivial (`blast`), but for the second Isabelle needs help to eliminate the case $z=35$. The second invocation of `subgoal_tac` leaves two subgoals:

```
 1. ⟦z < 37; 66 < 2 * z; z * z ≠ 1225; Q 34; Q 36;
     z ≠ 35⟧
     ⟹ z = 34 ∨ z = 36
 2. ⟦z < 37; 66 < 2 * z; z * z ≠ 1225; Q 34; Q 36⟧
     ⟹ z ≠ 35
```

Assuming that z is not 35, the first subgoal follows by linear arithmetic (`arith`). For the second subgoal we apply the method `force`, which proceeds by assuming that $z=35$ and arriving at a contradiction.

Summary of these methods:

- `insert` adds a theorem as a new assumption
- `subgoal_tac` adds a formula as a new assumption and leaves the subgoal of proving that formula

5.16 Managing Large Proofs

Naturally you should try to divide proofs into manageable parts. Look for lemmas that can be proved separately. Sometimes you will observe that they are instances of much simpler facts. On other occasions, no lemmas suggest themselves and you are forced to cope with a long proof involving many subgoals.

5.16.1 Tacticals, or Control Structures

If the proof is long, perhaps it at least has some regularity. Then you can express it more concisely using **tacticals**, which provide control structures. Here is a proof (it would be a one-liner using *blast*, but forget that) that contains a series of repeated commands:

lemma "$\llbracket P \longrightarrow Q; \ Q \longrightarrow R; \ R \longrightarrow S; \ P \rrbracket \implies S$"
apply *(drule mp, assumption)*
apply *(drule mp, assumption)*
apply *(drule mp, assumption)*
apply *(assumption)*
done

Each of the three identical commands finds an implication and proves its antecedent by assumption. The first one finds $P \longrightarrow Q$ and P, concluding Q; the second one concludes R and the third one concludes S. The final step matches the assumption S with the goal to be proved.

Suffixing a method with a plus sign (+) expresses one or more repetitions:

lemma "$\llbracket P \longrightarrow Q; \ Q \longrightarrow R; \ R \longrightarrow S; \ P \rrbracket \implies S$"
by *(drule mp, assumption)+*

Using **by** takes care of the final use of *assumption*. The new proof is more concise. It is also more general: the repetitive method works for a chain of implications having any length, not just three.

Choice is another control structure. Separating two methods by a vertical bar (*|*) gives the effect of applying the first method, and if that fails, trying the second. It can be combined with repetition, when the choice must be made over and over again. Here is a chain of implications in which most of the antecedents are proved by assumption, but one is proved by arithmetic:

lemma "$\llbracket Q \longrightarrow R; \ P \longrightarrow Q; \ x{<}5 \longrightarrow P; \ Suc \ x < 5 \rrbracket \implies R$"
by *(drule mp, (assumption|arith))+*

The *arith* method can prove $x < 5$ from $x{+}1 < 5$, but it cannot duplicate the effect of *assumption*. Therefore, we combine these methods using the choice operator.

A postfixed question mark (?) expresses zero or one repetitions of a method. It can also be viewed as the choice between executing a method and doing nothing. It is useless at top level but can be valuable within other control structures; for example, *(m+)?* performs zero or more repetitions of method *m*.

5.16.2 Subgoal Numbering

Another problem in large proofs is contending with huge subgoals or many subgoals. Induction can produce a proof state that looks like this:

```
1. bigsubgoal1
2. bigsubgoal2
3. bigsubgoal3
4. bigsubgoal4
5. bigsubgoal5
6. bigsubgoal6
```

If each `bigsubgoal` is 15 lines or so, the proof state will be too big to scroll through. By default, Isabelle displays at most 10 subgoals. The **pr** command lets you change this limit:

```
pr 2
1. bigsubgoal1
2. bigsubgoal2
A total of 6 subgoals...
```

All methods apply to the first subgoal. Sometimes, not only in a large proof, you may want to focus on some other subgoal. Then you should try the commands **defer** or **prefer**.

In the following example, the first subgoal looks hard, while the others look as if `blast` alone could prove them:

```
1. hard
2. ¬ ¬ P ⟹ P
3. Q ⟹ Q
```

The **defer** command moves the first subgoal into the last position.

```
defer 1
1. ¬ ¬ P ⟹ P
2. Q ⟹ Q
3. hard
```

Now we apply `blast` repeatedly to the easy subgoals:

```
apply blast+
1. hard
```

Using **defer**, we have cleared away the trivial parts of the proof so that we can devote attention to the difficult part.

The **prefer** command moves the specified subgoal into the first position. For example, if you suspect that one of your subgoals is invalid (not a theorem), then you should investigate that subgoal first. If it cannot be proved, then there is no point in proving the other subgoals.

```
1. ok1
2. ok2
3. doubtful
```

We decide to work on the third subgoal.

prefer *3*
```
 1. doubtful
 2. ok1
 3. ok2
```

If we manage to prove *doubtful*, then we can work on the other subgoals, confident that we are not wasting our time. Finally we revise the proof script to remove the **prefer** command, since we needed it only to focus our exploration. The previous example is different: its use of **defer** stops trivial subgoals from cluttering the rest of the proof. Even there, we should consider proving *hard* as a preliminary lemma. Always seek ways to streamline your proofs.

   Summary:

– the control structures +, ? and / help express complicated proofs
– the **pr** command can limit the number of subgoals to display
– the **defer** and **prefer** commands move a subgoal to the last or first position

Exercise 5.16.1 Explain the use of ? and + in this proof.

lemma *"⟦P∧Q⟶R; P⟶Q; P⟧ ⟹ R"*
by *(drule mp, intro?, assumption+)+*

5.17 Proving the Correctness of Euclid's Algorithm

A brief development will demonstrate the techniques of this chapter, including *blast* applied with additional rules. We shall also see *case_tac* used to perform a Boolean case split.

   Let us prove that *gcd* computes the greatest common divisor of its two arguments. We use induction: *gcd.induct* is the induction rule returned by *recdef*. We simplify using rules proved in Sect. 3.5.3, since rewriting by the definition of *gcd* can loop.

lemma *gcd_dvd_both:* *"(gcd(m,n) dvd m) ∧ (gcd(m,n) dvd n)"*

The induction formula must be a conjunction. In the inductive step, each conjunct establishes the other.

apply *(induct_tac m n rule: gcd.induct)*
```
 1. ⋀m n. n ≠ 0 ⟶
          gcd (n, m mod n) dvd n ∧ gcd (n, m mod n) dvd m mod n
          ⟹ gcd (m, n) dvd m ∧ gcd (m, n) dvd n
```

   The conditional induction hypothesis suggests doing a case analysis on *n=0*. We apply *case_tac* with type *bool* — and not with a datatype, as we have done until now. Since *nat* is a datatype, we could have written *case_tac n* instead of *case_tac "n=0"*. However, the definition of *gcd* makes a Boolean decision:

   "gcd (m,n) = (if n=0 then m else gcd(n, m mod n))"

Proofs about a function frequently follow the function's definition, so we perform case analysis over the same formula.

apply (case_tac "n=0")
 1. $\bigwedge$m n. $[\![$n $\neq$ 0 $\longrightarrow$
        gcd (n, m mod n) dvd n $\wedge$ gcd (n, m mod n) dvd m mod n;
        n = 0$]\!]$
      $\Longrightarrow$ gcd (m, n) dvd m $\wedge$ gcd (m, n) dvd n
 2. $\bigwedge$m n. $[\![$n $\neq$ 0 $\longrightarrow$
        gcd (n, m mod n) dvd n $\wedge$ gcd (n, m mod n) dvd m mod n;
        n $\neq$ 0$]\!]$
      $\Longrightarrow$ gcd (m, n) dvd m $\wedge$ gcd (m, n) dvd n

Simplification leaves one subgoal:

apply (simp_all)
 1. $\bigwedge$m n. $[\![$0 < n;
        gcd (n, m mod n) dvd n $\wedge$ gcd (n, m mod n) dvd m mod n$]\!]$
      $\Longrightarrow$ gcd (n, m mod n) dvd m

Here, we can use *blast*. One of the assumptions, the induction hypothesis, is a conjunction. The two divides relationships it asserts are enough to prove the conclusion, for we have the following theorem at our disposal:

$[\![$?k dvd (?m mod ?n); ?k dvd ?n$]\!]$ $\Longrightarrow$?k dvd ?m   (dvd_mod_imp_dvd)

This theorem can be applied in various ways. As an introduction rule, it would cause backward chaining from the conclusion (namely ?k dvd ?m) to the two premises, which also involve the divides relation. This process does not look promising and could easily loop. More sensible is to apply the rule in the forward direction; each step would eliminate an occurrence of the *mod* symbol, so the process must terminate.

apply (blast dest: dvd_mod_imp_dvd)
done

Attaching the *dest* attribute to *dvd_mod_imp_dvd* tells *blast* to use it as destruction rule; that is, in the forward direction.

We have proved a conjunction. Now, let us give names to each of the two halves:

lemmas gcd_dvd1 [iff] = gcd_dvd_both [THEN conjunct1]
lemmas gcd_dvd2 [iff] = gcd_dvd_both [THEN conjunct2]

Here we see **lemmas** used with the *iff* attribute, which supplies the new theorems to the classical reasoner and the simplifier. Recall that *THEN* is frequently used with destruction rules; *THEN conjunct1* extracts the first half of a conjunctive theorem. Given *gcd_dvd_both* it yields

    gcd (?m1, ?n1) dvd ?m1

The variable names *?m1* and *?n1* arise because Isabelle renames schematic variables to prevent clashes. The second **lemmas** declaration yields

    gcd (?m1, ?n1) dvd ?n1

To complete the verification of the *gcd* function, we must prove that it returns the greatest of all the common divisors of its arguments. The proof is by induction, case analysis and simplification.

lemma *gcd_greatest [rule_format]:*
    "k dvd m ⟶ k dvd n ⟶ k dvd gcd(m,n)"

The goal is expressed using HOL implication, ⟶, because the induction affects the two preconditions. The directive *rule_format* tells Isabelle to replace each ⟶ by ⟹ before storing the eventual theorem. This directive can also remove outer universal quantifiers, converting the theorem into the usual format for inference rules. It can replace any series of applications of THEN to the rules *mp* and *spec*. We did not have to write this:

    lemma *gcd_greatest [THEN mp, THEN mp]:*
       "k dvd m ⟶ k dvd n ⟶ k dvd gcd(m,n)"

Because we are again reasoning about *gcd*, we perform the same induction and case analysis as in the previous proof:

apply (*induct_tac m n rule: gcd.induct*)
apply (*case_tac "n=0"*)
 1. ⋀m n. ⟦n ≠ 0 ⟶
         k dvd n ⟶ k dvd m mod n ⟶ k dvd gcd (n, m mod n);
         n = 0⟧
       ⟹ k dvd m ⟶ k dvd n ⟶ k dvd gcd (m, n)
 2. ⋀m n. ⟦n ≠ 0 ⟶
         k dvd n ⟶ k dvd m mod n ⟶ k dvd gcd (n, m mod n);
         n ≠ 0⟧
       ⟹ k dvd m ⟶ k dvd n ⟶ k dvd gcd (m, n)

Simplification proves both subgoals.

apply (*simp_all add: dvd_mod*)
done

In the first, where *n=0*, the implication becomes trivial: *k dvd gcd (m, n)* goes to *k dvd m*. The second subgoal is proved by an unfolding of *gcd*, using this rule about divides:

⟦?f dvd ?m; ?f dvd ?n⟧ ⟹ ?f dvd ?m mod ?n   (dvd_mod)

The facts proved above can be summarized as a single logical equivalence. This step gives us a chance to see another application of *blast*.

theorem *gcd_greatest_iff [iff]:*
      "(k dvd gcd(m,n)) = (k dvd m ∧ k dvd n)"
by (*blast intro!: gcd_greatest intro: dvd_trans*)

This theorem concisely expresses the correctness of the *gcd* function. We state it with the *iff* attribute so that Isabelle can use it to remove some occurrences of *gcd*. The theorem has a one-line proof using *blast* supplied with two additional introduction rules. The exclamation mark (*intro!*) signifies safe rules, which are applied aggressively. Rules given without the exclamation mark are applied reluctantly and their uses can be undone if the search backtracks. Here the unsafe rule expresses transitivity of the divides relation:

$$[\![?m \; dvd \; ?n; \; ?n \; dvd \; ?p]\!] \implies ?m \; dvd \; ?p \hspace{3cm} (dvd\_trans)$$

Applying *dvd_trans* as an introduction rule entails a risk of looping, for it multiplies occurrences of the divides symbol. However, this proof relies on transitivity reasoning. The rule *gcd_greatest* is safe to apply aggressively because it yields simpler subgoals. The proof implicitly uses *gcd_dvd1* and *gcd_dvd2* as safe rules, because they were declared using *iff*.

6. Sets, Functions, and Relations

This chapter describes the formalization of typed set theory, which is the basis of much else in HOL. For example, an inductive definition yields a set, and the abstract theories of relations regard a relation as a set of pairs. The chapter introduces the well-known constants such as union and intersection, as well as the main operations on relations, such as converse, composition and transitive closure. Functions are also covered. They are not sets in HOL, but many of their properties concern sets: the range of a function is a set, and the inverse image of a function maps sets to sets.

This chapter will be useful to anybody who plans to develop a substantial proof. sets are convenient for formalizing computer science concepts such as grammars, logical calculi and state transition systems. Isabelle can prove many statements involving sets automatically.

This chapter ends with a case study concerning model checking for the temporal logic CTL. Most of the other examples are simple. The chapter presents a small selection of built-in theorems in order to point out some key properties of the various constants and to introduce you to the notation.

Natural deduction rules are provided for the set theory constants, but they are seldom used directly, so only a few are presented here.

6.1 Sets

HOL's set theory should not be confused with traditional, untyped set theory, in which everything is a set. Our sets are typed. In a given set, all elements have the same type, say τ, and the set itself has type τ *set*.

We begin with **intersection**, **union** and **complement**. In addition to the **membership relation**, there is a symbol for its negation. These points can be seen below.

Here are the natural deduction rules for intersection. Note the resemblance to those for conjunction.

$$\llbracket c \in A; \ c \in B \rrbracket \implies c \in A \cap B \qquad\qquad (IntI)$$
$$c \in A \cap B \implies c \in A \qquad\qquad (IntD1)$$
$$c \in A \cap B \implies c \in B \qquad\qquad (IntD2)$$

Here are two of the many installed theorems concerning set complement. Note that it is denoted by a minus sign.

T. Nipkow, L.C. Paulson, and M. Wenzel: Isabelle/HOL, LNCS 2283, pp. 105–126, 2002.
© Springer-Verlag Berlin Heidelberg 2002

$$(c \in - A) = (c \notin A) \qquad\qquad\qquad (Compl\_iff)$$
$$- (A \cup B) = - A \cap - B \qquad\qquad\qquad (Compl\_Un)$$

Set **difference** is the intersection of a set with the complement of another set. Here we also see the syntax for the empty set and for the universal set.

$$A \cap (B - A) = \{\} \qquad\qquad\qquad\qquad (Diff\_disjoint)$$
$$A \cup - A = UNIV \qquad\qquad\qquad\qquad (Compl\_partition)$$

The **subset relation** holds between two sets just if every element of one is also an element of the other. This relation is reflexive. These are its natural deduction rules:

$$(\bigwedge x.\ x \in A \implies x \in B) \implies A \subseteq B \qquad\qquad (subsetI)$$
$$[\![A \subseteq B;\ c \in A]\!] \implies c \in B \qquad\qquad\qquad (subsetD)$$

In harder proofs, you may need to apply $subsetD$ giving a specific term for c. However, $blast$ can instantly prove facts such as this one:

$$(A \cup B \subseteq C) = (A \subseteq C \wedge B \subseteq C) \qquad\qquad (Un\_subset\_iff)$$

Here is another example, also proved automatically:

lemma $"(A \subseteq -B) = (B \subseteq -A)"$
by blast

This is the same example using ASCII syntax, illustrating a pitfall:

lemma $"(A <= -B) = (B <= -A)"$

The proof fails. It is not a statement about sets, due to overloading; the relation symbol <= can be any relation, not just subset. In this general form, the statement is not valid. Putting in a type constraint forces the variables to denote sets, allowing the proof to succeed:

lemma $"((A:: \ 'a \ set) <= -B) = (B <= -A)"$

Section 8.4 below describes overloading. Incidentally, $A \subseteq -B$ asserts that the sets A and B are disjoint.

Two sets are **equal** if they contain the same elements. This is the principle of **extensionality** for sets.

$$(\bigwedge x.\ (x \in A) = (x \in B)) \implies A = B \qquad\qquad (set\_ext)$$

Extensionality can be expressed as $A = B \iff (A \subseteq B) \wedge (B \subseteq A)$. The following rules express both directions of this equivalence. Proving a set equation using $equalityI$ allows the two inclusions to be proved independently.

$$[\![A \subseteq B;\ B \subseteq A]\!] \implies A = B \qquad\qquad\qquad (equalityI)$$
$$[\![A = B;\ [\![A \subseteq B;\ B \subseteq A]\!] \implies P]\!] \implies P \qquad\qquad (equalityE)$$

6.1.1 Finite Set Notation

Finite sets are expressed using the constant *insert*, which is a form of union:

insert a A = {a} ∪ A   (*insert_is_Un*)

The finite set expression *{a,b}* abbreviates *insert a (insert b {})*. Many facts about finite sets can be proved automatically:

lemma *"{a,b} ∪ {c,d} = {a,b,c,d}"*
by *blast*

Not everything that we would like to prove is valid. Consider this attempt:

lemma *"{a,b} ∩ {b,c} = {b}"*
apply *auto*

The proof fails, leaving the subgoal *b=c*. To see why it fails, consider a correct version:

lemma *"{a,b} ∩ {b,c} = (if a=c then {a,b} else {b})"*
apply *simp*
by *blast*

Our mistake was to suppose that the various items were distinct. Another remark: this proof uses two methods, namely *simp* and *blast*. Calling *simp* eliminates the *if-then-else* expression, which *blast* cannot break down. The combined methods (namely *force* and *auto*) can prove this fact in one step.

6.1.2 Set Comprehension

The set comprehension *{x. P}* expresses the set of all elements that satisfy the predicate *P*. Two laws describe the relationship between set comprehension and the membership relation:

(a ∈ {x. P x}) = P a   (*mem_Collect_eq*)
{x. x ∈ A} = A   (*Collect_mem_eq*)

Facts such as these have trivial proofs:

lemma *"{x. P x ∨ x ∈ A} = {x. P x} ∪ A"*
lemma *"{x. P x ⟶ Q x} = -{x. P x} ∪ {x. Q x}"*

Isabelle has a general syntax for comprehension, which is best described through an example:

lemma *"{p*q | p q. p∈prime ∧ q∈prime} =*
         *{z. ∃p q. z = p*q ∧ p∈prime ∧ q∈prime}"*

The left and right hand sides of this equation are identical. The syntax used in the left-hand side abbreviates the right-hand side: in this case, all numbers that are the product of two primes. The syntax provides a neat way of expressing any set given by an expression built up from variables under specific constraints. The drawback is that it hides the true form of the expression, with its existential quantifiers.

Remark. We do not need sets at all. They are essentially equivalent to predicate variables, which are allowed in higher-order logic. The main benefit of sets is their notation; we can write $x \in A$ and $\{z.\ P\}$ where predicates would require writing $A(x)$ and $\lambda z.\ P$.

6.1.3 Binding Operators

Universal and existential quantifications may range over sets, with the obvious meaning. Here are the natural deduction rules for the bounded universal quantifier. Occasionally you will need to apply *bspec* with an explicit instantiation of the variable x:

$$(\bigwedge x.\ x \in A \implies P\ x) \implies \forall x \in A.\ P\ x \qquad \text{(ballI)}$$
$$[\![\forall x \in A.\ P\ x;\ x \in A]\!] \implies P\ x \qquad \text{(bspec)}$$

Dually, here are the natural deduction rules for the bounded existential quantifier. You may need to apply *bexI* with an explicit instantiation:

$$[\![P\ x;\ x \in A]\!] \implies \exists x \in A.\ P\ x \qquad \text{(bexI)}$$
$$[\![\exists x \in A.\ P\ x;\ \bigwedge x.\ [\![x \in A;\ P\ x]\!] \implies Q]\!] \implies Q \qquad \text{(bexE)}$$

Unions can be formed over the values of a given set. The syntax is $\bigcup x \in A.\ B$ or *UN* $x \in A.\ B$ in ASCII. Indexed union satisfies this basic law:

$$(b \in (\textstyle\bigcup x \in A.\ B\ x)) = (\exists x \in A.\ b \in B\ x) \qquad \text{(UN\_iff)}$$

It has two natural deduction rules similar to those for the existential quantifier. Sometimes *UN_I* must be applied explicitly:

$$[\![a \in A;\ b \in B\ a]\!] \implies b \in (\textstyle\bigcup x \in A.\ B\ x) \qquad \text{(UN\_I)}$$
$$[\![b \in (\textstyle\bigcup x \in A.\ B\ x);\ \bigwedge x.\ [\![x \in A;\ b \in B\ x]\!] \implies R]\!] \implies R \qquad \text{(UN\_E)}$$

The following built-in syntax translation (see Sect. 4.1.4) lets us express the union over a *type*:

$$(\textstyle\bigcup x.\ B\ x) \rightleftharpoons (\textstyle\bigcup x \in UNIV.\ B\ x)$$

We may also express the union of a set of sets, written *Union C* in ASCII:

$$(A \in \textstyle\bigcup C) = (\exists X \in C.\ A \in X) \qquad \text{(Union\_iff)}$$

Intersections are treated dually, although they seem to be used less often than unions. The syntax below would be *INT x: A. B* and *Inter C* in ASCII. Among others, these theorems are available:

$$(b \in (\textstyle\bigcap x \in A.\ B\ x)) = (\forall x \in A.\ b \in B\ x) \qquad \text{(INT\_iff)}$$
$$(A \in \textstyle\bigcap C) = (\forall X \in C.\ A \in X) \qquad \text{(Inter\_iff)}$$

Isabelle uses logical equivalences such as those above in automatic proof. Unions, intersections and so forth are not simply replaced by their definitions. Instead, membership tests are simplified. For example, $x \in A \cup B$ is replaced by $x \in A \lor x \in B$.

The internal form of a comprehension involves the constant *Collect*, which occasionally appears when a goal or theorem is displayed. For example, *Collect P* is the same term as *{x. P x}*. The same thing can happen with quantifiers: *All P* is $\forall z.\ P\ x$ and *Ex P* is $\exists z.\ P\ x$; also *Ball A P* is $\forall z \in A.\ P\ x$ and *Bex A P* is $\exists z \in A.\ P\ x$. For indexed unions and intersections, you may see the constants *UNION* and *INTER*. The internal constant for $\varepsilon x.P(x)$ is *Eps*.

We have only scratched the surface of Isabelle/HOL's set theory, which provides hundreds of theorems for your use.

6.1.4 Finiteness and Cardinality

The predicate *finite* holds of all finite sets. Isabelle/HOL includes many familiar theorems about finiteness and cardinality (*card*). For example, we have theorems concerning the cardinalities of unions, intersections and the powerset:

$\llbracket$*finite A; finite B*$\rrbracket$
$\implies$ *card A + card B = card (A $\cup$ B) + card (A $\cap$ B)*   (card_Un_Int)

finite A $\implies$ *card (Pow A) = 2 ^ card A*   (card_Pow)

finite A $\implies$
card {B. B $\subseteq$ A $\wedge$ card B = k} = card A choose k   (n_subsets)

Writing $|A|$ as n, the last of these theorems says that the number of k-element subsets of A is $\binom{n}{k}$.

! The term *finite A* is defined via a syntax translation as an abbreviation for **•** *A $\in$ Finites*, where the constant *Finites* denotes the set of all finite sets of a given type. There is no constant *finite*.

6.2 Functions

This section describes a few concepts that involve functions. Some of the more important theorems are given along with the names. A few sample proofs appear. Unlike with set theory, however, we cannot simply state lemmas and expect them to be proved using *blast*.

6.2.1 Function Basics

Two functions are **equal** if they yield equal results given equal arguments. This is the principle of **extensionality** for functions:

$(\bigwedge x.\ f\ x = g\ x) \implies f = g$ (ext)

Function **update** is useful for modelling machine states. It has the obvious definition and many useful facts are proved about it. In particular, the following equation is installed as a simplification rule:

```
(f(x:=y)) z = (if z = x then y else f z)              (fun_upd_apply)
```

Two syntactic points must be noted. In $(f(x:=y))$ z we are applying an updated function to an argument; the outer parentheses are essential. A series of two or more updates can be abbreviated as shown on the left-hand side of this theorem:

```
f(x:=y, x:=z) = f(x:=z)                               (fun_upd_upd)
```

Note also that we can write $f(x:=z)$ with only one pair of parentheses when it is not being applied to an argument.

The **identity function** and function **composition** are defined:

```
id ≡ λx. x                                            (id_def)
f ○ g ≡ λx. f (g x)                                   (o_def)
```

Many familiar theorems concerning the identity and composition are proved. For example, we have the associativity of composition:

```
f ○ (g ○ h) = f ○ g ○ h                               (o_assoc)
```

6.2.2 Injections, Surjections, Bijections

A function may be **injective**, **surjective** or **bijective**:

```
inj_on f A ≡ ∀x∈A. ∀y∈A. f x = f y ⟶ x = y          (inj_on_def)
surj f ≡ ∀y. ∃x. y = f x                              (surj_def)
bij f ≡ inj f ∧ surj f                                (bij_def)
```

The second argument of `inj_on` lets us express that a function is injective over a given set. This refinement is useful in higher-order logic, where functions are total; in some cases, a function's natural domain is a subset of its domain type. Writing `inj f` abbreviates `inj_on f UNIV`, for when `f` is injective everywhere.

The operator `inv` expresses the **inverse** of a function. In general the inverse may not be well behaved. We have the usual laws, such as these:

```
inj f  ⟹  inv f (f x) = x                             (inv_f_f)
surj f ⟹  f (inv f y) = y                             (surj_f_inv_f)
bij f  ⟹  inv (inv f) = f                             (inv_inv_eq)
```

Theorems involving these concepts can be hard to prove. The following example is easy, but it cannot be proved automatically. To begin with, we need a law that relates the equality of functions to equality over all arguments:

```
(f = g) = (∀x. f x = g x)                             (expand_fun_eq)
```

This is just a restatement of extensionality. Our lemma states that an injection can be cancelled from the left side of function composition:

```
lemma "inj f ⟹ (f ○ g = f ○ h) = (g = h)"
apply (simp add: expand_fun_eq inj_on_def)
apply auto
done
```

The first step of the proof invokes extensionality and the definitions of injectiveness and composition. It leaves one subgoal:

1. $\forall x\ y.\ f\ x = f\ y \longrightarrow x = y \implies$
   $(\forall x.\ f\ (g\ x) = f\ (h\ x)) = (\forall x.\ g\ x = h\ x)$

This can be proved using the `auto` method.

6.2.3 Function Image

The **image** of a set under a function is a most useful notion. It has the obvious definition:

$f\ `\ A \equiv \{y.\ \exists x \in A.\ y = f\ x\}$ *(image_def)*

Here are some of the many facts proved about image:

$(f \circ g)\ `\ r = f\ `\ g\ `\ r$ *(image_compose)*
$f`(A\ \cup\ B) = f`A\ \cup\ f`B$ *(image_Un)*
$inj\ f \implies f`(A\ \cap\ B) = f`A\ \cap\ f`B$ *(image_Int)*

Laws involving image can often be proved automatically. Here are two examples, illustrating connections with indexed union and with the general syntax for comprehension:

lemma "$f`A\ \cup\ g`A = (\bigcup x \in A.\ \{f\ x,\ g\ x\})$"
lemma "$f\ `\ \{(x,y).\ P\ x\ y\} = \{f(x,y)\ |\ x\ y.\ P\ x\ y\}$"

A function's **range** is the set of values that the function can take on. It is, in fact, the image of the universal set under that function. There is no constant `range`. Instead, `range` abbreviates an application of image to `UNIV`:

   $range\ f \rightleftharpoons f`UNIV$

Few theorems are proved specifically for `range`; in most cases, you should look for a more general theorem concerning images.

Inverse image is also useful. It is defined as follows:

$f\ -`\ B \equiv \{x.\ f\ x \in B\}$ *(vimage_def)*

This is one of the facts proved about it:

$f\ -`\ (-\ A) = -\ f\ -`\ A$ *(vimage_Compl)*

6.3 Relations

A **relation** is a set of pairs. As such, the set operations apply to them. For instance, we may form the union of two relations. Other primitives are defined specifically for relations.

6.3.1 Relation Basics

The **identity relation**, also known as equality, has the obvious definition:

$$Id \equiv \{p.\ \exists x.\ p = (x,x)\} \tag{Id\_def}$$

Composition of relations (the infix O) is also available:

$$r\ O\ s \equiv \{(x,z).\ \exists y.\ (x,y) \in s \land (y,z) \in r\} \tag{rel\_comp\_def}$$

This is one of the many lemmas proved about these concepts:

$$R\ O\ Id = R \tag{R\_O\_Id}$$

Composition is monotonic, as are most of the primitives appearing in this chapter. We have many theorems similar to the following one:

$$[\![r' \subseteq r;\ s' \subseteq s]\!] \implies r'\ O\ s' \subseteq r\ O\ s \tag{rel\_comp\_mono}$$

The **converse** or inverse of a relation exchanges the roles of the two operands. We use the postfix notation r^{-1} or $r\char`^-1$ in ASCII.

$$((a,b) \in r^{-1}) = ((b,a) \in r) \tag{converse\_iff}$$

Here is a typical law proved about converse and composition:

$$(r\ O\ s)^{-1} = s^{-1}\ O\ r^{-1} \tag{converse\_rel\_comp}$$

The **image** of a set under a relation is defined analogously to image under a function:

$$(b \in r\ ''\ A) = (\exists x \in A.\ (x,b) \in r) \tag{Image\_iff}$$

It satisfies many similar laws.

The **domain** and **range** of a relation are defined in the standard way:

$$(a \in Domain\ r) = (\exists y.\ (a,y) \in r) \tag{Domain\_iff}$$
$$(a \in Range\ r) = (\exists y.\ (y,a) \in r) \tag{Range\_iff}$$

Iterated composition of a relation is available. The notation overloads that of exponentiation. Two simplification rules are installed:

$$R\ \char`^\ 0 = Id$$
$$R\ \char`^\ Suc\ n = R\ O\ R\char`^n$$

6.3.2 The Reflexive and Transitive Closure

The **reflexive and transitive closure** of the relation r is written with a postfix syntax. In ASCII we write $r\char`^*$ and in symbol notation r^*. It is the least solution of the equation

$$r^* = Id \cup (r\ O\ r^*) \tag{rtrancl\_unfold}$$

Among its basic properties are three that serve as introduction rules:

$$(a,\ a) \in r^* \tag{rtrancl\_refl}$$
$$p \in r \implies p \in r^* \tag{r\_into\_rtrancl}$$
$$[\![(a,b) \in r^*;\ (b,c) \in r^*]\!] \implies (a,c) \in r^* \tag{rtrancl\_trans}$$

Induction over the reflexive transitive closure is available:

$$[(a, b) \in r^*; P\ a; \bigwedge y\ z.\ [(a, y) \in r^*;\ (y, z) \in r;\ P\ y] \Longrightarrow P\ z]$$
$$\Longrightarrow P\ b \qquad\qquad\qquad\qquad\qquad\qquad\qquad\qquad\qquad \text{(rtrancl\_induct)}$$

Idempotence is one of the laws proved about the reflexive transitive closure:

$$(r^*)^* = r^* \qquad\qquad\qquad\qquad\qquad\qquad\qquad\qquad\qquad \text{(rtrancl\_idemp)}$$

The transitive closure is similar. The ASCII syntax is r^+. It has two introduction rules:

$$p \in r \Longrightarrow p \in r^+ \qquad\qquad\qquad\qquad\qquad\qquad\qquad \text{(r\_into\_trancl)}$$
$$[(a, b) \in r^+;\ (b, c) \in r^+] \Longrightarrow (a, c) \in r^+ \qquad\qquad \text{(trancl\_trans)}$$

The induction rule resembles the one shown above. A typical lemma states that transitive closure commutes with the converse operator:

$$(r^{-1})^+ = (r^+)^{-1} \qquad\qquad\qquad\qquad\qquad\qquad\qquad \text{(trancl\_converse)}$$

6.3.3 A Sample Proof

The reflexive transitive closure also commutes with the converse operator. Let us examine the proof. Each direction of the equivalence is proved separately. The two proofs are almost identical. Here is the first one:

```
lemma rtrancl_converseD: "(x,y) ∈ (r⁻¹)* ⟹ (y,x) ∈ r*"
apply (erule rtrancl_induct)
 apply (rule rtrancl_refl)
apply (blast intro: rtrancl_trans)
done
```

The first step of the proof applies induction, leaving these subgoals:

1. $(x, x) \in r^*$
2. $\bigwedge y\ z.\ [(x,y) \in (r^{-1})^*;\ (y,z) \in r^{-1};\ (y,x) \in r^*]$
    $\Longrightarrow (z,x) \in r^*$

The first subgoal is trivial by reflexivity. The second follows by first eliminating the converse operator, yielding the assumption $(z,y) \in r$, and then applying the introduction rules shown above. The same proof script handles the other direction:

```
lemma rtrancl_converseI: "(y,x) ∈ r* ⟹ (x,y) ∈ (r⁻¹)*"
apply (erule rtrancl_induct)
 apply (rule rtrancl_refl)
apply (blast intro: rtrancl_trans)
done
```

Finally, we combine the two lemmas to prove the desired equation:

```
lemma rtrancl_converse: "(r⁻¹)* = (r*)⁻¹"
by (auto intro: rtrancl_converseI dest: rtrancl_converseD)
```

! This trivial proof requires `auto` rather than `blast` because of a subtle issue
   • involving ordered pairs. Here is a subgoal that arises internally after the rules
`equalityI` and `subsetI` have been applied:

1. $\bigwedge x.\ x \in (r^{-1})^{*} \implies x \in (r^{*})^{-1}$

We cannot apply `rtrancl_converseD`. It refers to ordered pairs, while x is a variable of product type. The `simp` and `blast` methods can do nothing, so let us try
`clarify`:

1. $\bigwedge a\ b.\ (a,b) \in (r^{-1})^{*} \implies (b,a) \in r^{*}$

Now that x has been replaced by the pair (a,b), we can proceed. Other methods
that split variables in this way are `force`, `auto`, `fast` and `best`. Section 8.2 will
discuss proof techniques for ordered pairs in more detail.

6.4 Well-Founded Relations and Induction

A well-founded relation captures the notion of a terminating process. Each
recdef declaration must specify a well-founded relation that justifies the
termination of the desired recursive function. Most of the forms of induction found in mathematics are merely special cases of induction over a well-founded relation.

Intuitively, the relation $\prec$ is **well-founded** if it admits no infinite descending chains

$$\cdots \prec a_2 \prec a_1 \prec a_0.$$

Well-foundedness can be hard to show. The various formulations are all complicated. However, often a relation is well-founded by construction. HOL provides theorems concerning ways of constructing a well-founded relation. The
most familiar way is to specify a **measure function** f into the natural numbers, when $x \prec y \iff f\ x < f\ y$; we write this particular relation as
`measure f`.

! You may want to skip the rest of this section until you need to perform a
   • complex recursive function definition or induction. The induction rule returned
by **recdef** is good enough for most purposes. We use an explicit well-founded
induction only in Sect. 9.3.4.

Isabelle/HOL declares `less_than` as a relation object, that is, a set of
pairs of natural numbers. Two theorems tell us that this relation behaves as
expected and that it is well-founded:

$((x,y) \in \mathtt{less\_than}) = (x < y)$	(`less_than_iff`)
`wf less_than`	(`wf_less_than`)

The notion of measure generalizes to the **inverse image** of a relation.
Given a relation r and a function f, we express a new relation using f as a
measure. An infinite descending chain on this new relation would give rise
to an infinite descending chain on r. Isabelle/HOL defines this concept and
proves a theorem stating that it preserves well-foundedness:

```
inv_image r f ≡ {(x,y). (f x, f y) ∈ r}                    (inv_image_def)
wf r ⟹ wf (inv_image r f)                                  (wf_inv_image)
```

A measure function involves the natural numbers. The relation `measure size` justifies primitive recursion and structural induction over a datatype. Isabelle/HOL defines `measure` as shown:

```
measure ≡ inv_image less_than                              (measure_def)
wf (measure f)                                             (wf_measure)
```

Of the other constructions, the most important is the **lexicographic product** of two relations. It expresses the standard dictionary ordering over pairs. We write `ra <*lex*> rb`, where `ra` and `rb` are the two operands. The lexicographic product satisfies the usual definition and it preserves well-foundedness:

```
ra <*lex*> rb ≡
  {((a,b),(a',b')). (a,a') ∈ ra ∨
                    a=a' ∧ (b,b') ∈ rb}                    (lex_prod_def)
⟦wf ra; wf rb⟧ ⟹ wf (ra <*lex*> rb)                        (wf_lex_prod)
```

These constructions can be used in a **recdef** declaration (Sect. 3.5.3) to define the well-founded relation used to prove termination.

The **multiset ordering**, useful for hard termination proofs, is available in the Library [4]. Baader and Nipkow [3, Sect. 2.5] discuss it.

Induction comes in many forms, including traditional mathematical induction, structural induction on lists and induction on size. All are instances of the following rule, for a suitable well-founded relation $\prec$:

$$\frac{\begin{array}{c}[\forall y.\ y \prec x \to P(y)] \\ \vdots \\ P(x)\end{array}}{P(a)}$$

To show $P(a)$ for a particular term a, it suffices to show $P(x)$ for arbitrary x under the assumption that $P(y)$ holds for $y \prec x$. Intuitively, the well-foundedness of $\prec$ ensures that the chains of reasoning are finite.

In Isabelle, the induction rule is expressed like this:

```
⟦wf r; ⋀x. ∀y. (y,x) ∈ r ⟶ P y ⟹ P x⟧ ⟹ P a              (wf_induct)
```

Here `wf r` expresses that the relation `r` is well-founded.

Many familiar induction principles are instances of this rule. For example, the predecessor relation on the natural numbers is well-founded; induction over it is mathematical induction. The "tail of" relation on lists is well-founded; induction over it is structural induction.

6.5 Fixed Point Operators

Fixed point operators define sets recursively. They are invoked implicitly when making an inductive definition, as discussed in Chap. 7 below. However, they can be used directly, too. The *least* or *strongest* fixed point yields an inductive definition; the *greatest* or *weakest* fixed point yields a coinductive definition. Mathematicians may wish to note that the existence of these fixed points is guaranteed by the Knaster-Tarski theorem.

! Casual readers should skip the rest of this section. We use fixed point operators
• only in Sect. 6.6.

The theory applies only to monotonic functions. Isabelle's definition of monotone is overloaded over all orderings:

$$mono\ f \equiv \forall A\ B.\ A \leq B \longrightarrow f\ A \leq f\ B \qquad (mono\_def)$$

For fixed point operators, the ordering will be the subset relation: if $A \subseteq B$ then we expect $f(A) \subseteq f(B)$. In addition to its definition, monotonicity has the obvious introduction and destruction rules:

$$(\bigwedge A\ B.\ A \leq B \implies f\ A \leq f\ B) \implies mono\ f \qquad (monoI)$$
$$[\![mono\ f;\ A \leq B]\!] \implies f\ A \leq f\ B \qquad (monoD)$$

The most important properties of the least fixed point are that it is a fixed point and that it enjoys an induction rule:

$$mono\ f \implies lfp\ f = f\ (lfp\ f) \qquad (lfp\_unfold)$$
$$[\![a \in lfp\ f;\ mono\ f;$$
$$\bigwedge x.\ x \in f\ (lfp\ f \cap \{x.\ P\ x\}) \implies P\ x]\!] \implies P\ a \qquad (lfp\_induct)$$

The induction rule shown above is more convenient than the basic one derived from the minimality of `lfp`. Observe that both theorems demand `mono f` as a premise.

The greatest fixed point is similar, but it has a **coinduction** rule:

$$mono\ f \implies gfp\ f = f\ (gfp\ f) \qquad (gfp\_unfold)$$
$$[\![mono\ f;\ a \in X;\ X \subseteq f\ (X \cup gfp\ f)]\!] \implies a \in gfp\ f \qquad (coinduct)$$

A **bisimulation** is perhaps the best-known concept defined as a greatest fixed point. Exhibiting a bisimulation to prove the equality of two agents in a process algebra is an example of coinduction. The coinduction rule can be strengthened in various ways.

6.6 Case Study: Verified Model Checking

This chapter ends with a case study concerning model checking for Computation Tree Logic (CTL), a temporal logic. Model checking is a popular technique for the verification of finite state systems (implementations) with respect to temporal logic formulae (specifications) [7, 14]. Its foundations are set theoretic and this section will explore them in HOL. This is done in two steps. First we consider a simple modal logic called propositional dynamic logic (PDL). We then proceed to the temporal logic CTL, which is used in many real model checkers. In each case we give both a traditional semantics ($\models$) and a recursive function mc that maps a formula into the set of all states of the system where the formula is valid. If the system has a finite number of states, mc is directly executable: it is a model checker, albeit an inefficient one. The main proof obligation is to show that the semantics and the model checker agree.

Our models are *transition systems*: sets of *states* with transitions between them. Here is a simple example:

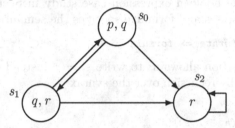

Each state has a unique name or number (s_0, s_1, s_2), and in each state certain *atomic propositions* (p, q, r) hold. The aim of temporal logic is to formalize statements such as "there is no path starting from s_2 leading to a state where p or q holds," which is true, and "on all paths starting from s_0, q always holds," which is false.

Abstracting from this concrete example, we assume there is a type of states:

typedecl `state`

Command **typedecl** merely declares a new type but without defining it (see Sect. 8.5.1). Thus we know nothing about the type other than its existence. That is exactly what we need because `state` really is an implicit parameter of our model. Of course it would have been more generic to make `state` a type parameter of everything but declaring `state` globally as above reduces clutter. Similarly we declare an arbitrary but fixed transition system, i.e. a relation between states:

consts `M ::` `"(state × state)set"`

Again, we could have made `M` a parameter of everything. Finally we introduce a type of atomic propositions

typedecl `atom`

and a *labelling function*

consts `L ::` `"state ⇒ atom set"`

telling us which atomic propositions are true in each state.

6.6.1 Propositional Dynamic Logic — PDL

The formulae of PDL are built up from atomic propositions via negation and conjunction and the two temporal connectives AX and EF. Since formulae are essentially syntax trees, they are naturally modelled as a datatype:[1]

```
datatype formula = Atom atom
                 | Neg formula
                 | And formula formula
                 | AX formula
                 | EF formula
```

This resembles the boolean expression case study in Sect. 2.4.6. A validity relation between states and formulae specifies the semantics:

```
consts valid :: "state ⇒ formula ⇒ bool"   ("(_ |= _)" [80,80] 80)
```

The syntax annotation allows us to write $s \models f$ instead of valid s f. The definition of $\models$ is by recursion over the syntax:

```
primrec
"s |= Atom a  = (a ∈ L s)"
"s |= Neg f   = (¬(s |= f))"
"s |= And f g = (s |= f ∧ s |= g)"
"s |= AX f    = (∀t. (s,t) ∈ M ⟶ t |= f)"
"s |= EF f    = (∃t. (s,t) ∈ M* ∧ t |= f)"
```

The first three equations should be self-explanatory. The temporal formula AX f means that f is true in All neXt states whereas EF f means that there Exists some Future state in which f is true. The future is expressed via *, the reflexive transitive closure. Because of reflexivity, the future includes the present.

Now we come to the model checker itself. It maps a formula into the set of states where the formula is true. It too is defined by recursion over the syntax:

```
consts mc :: "formula ⇒ state set"
primrec
"mc(Atom a)  = {s. a ∈ L s}"
"mc(Neg f)   = -mc f"
"mc(And f g) = mc f ∩ mc g"
"mc(AX f)    = {s. ∀t. (s,t) ∈ M ⟶ t ∈ mc f}"
"mc(EF f)    = lfp(λT. mc f ∪ (M⁻¹ '' T))"
```

Only the equation for EF deserves some comments. Remember that the postfix $^{-1}$ and the infix '' are predefined and denote the converse of a relation and the image of a set under a relation. Thus M^{-1} '' T is the set of all predecessors

---

[1] The customary definition of PDL [11] looks quite different from ours, but the two are easily shown to be equivalent.

of T and the least fixed point (`lfp`) of $\lambda T.$ `mc f` $\cup$ M^{-1} `'' T` is the least set
T containing `mc f` and all predecessors of T. If you find it hard to see that
`mc (EF f)` contains exactly those states from which there is a path to a state
where `f` is true, do not worry — this will be proved in a moment.

First we prove monotonicity of the function inside `lfp` in order to make
sure it really has a least fixed point.

lemma `mono_ef: "mono(`$\lambda T.$` A` $\cup$ `(`M^{-1}` '' T))"`
apply`(rule monoI)`
apply `blast`
done

Now we can relate model checking and semantics. For the `EF` case we need a
separate lemma:

lemma `EF_lemma:`
   `"lfp(`$\lambda T.$` A` $\cup$ `(`M^{-1}` '' T)) = {s.` $\exists t.$ `(s,t)` $\in M^*$ $\wedge$ `t` $\in$ `A}"`

The equality is proved in the canonical fashion by proving that each set
includes the other; the inclusion is shown pointwise:

apply`(rule equalityI)`
 apply`(rule subsetI)`
 apply`(simp)`

Simplification leaves us with the following first subgoal

   1. $\bigwedge s.$ `s` $\in$ `lfp (`$\lambda T.$` A` $\cup M^{-1}$ `'' T)` $\implies \exists t.$ `(s, t)` $\in M^*$ $\wedge$ `t` $\in$ `A`

which is proved by `lfp`-induction:

 apply`(erule lfp_induct)`
  apply`(rule mono_ef)`
 apply`(simp)`

Having disposed of the monotonicity subgoal, simplification leaves us with
the following goal:

   1. $\bigwedge x.$ `x` $\in$ `A` $\vee$
         `x` $\in M^{-1}$ `'' (lfp ( ... )` $\cap$ `{x.` $\exists t.$ `(x, t)` $\in M^*$ $\wedge$ `t` $\in$ `A})`
         $\implies \exists t.$ `(x, t)` $\in M^*$ $\wedge$ `t` $\in$ `A`

It is proved by `blast`, using the transitivity of M^*.

 apply`(blast intro: rtrancl_trans)`

We now return to the second set inclusion subgoal, which is again proved
pointwise:

apply`(rule subsetI)`
apply`(simp, clarify)`

After simplification and clarification we are left with

   1. $\bigwedge x\ t.$ $[\![$`(x, t)` $\in M^*$`; t` $\in$ `A`$]\!]$ $\implies$ `x` $\in$ `lfp (`$\lambda T.$` A` $\cup M^{-1}$ `'' T)`

This goal is proved by induction on $(s, t) \in M^*$. But since the model checker works backwards (from t to s), we cannot use the induction theorem `rtrancl_induct`: it works in the forward direction. Fortunately the converse induction theorem `converse_rtrancl_induct` already exists:

$$\llbracket (a, b) \in r^*;\ P\ b;$$
$$\quad \bigwedge y\ z.\ \llbracket (y, z) \in r;\ (z, b) \in r^*;\ P\ z \rrbracket \Longrightarrow P\ y \rrbracket$$
$$\Longrightarrow P\ a$$

It says that if $(a, b) \in r^*$ and we know $P\ b$ then we can infer $P\ a$ provided each step backwards from a predecessor z of b preserves P.

apply (`erule converse_rtrancl_induct`)

The base case

1. $\bigwedge x\ t.\ t \in A \Longrightarrow t \in lfp\ (\lambda T.\ A \cup M^{-1}\ ''\ T)$

is solved by unrolling `lfp` once

apply (`subst lfp_unfold[OF mono_ef]`)

1. $\bigwedge x\ t.\ t \in A \Longrightarrow t \in A \cup M^{-1}\ ''\ lfp\ (\lambda T.\ A \cup M^{-1}\ ''\ T)$

and disposing of the resulting trivial subgoal automatically:

apply (`blast`)

The proof of the induction step is identical to the one for the base case:

apply (`subst lfp_unfold[OF mono_ef]`)
apply (`blast`)
done

The main theorem is proved in the familiar manner: induction followed by `auto` augmented with the lemma as a simplification rule.

theorem `"mc f = {s. s ⊨ f}"`
apply (`induct_tac f`)
apply (`auto simp add: EF_lemma`)
done

Exercise 6.6.1 `AX` has a dual operator `EN` ("there exists a next state such that")[2] with the intended semantics

$$s \models EN\ f = (\exists t.\ (s, t) \in M \wedge t \models f)$$

Fortunately, `EN f` can already be expressed as a PDL formula. How?

Show that the semantics for `EF` satisfies the following recursion equation:

$$s \models EF\ f = (s \models f \vee s \models EN\ (EF\ f))$$

---

[2] We cannot use the customary `EX`: it is reserved as the ASCII-equivalent of $\exists$.

6.6.2 Computation Tree Logic — CTL

The semantics of PDL only needs reflexive transitive closure. Let us be adventurous and introduce a more expressive temporal operator. We extend the datatype `formula` by a new constructor

```
| AF formula
```

which stands for "*A*lways in the *F*uture": on all infinite paths, at some point the formula holds. Formalizing the notion of an infinite path is easy in HOL: it is simply a function from `nat` to `state`.

constdefs Paths :: "state ⇒ (nat ⇒ state)set"
　　　　　"Paths s ≡ {p. s = p 0 ∧ (∀i. (p i, p(i+1)) ∈ M)}"

This definition allows a succinct statement of the semantics of `AF`: [3]

"s ⊨ AF f　 = (∀p ∈ Paths s. ∃i. p i ⊨ f)"

Model checking `AF` involves a function which is just complicated enough to warrant a separate definition:

constdefs af :: "state set ⇒ state set ⇒ state set"
　　　　　"af A T ≡ A ∪ {s. ∀t. (s, t) ∈ M ⟶ t ∈ T}"

Now we define `mc (AF f)` as the least set `T` that includes `mc f` and all states all of whose direct successors are in `T`:

"mc(AF f)　 = lfp(af(mc f))"

Because `af` is monotone in its second argument (and also its first, but that is irrelevant), `af A` has a least fixed point:

lemma mono_af: "mono(af A)"
apply(simp add: mono_def af_def)
apply blast
done

　All we need to prove now is `mc (AF f)` = {s. s ⊨ AF f}, which states that `mc` and ⊨ agree for `AF`. This time we prove the two inclusions separately, starting with the easy one:

theorem AF_lemma1:
　"lfp(af A) ⊆ {s. ∀p ∈ Paths s. ∃i. p i ∈ A}"

In contrast to the analogous proof for `EF`, and just for a change, we do not use fixed point induction. Park-induction, named after David Park, is weaker but sufficient for this proof:

f S ⊆ S ⟹ lfp f ⊆ S　　　　　　　　　　　　　(lfp_lowerbound)

---

[3] Do not be misled: neither datatypes nor recursive functions can be extended by new constructors or equations. This is just a trick of the presentation (see Sect. 4.2.5). In reality one has to define a new datatype and a new function.

The instance of the premise $f\ S \subseteq S$ is proved pointwise, a decision that clarification takes for us:

apply *(rule lfp_lowerbound)*
apply *(clarsimp simp add: af_def Paths_def)*

1. $\bigwedge p.\ [\![p\ 0 \in A\ \vee$
$(\forall t.\ (p\ 0,\ t) \in M \longrightarrow$
$(\forall p.\ t = p\ 0 \wedge (\forall i.\ (p\ i,\ p\ (Suc\ i)) \in M) \longrightarrow$
$(\exists i.\ p\ i \in A)));$
$\forall i.\ (p\ i,\ p\ (Suc\ i)) \in M]\!]$
$\implies \exists i.\ p\ i \in A$

Now we eliminate the disjunction. The case $p\ 0 \in A$ is trivial:

apply *(erule disjE)*
 apply *(blast)*

In the other case we set t to $p\ 1$ and simplify matters:

apply *(erule_tac x = "p 1" in allE)*
apply *(clarsimp)*

1. $\bigwedge p.\ [\![\forall i.\ (p\ i,\ p\ (Suc\ i)) \in M;$
$\forall pa.\ p\ (Suc\ 0) = pa\ 0 \wedge (\forall i.\ (pa\ i,\ pa\ (Suc\ i)) \in M) \longrightarrow$
$(\exists i.\ pa\ i \in A)]\!]$
$\implies \exists i.\ p\ i \in A$

It merely remains to set pa to $\lambda i.\ p\ (i + 1)$, that is, p without its first element. The rest is automatic:

apply *(erule_tac x = "λi. p(i+1)" in allE)*
apply *force*
done

The opposite inclusion is proved by contradiction: if some state s is not in *lfp (af A)*, then we can construct an infinite *A*-avoiding path starting from s. The reason is that by unfolding *lfp* we find that if s is not in *lfp (af A)*, then s is not in *A* and there is a direct successor of s that is again not in *lfp (af A)*. Iterating this argument yields the promised infinite *A*-avoiding path. Let us formalize this sketch.

The one-step argument in the sketch above is proved by a variant of contraposition:

lemma *not_in_lfp_afD:*
 "$s \notin lfp(af\ A) \implies s \notin A \wedge (\exists\ t.\ (s,t) \in M \wedge t \notin lfp(af\ A))$"
apply *(erule contrapos_np)*
apply *(subst lfp_unfold[OF mono_af])*
apply *(simp add: af_def)*
done

We assume the negation of the conclusion and prove $s \in lfp$ (af A). Unfolding lfp once and simplifying with the definition of af finishes the proof.

Now we iterate this process. The following construction of the desired path is parameterized by a predicate Q that should hold along the path:

```
consts path :: "state ⇒ (state ⇒ bool) ⇒ (nat ⇒ state)"
primrec
"path s Q 0 = s"
"path s Q (Suc n) = (SOME t. (path s Q n,t) ∈ M ∧ Q t)"
```

Element $n + 1$ on this path is some arbitrary successor t of element n such that $Q t$ holds. Remember that $SOME \ t. \ R \ t$ is some arbitrary but fixed t such that $R \ t$ holds (see Sect. 5.10). Of course, such a t need not exist, but that is of no concern to us since we will only use $path$ when a suitable t does exist.

Let us show that if each state s that satisfies Q has a successor that again satisfies Q, then there exists an infinite Q-path:

lemma `infinity_lemma`:
  "⟦ Q s; ∀s. Q s ⟶ (∃ t. (s,t) ∈ M ∧ Q t) ⟧ ⟹
   ∃p∈Paths s. ∀i. Q(p i)"

First we rephrase the conclusion slightly because we need to prove simultaneously both the path property and the fact that Q holds:

```
apply(subgoal_tac
  "∃p. s = p 0 ∧ (∀i::nat. (p i, p(i+1)) ∈ M ∧ Q(p i))")
```

From this proposition the original goal follows easily:

```
 apply(simp add: Paths_def, blast)
```

The new subgoal is proved by providing the witness $path \ s \ Q$ for p:

```
apply(rule_tac x = "path s Q" in exI)
apply(clarsimp)
```

After simplification and clarification, the subgoal has the following form:

1. ⋀i. ⟦Q s; ∀s. Q s ⟶ (∃t. (s, t) ∈ M ∧ Q t)⟧
        ⟹ (path s Q i, SOME t. (path s Q i, t) ∈ M ∧ Q t) ∈ M ∧
        Q (path s Q i)

It invites a proof by induction on i:

```
apply(induct_tac i)
 apply(simp)
```

After simplification, the base case boils down to

1. ⟦Q s; ∀s. Q s ⟶ (∃t. (s, t) ∈ M ∧ Q t)⟧
    ⟹ (s, SOME t. (s, t) ∈ M ∧ Q t) ∈ M

The conclusion looks exceedingly trivial: after all, t is chosen such that $(s, t) \in M$ holds. However, we first have to show that such a t actually exists! This reasoning is embodied in the theorem *someI2_ex*:

$$\llbracket \exists a. ~?P~a; ~\bigwedge x. ~?P~x \implies ?Q~x \rrbracket \implies ?Q~(SOME~x. ~?P~x)$$

When we apply this theorem as an introduction rule, $?P~x$ becomes $(s, x) \in M \wedge Q~x$ and $?Q~x$ becomes $(s, x) \in M$ and we have to prove two subgoals: $\exists a. ~(s, a) \in M \wedge Q~a$, which follows from the assumptions, and $(s, x) \in M \wedge Q~x \implies (s, x) \in M$, which is trivial. Thus it is not surprising that *fast* can prove the base case quickly:

apply *(fast intro: someI2_ex)*

What is worth noting here is that we have used *fast* rather than *blast*. The reason is that *blast* would fail because it cannot cope with *someI2_ex*: unifying its conclusion with the current subgoal is non-trivial because of the nested schematic variables. For efficiency reasons *blast* does not even attempt such unifications. Although *fast* can in principle cope with complicated unification problems, in practice the number of unifiers arising is often prohibitive and the offending rule may need to be applied explicitly rather than automatically. This is what happens in the step case.

The induction step is similar, but more involved, because now we face nested occurrences of *SOME*. As a result, *fast* is no longer able to solve the subgoal and we apply *someI2_ex* by hand. We merely show the proof commands but do not describe the details:

apply *(simp)*
apply *(rule someI2_ex)*
 apply *(blast)*
apply *(rule someI2_ex)*
 apply *(blast)*
apply *(blast)*
done

Function *path* has fulfilled its purpose now and can be forgotten. It was merely defined to provide the witness in the proof of the *infinity_lemma*. Aficionados of minimal proofs might like to know that we could have given the witness without having to define a new function: the term

$$nat\_rec~s~(\lambda n~t.~SOME~u.~(t,~u) \in M \wedge Q~u)$$

is extensionally equal to *path s Q*, where *nat_rec* is the predefined primitive recursor on *nat*.

At last we can prove the opposite direction of *AF_lemma1*:

theorem *AF_lemma2:* "{s. $\forall p \in$ Paths s. $\exists i.~p~i \in A$} $\subseteq$ lfp(af A)"

The proof is again pointwise and then by contraposition:

```
apply(rule subsetI)
apply(erule contrapos_pp)
apply simp
```

1. $\bigwedge x.\ x \notin$ lfp (af A) $\Longrightarrow \exists p \in$ Paths x. $\forall i.\ p\ i \notin A$

Applying the `infinity_lemma` as a destruction rule leaves two subgoals, the second premise of `infinity_lemma` and the original subgoal:

```
apply(drule infinity_lemma)
```

1. $\bigwedge x.\ \forall s.\ s \notin$ lfp (af A) $\longrightarrow (\exists t.\ (s,\ t) \in M \wedge t \notin$ lfp (af A))
2. $\bigwedge x.\ \exists p \in$ Paths x. $\forall i.\ p\ i \notin$ lfp (af A) $\Longrightarrow$
   $\exists p \in$ Paths x. $\forall i.\ p\ i \notin A$

Both are solved automatically:

```
 apply(auto dest: not_in_lfp_afD)
done
```

If you find these proofs too complicated, we recommend that you read Sect. 9.3.4, where we show how inductive definitions lead to simpler arguments.

The main theorem is proved as for PDL, except that we also derive the necessary equality `lfp(af A) = ...` by combining `AF_lemma1` and `AF_lemma2` on the spot:

```
theorem "mc f = {s. s ⊨ f}"
apply(induct_tac f)
apply(auto simp add: EF_lemma equalityI[OF AF_lemma1 AF_lemma2])
done
```

The language defined above is not quite CTL. The latter also includes an until-operator `EU f g` with semantics "there Exists a path where `f` is true Until `g` becomes true". We need an auxiliary function:

```
consts until:: "state set ⇒ state set ⇒ state ⇒ state list ⇒ bool"
primrec
"until A B s []      = (s ∈ B)"
"until A B s (t#p) = (s ∈ A ∧ (s,t) ∈ M ∧ until A B t p)"
```

Expressing the semantics of `EU` is now straightforward:

$$s \models EU\ f\ g = (\exists p.\ until\ \{t.\ t \models f\}\ \{t.\ t \models g\}\ s\ p)$$

Note that `EU` is not definable in terms of the other operators!

Model checking `EU` is again a least fixed point construction:

$$mc(EU\ f\ g) = lfp(\lambda T.\ mc\ g \cup mc\ f \cap (M^{-1}\ ``\ T))$$

Exercise 6.6.2 Extend the datatype of formulae by the above until operator and prove the equivalence between semantics and model checking, i.e. that

$$mc \ (EU \ f \ g) \ = \ \{s. \ s \models EU \ f \ g\}$$

For more CTL exercises see, for example, Huth and Ryan [14].

Let us close this section with a few words about the executability of our model checkers. It is clear that if all sets are finite, they can be represented as lists and the usual set operations are easily implemented. Only `lfp` requires a little thought. Fortunately, theory `While_Combinator` in the Library [4] provides a theorem stating that in the case of finite sets and a monotone function `F`, the value of `lfp F` can be computed by iterated application of `F` to `{}` until a fixed point is reached. It is actually possible to generate executable functional programs from HOL definitions, but that is beyond the scope of the tutorial.

7. Inductively Defined Sets

This chapter is dedicated to the most important definition principle after recursive functions and datatypes: inductively defined sets.

We start with a simple example: the set of even numbers. A slightly more complicated example, the reflexive transitive closure, is the subject of Sect. 7.2. In particular, some standard induction heuristics are discussed. Advanced forms of inductive definitions are discussed in Sect. 7.3. To demonstrate the versatility of inductive definitions, the chapter closes with a case study from the realm of context-free grammars. The first two sections are required reading for anybody interested in mathematical modelling.

7.1 The Set of Even Numbers

The set of even numbers can be inductively defined as the least set containing 0 and closed under the operation +2. Obviously, *even* can also be expressed using the divides relation (`dvd`). We shall prove below that the two formulations coincide. On the way we shall examine the primary means of reasoning about inductively defined sets: rule induction.

7.1.1 Making an Inductive Definition

Using **consts**, we declare the constant *even* to be a set of natural numbers. The **inductive** declaration gives it the desired properties.

```
consts even :: "nat set"
inductive even
intros
zero[intro!]: "0 ∈ even"
step[intro!]: "n ∈ even ⟹ (Suc (Suc n)) ∈ even"
```

An inductive definition consists of introduction rules. The first one above states that 0 is even; the second states that if n is even, then so is $n+2$. Given this declaration, Isabelle generates a fixed point definition for *even* and proves theorems about it, thus following the definitional approach (see Sect. 2.7). These theorems include the introduction rules specified in the declaration, an elimination rule for case analysis and an induction rule. We can refer to these theorems by automatically-generated names. Here are two examples:

T. Nipkow, L.C. Paulson, and M. Wenzel: Isabelle/HOL, LNCS 2283, pp. 127–145, 2002.
© Springer-Verlag Berlin Heidelberg 2002

```
0 ∈ even                                                  (even.zero)
n ∈ even ⟹ Suc (Suc n) ∈ even                            (even.step)
```

The introduction rules can be given attributes. Here both rules are specified as *intro!*, directing the classical reasoner to apply them aggressively. Obviously, regarding 0 as even is safe. The *step* rule is also safe because $n + 2$ is even if and only if n is even. We prove this equivalence later.

7.1.2 Using Introduction Rules

Our first lemma states that numbers of the form $2 \times k$ are even. Introduction rules are used to show that specific values belong to the inductive set. Such proofs typically involve induction, perhaps over some other inductive set.

```
lemma two_times_even[intro!]: "2*k ∈ even"
apply (induct_tac k)
 apply auto
done
```

The first step is induction on the natural number k, which leaves two subgoals:

```
1. 2 * 0 ∈ even
2. ⋀n. 2 * n ∈ even ⟹ 2 * Suc n ∈ even
```

Here auto simplifies both subgoals so that they match the introduction rules, which are then applied automatically.

Our ultimate goal is to prove the equivalence between the traditional definition of *even* (using the divides relation) and our inductive definition. One direction of this equivalence is immediate by the lemma just proved, whose *intro!* attribute ensures it is applied automatically.

```
lemma dvd_imp_even: "2 dvd n ⟹ n ∈ even"
by (auto simp add: dvd_def)
```

7.1.3 Rule Induction

From the definition of the set *even*, Isabelle has generated an induction rule:

```
⟦xa ∈ even;
 P 0;
 ⋀n. ⟦n ∈ even; P n⟧ ⟹ P (Suc (Suc n))⟧
 ⟹ P xa                                                  (even.induct)
```

A property P holds for every even number provided it holds for 0 and is closed under the operation $Suc(Suc \cdot)$. Then P is closed under the introduction rules for *even*, which is the least set closed under those rules. This type of inductive argument is called **rule induction**.

Apart from the double application of *Suc*, the induction rule above resembles the familiar mathematical induction, which indeed is an instance of rule induction; the natural numbers can be defined inductively to be the least set containing 0 and closed under *Suc*.

Induction is the usual way of proving a property of the elements of an inductively defined set. Let us prove that all members of the set *even* are multiples of two.

lemma *even_imp_dvd:* *"n ∈ even ⟹ 2 dvd n"*

We begin by applying induction. Note that *even.induct* has the form of an elimination rule, so we use the method *erule*. We get two subgoals:

apply *(erule even.induct)*

```
1. 2 dvd 0
2. ⋀n. ⟦n ∈ even; 2 dvd n⟧ ⟹ 2 dvd Suc (Suc n)
```

We unfold the definition of *dvd* in both subgoals, proving the first one and simplifying the second:

apply *(simp_all add: dvd_def)*

```
1. ⋀n. ⟦n ∈ even; ∃k. n = 2 * k⟧ ⟹ ∃k. Suc (Suc n) = 2 * k
```

The next command eliminates the existential quantifier from the assumption and replaces *n* by *2 * k*.

apply *clarify*

```
1. ⋀n k. 2 * k ∈ even ⟹ ∃ka. Suc (Suc (2 * k)) = 2 * ka
```

To conclude, we tell Isabelle that the desired value is *Suc k*. With this hint, the subgoal falls to *simp*.

apply *(rule_tac x = "Suc k" in exI, simp)*

Combining the previous two results yields our objective, the equivalence relating *even* and *dvd*.

theorem *even_iff_dvd:* *"(n ∈ even) = (2 dvd n)"*
by *(blast intro: dvd_imp_even even_imp_dvd)*

7.1.4 Generalization and Rule Induction

Before applying induction, we typically must generalize the induction formula. With rule induction, the required generalization can be hard to find and sometimes requires a complete reformulation of the problem. In this example, our first attempt uses the obvious statement of the result. It fails:

lemma *"Suc (Suc n) ∈ even ⟹ n ∈ even"*
apply *(erule even.induct)*
oops

Rule induction finds no occurrences of *Suc(Suc n)* in the conclusion, which it therefore leaves unchanged. (Look at *even.induct* to see why this happens.) We have these subgoals:

```
1. n ∈ even
2. ⋀na. [na ∈ even; n ∈ even] ⟹ n ∈ even
```

The first one is hopeless. Rule inductions involving non-trivial terms usually fail. How to deal with such situations in general is described in Sect. 9.3.1 below. In the current case the solution is easy because we have the necessary inverse, subtraction:

lemma even_imp_even_minus_2: "n ∈ even ⟹ n-2 ∈ even"
apply (erule even.induct)
 apply auto
done

This lemma is trivially inductive. Here are the subgoals:

```
1. 0 - 2 ∈ even
2. ⋀n. [n ∈ even; n - 2 ∈ even] ⟹ Suc (Suc n) - 2 ∈ even
```

The first is trivial because 0 - 2 simplifies to 0, which is even. The second is trivial too: Suc (Suc n) - 2 simplifies to n, matching the assumption.

Using our lemma, we can easily prove the result we originally wanted:

lemma Suc_Suc_even_imp_even: "Suc (Suc n) ∈ even ⟹ n ∈ even"
by (drule even_imp_even_minus_2, simp)

We have just proved the converse of the introduction rule even.step. This suggests proving the following equivalence. We give it the iff attribute because of its obvious value for simplification.

lemma [iff]: "((Suc (Suc n)) ∈ even) = (n ∈ even)"
by (blast dest: Suc_Suc_even_imp_even)

7.1.5 Rule Inversion

Case analysis on an inductive definition is called **rule inversion**. It is frequently used in proofs about operational semantics. It can be highly effective when it is applied automatically. Let us look at how rule inversion is done in Isabelle/HOL.

Recall that even is the minimal set closed under these two rules:

```
0 ∈ even
n ∈ even ⟹ Suc (Suc n) ∈ even
```

Minimality means that even contains only the elements that these rules force it to contain. If we are told that a belongs to even then there are only two possibilities. Either a is 0 or else a has the form Suc(Suc n), for some suitable n that belongs to even. That is the gist of the cases rule, which Isabelle proves for us when it accepts an inductive definition:

```
[a ∈ even;
  a = 0 ⟹ P;
  ⋀n. [a = Suc(Suc n); n ∈ even] ⟹ P] ⟹ P                    (even.cases)
```

This general rule is less useful than instances of it for specific patterns. For example, if a has the form `Suc(Suc n)` then the first case becomes irrelevant, while the second case tells us that n belongs to `even`. Isabelle will generate this instance for us:

inductive_cases `Suc_Suc_cases` `[elim!]`:   `"Suc(Suc n) ∈ even"`

The **inductive_cases** command generates an instance of the `cases` rule for the supplied pattern and gives it the supplied name:

[[`Suc(Suc n) ∈ even; n ∈ even ⟹ P`]] ⟹ `P`   (`Suc_Suc_cases`)

Applying this as an elimination rule yields one case where `even.cases` would yield two. Rule inversion works well when the conclusions of the introduction rules involve datatype constructors like `Suc` and `#` (list "cons"); freeness reasoning discards all but one or two cases.

In the **inductive_ cases** command we supplied an attribute, `elim!`, indicating that this elimination rule can be applied aggressively. The original `cases` rule would loop if used in that manner because the pattern a matches everything.

The rule `Suc_Suc_cases` is equivalent to the following implication:

`Suc (Suc n) ∈ even ⟹ n ∈ even`

Just above we devoted some effort to reaching precisely this result. Yet we could have obtained it by a one-line declaration, dispensing with the lemma `even_imp_even_minus_2`. This example also justifies the terminology **rule inversion**: the new rule inverts the introduction rule `even.step`. In general, a rule can be inverted when the set of elements it introduces is disjoint from those of the other introduction rules.

For one-off applications of rule inversion, use the `ind_cases` method. Here is an example:

apply (`ind_cases` `"Suc(Suc n) ∈ even"`)

The specified instance of the `cases` rule is generated, then applied as an elimination rule.

To summarize, every inductive definition produces a `cases` rule. The **inductive_cases** command stores an instance of the `cases` rule for a given pattern. Within a proof, the `ind_cases` method applies an instance of the `cases` rule.

The even numbers example has shown how inductive definitions can be used. Later examples will show that they are actually worth using.

7.1.6 Mutually Inductive Definitions

Just as there are datatypes defined by mutual recursion, there are sets defined by mutual induction. As a trivial example we consider the even and odd natural numbers:

```
consts even :: "nat set"
       odd  :: "nat set"
```

```
inductive even odd
intros
zero:  "0 ∈ even"
evenI: "n ∈ odd ⟹ Suc n ∈ even"
oddI:  "n ∈ even ⟹ Suc n ∈ odd"
```

The mutually inductive definition of multiple sets is no different from that of a single set, except for induction: just as for mutually recursive datatypes, induction needs to involve all the simultaneously defined sets. In the above case, the induction rule is called `even_odd.induct` (simply concatenate the names of the sets involved) and has the conclusion

$$(?x \in even \longrightarrow ?P\ ?x) \land (?y \in odd \longrightarrow ?Q\ ?y)$$

If we want to prove that all even numbers are divisible by two, we have to generalize the statement as follows:

lemma `"(m ∈ even ⟶ 2 dvd m) ∧ (n ∈ odd ⟶ 2 dvd (Suc n))"`

The proof is by rule induction. Because of the form of the induction theorem, it is applied by `rule` rather than `erule` as for ordinary inductive definitions:

apply`(rule even_odd.induct)`

```
 1. 2 dvd 0
 2. ⋀n. ⟦n ∈ odd; 2 dvd Suc n⟧ ⟹ 2 dvd Suc n
 3. ⋀n. ⟦n ∈ even; 2 dvd n⟧ ⟹ 2 dvd Suc (Suc n)
```

The first two subgoals are proved by simplification and the final one can be proved in the same manner as in Sect. 7.1.3 where the same subgoal was encountered before. We do not show the proof script.

7.2 The Reflexive Transitive Closure

An inductive definition may accept parameters, so it can express functions that yield sets. Relations too can be defined inductively, since they are just sets of pairs. A perfect example is the function that maps a relation to its reflexive transitive closure. This concept was already introduced in Sect. 6.3, where the operator * was defined as a least fixed point because inductive definitions were not yet available. But now they are:

consts `rtc :: "('a × 'a)set ⇒ ('a × 'a)set"    ("_*" [1000] 999)`
inductive `"r*"`
intros

```
rtc_refl[iff]:    "(x,x) ∈ r*"
rtc_step:         "[ (x,y) ∈ r; (y,z) ∈ r* ] ⟹ (x,z) ∈ r*"
```

The function `rtc` is annotated with concrete syntax: instead of `rtc r` we can write `r*`. The actual definition consists of two rules. Reflexivity is obvious and is immediately given the `iff` attribute to increase automation. The second rule, `rtc_step`, says that we can always add one more `r`-step to the left. Although we could make `rtc_step` an introduction rule, this is dangerous: the recursion in the second premise slows down and may even kill the automatic tactics.

The above definition of the concept of reflexive transitive closure may be sufficiently intuitive but it is certainly not the only possible one: for a start, it does not even mention transitivity. The rest of this section is devoted to proving that it is equivalent to the standard definition. We start with a simple lemma:

lemma [intro]: "(x,y) ∈ r ⟹ (x,y) ∈ r*"
by(blast intro: rtc_step)

Although the lemma itself is an unremarkable consequence of the basic rules, it has the advantage that it can be declared an introduction rule without the danger of killing the automatic tactics because `r*` occurs only in the conclusion and not in the premise. Thus some proofs that would otherwise need `rtc_step` can now be found automatically. The proof also shows that `blast` is able to handle `rtc_step`. But some of the other automatic tactics are more sensitive, and even `blast` can be lead astray in the presence of large numbers of rules.

To prove transitivity, we need rule induction, i.e. theorem `rtc.induct`:

```
[(?xb, ?xa) ∈ ?r*; ⋀x. ?P x x;
    ⋀x y z. [(x, y) ∈ ?r; (y, z) ∈ ?r*; ?P y z] ⟹ ?P x z]
⟹ ?P ?xb ?xa
```

It says that `?P` holds for an arbitrary pair `(?xb,?xa) ∈ ?r*` if `?P` is preserved by all rules of the inductive definition, i.e. if `?P` holds for the conclusion provided it holds for the premises. In general, rule induction for an n-ary inductive relation R expects a premise of the form $(x_1, \ldots, x_n) \in R$.

Now we turn to the inductive proof of transitivity:

lemma rtc_trans: "[(x,y) ∈ r*; (y,z) ∈ r*] ⟹ (x,z) ∈ r*"
apply(erule rtc.induct)

Unfortunately, even the base case is a problem:

```
1. ⋀x. (y, z) ∈ r* ⟹ (x, z) ∈ r*
```

We have to abandon this proof attempt. To understand what is going on, let us look again at `rtc.induct`. In the above application of `erule`, the first premise of `rtc.induct` is unified with the first suitable assumption, which is `(x, y) ∈ r*` rather than `(y, z) ∈ r*`. Although that is what we want, it is merely due to the order in which the assumptions occur in the subgoal, which it is not good practice to rely on. As a result, ?xb becomes x, ?xa becomes y and ?P becomes λu v. (u, z) ∈ r*, thus yielding the above subgoal. So what went wrong?

When looking at the instantiation of ?P we see that it does not depend on its second parameter at all. The reason is that in our original goal, of the pair (x, y) only x appears also in the conclusion, but not y. Thus our induction statement is too weak. Fortunately, it can easily be strengthened: transfer the additional premise (y, z) ∈ r* into the conclusion:

lemma rtc_trans[rule_format]:
  "(x,y) ∈ r* ⟹ (y,z) ∈ r* ⟶ (x,z) ∈ r*"

This is not an obscure trick but a generally applicable heuristic:

> *When proving a statement by rule induction on $(x_1, \ldots, x_n) \in R$, pull all other premises containing any of the x_i into the conclusion using*
> ⟶.

A similar heuristic for other kinds of inductions is formulated in Sect. 9.3.1. The rule_format directive turns ⟶ back into ⟹: in the end we obtain the original statement of our lemma.

apply(erule rtc.induct)

Now induction produces two subgoals which are both proved automatically:

```
1. ⋀x. (x, z) ∈ r* ⟶ (x, z) ∈ r*
2. ⋀x y za.
     ⟦(x, y) ∈ r; (y, za) ∈ r*; (za, z) ∈ r* ⟶ (y, z) ∈ r*⟧
     ⟹ (za, z) ∈ r* ⟶ (x, z) ∈ r*
```

apply(blast)
apply(blast intro: rtc_step)
done

Let us now prove that r* is really the reflexive transitive closure of r, i.e. the least reflexive and transitive relation containing r. The latter is easily formalized

consts rtc2 :: "('a × 'a)set ⟹ ('a × 'a)set"
inductive "rtc2 r"
intros
"(x,y) ∈ r ⟹ (x,y) ∈ rtc2 r"
"(x,x) ∈ rtc2 r"
"⟦ (x,y) ∈ rtc2 r; (y,z) ∈ rtc2 r ⟧ ⟹ (x,z) ∈ rtc2 r"

and the equivalence of the two definitions is easily shown by the obvious rule inductions:

lemma "(x,y) ∈ rtc2 r ⟹ (x,y) ∈ r*"
apply(erule rtc2.induct)

```
  apply(blast)
 apply(blast)
apply(blast intro: rtc_trans)
done

lemma "(x,y) ∈ r* ⟹ (x,y) ∈ rtc2 r"
apply(erule rtc.induct)
 apply(blast intro: rtc2.intros)
apply(blast intro: rtc2.intros)
done
```

So why did we start with the first definition? Because it is simpler. It contains only two rules, and the single step rule is simpler than transitivity. As a consequence, `rtc.induct` is simpler than `rtc2.induct`. Since inductive proofs are hard enough anyway, we should always pick the simplest induction schema available. Hence `rtc` is the definition of choice.

Exercise 7.2.1 Show that the converse of `rtc_step` also holds:

$$[\![(x, \ y) \in r*; \ (y, \ z) \in r]\!] \implies (x, \ z) \in r*$$

Exercise 7.2.2 Repeat the development of this section, but starting with a definition of `rtc` where `rtc_step` is replaced by its converse as shown in exercise 7.2.1.

7.3 Advanced Inductive Definitions

The premises of introduction rules may contain universal quantifiers and monotone functions. A universal quantifier lets the rule refer to any number of instances of the inductively defined set. A monotone function lets the rule refer to existing constructions (such as "list of") over the inductively defined set. The examples below show how to use the additional expressiveness and how to reason from the resulting definitions.

7.3.1 Universal Quantifiers in Introduction Rules

As a running example, this section develops the theory of **ground terms**: terms constructed from constant and function symbols but not variables. To simplify matters further, we regard a constant as a function applied to the null argument list. Let us declare a datatype `gterm` for the type of ground terms. It is a type constructor whose argument is a type of function symbols.

```
datatype 'f gterm = Apply 'f "'f gterm list"
```

To try it out, we declare a datatype of some integer operations: integer constants, the unary minus operator and the addition operator.

datatype `integer_op` = `Number int | UnaryMinus | Plus`

Now the type `integer_op gterm` denotes the ground terms built over those symbols.

The type constructor `gterm` can be generalized to a function over sets. It returns the set of ground terms that can be formed over a set `F` of function symbols. For example, we could consider the set of ground terms formed from the finite set `{Number 2, UnaryMinus, Plus}`.

This concept is inductive. If we have a list `args` of ground terms over `F` and a function symbol `f` in `F`, then we can apply `f` to `args` to obtain another ground term. The only difficulty is that the argument list may be of any length. Hitherto, each rule in an inductive definition referred to the inductively defined set a fixed number of times, typically once or twice. A universal quantifier in the premise of the introduction rule expresses that every element of `args` belongs to our inductively defined set: is a ground term over `F`. The function `set` denotes the set of elements in a given list.

consts `gterms` `::` `"'f set ⇒ 'f gterm set"`
inductive `"gterms F"`
intros
`step[intro!]:` `"⟦∀ t ∈ set args. t ∈ gterms F; f ∈ F⟧`
`⟹ (Apply f args) ∈ gterms F"`

To demonstrate a proof from this definition, let us show that the function `gterms` is **monotone**. We shall need this concept shortly.

lemma `gterms_mono:` `"F⊆G ⟹ gterms F ⊆ gterms G"`
apply `clarify`
apply `(erule gterms.induct)`
apply `blast`
done

Intuitively, this theorem says that enlarging the set of function symbols enlarges the set of ground terms. The proof is a trivial rule induction. First we use the `clarify` method to assume the existence of an element of `gterms F`. (We could have used `intro subsetI`.) We then apply rule induction. Here is the resulting subgoal:

1. ⋀x args f.
    ⟦F ⊆ G; ∀t∈set args. t ∈ gterms F ∧ t ∈ gterms G; f ∈ F⟧
    ⟹ Apply f args ∈ gterms G

The assumptions state that `f` belongs to `F`, which is included in `G`, and that every element of the list `args` is a ground term over `G`. The `blast` method finds this chain of reasoning easily.

! Why do we call this function `gterms` instead of `gterm`? A constant may have the same name as a type. However, name clashes could arise in the theorems that Isabelle generates. Our choice of names keeps `gterms.induct` separate from `gterm.induct`.

Call a term **well-formed** if each symbol occurring in it is applied to the correct number of arguments. (This number is called the symbol's **arity**.) We can express well-formedness by generalizing the inductive definition of *gterms*. Suppose we are given a function called `arity`, specifying the arities of all symbols. In the inductive step, we have a list `args` of such terms and a function symbol `f`. If the length of the list matches the function's arity then applying `f` to `args` yields a well-formed term.

```
consts well_formed_gterm :: "('f ⇒ nat) ⇒ 'f gterm set"
inductive "well_formed_gterm arity"
intros
step[intro!]: "[[∀t ∈ set args. t ∈ well_formed_gterm arity;
                length args = arity f]]
               ⟹ (Apply f args) ∈ well_formed_gterm arity"
```

The inductive definition neatly captures the reasoning above. The universal quantification over the `set` of arguments expresses that all of them are well-formed.

7.3.2 Alternative Definition Using a Monotone Function

An inductive definition may refer to the inductively defined set through an arbitrary monotone function. To demonstrate this powerful feature, let us change the inductive definition above, replacing the quantifier by a use of the function `lists`. This function, from the Isabelle theory of lists, is analogous to the function *gterms* declared above: if A is a set then `lists A` is the set of lists whose elements belong to A.

In the inductive definition of well-formed terms, examine the one introduction rule. The first premise states that `args` belongs to the `lists` of well-formed terms. This formulation is more direct, if more obscure, than using a universal quantifier.

```
consts well_formed_gterm' :: "('f ⇒ nat) ⇒ 'f gterm set"
inductive "well_formed_gterm' arity"
intros
step[intro!]: "[[args ∈ lists (well_formed_gterm' arity);
                length args = arity f]]
               ⟹ (Apply f args) ∈ well_formed_gterm' arity"
monos lists_mono
```

We cite the theorem `lists_mono` to justify using the function `lists`.[1]

$$A \subseteq B \implies lists\ A \subseteq lists\ B \qquad\qquad (lists\_mono)$$

Why must the function be monotone? An inductive definition describes an iterative construction: each element of the set is constructed by a finite number of introduction rule applications. For example, the elements of *even* are constructed by finitely many applications of the rules

---

[1] This particular theorem is installed by default already, but we include the **monos** declaration in order to illustrate its syntax.

```
0 ∈ even
n ∈ even ⟹ (Suc (Suc n)) ∈ even
```

All references to a set in its inductive definition must be positive. Applications of an introduction rule cannot invalidate previous applications, allowing the construction process to converge. The following pair of rules do not constitute an inductive definition:

```
0 ∈ even
n ∉ even ⟹ (Suc n) ∈ even
```

Showing that 4 is even using these rules requires showing that 3 is not even. It is far from trivial to show that this set of rules characterizes the even numbers.

Even with its use of the function *lists*, the premise of our introduction rule is positive:

```
args ∈ lists (well_formed_gterm' arity)
```

To apply the rule we construct a list `args` of previously constructed well-formed terms. We obtain a new term, `Apply f args`. Because `lists` is monotone, applications of the rule remain valid as new terms are constructed. Further lists of well-formed terms become available and none are taken away.

7.3.3 A Proof of Equivalence

We naturally hope that these two inductive definitions of "well-formed" coincide. The equality can be proved by separate inclusions in each direction. Each is a trivial rule induction.

```
lemma "well_formed_gterm arity ⊆ well_formed_gterm' arity"
apply clarify
apply (erule well_formed_gterm.induct)
apply auto
done
```

The `clarify` method gives us an element of `well_formed_gterm` arity on which to perform induction. The resulting subgoal can be proved automatically:

```
1. ⋀x args f.
     ⟦∀t∈set args.
         t ∈ well_formed_gterm arity ∧ t ∈ well_formed_gterm' arity;
       length args = arity f⟧
     ⟹ Apply f args ∈ well_formed_gterm' arity
```

This proof resembles the one given in Sect. 7.3.1 above, especially in the form of the induction hypothesis. Next, we consider the opposite inclusion:

```
lemma "well_formed_gterm' arity ⊆ well_formed_gterm arity"
apply clarify
apply (erule well_formed_gterm'.induct)
apply auto
done
```

The proof script is identical, but the subgoal after applying induction may be surprising:

```
1. ⋀x args f.
      ⟦args ∈ lists (well_formed_gterm' arity ∩
                      {u. u ∈ well_formed_gterm arity});
        length args = arity f⟧
        ⟹ Apply f args ∈ well_formed_gterm arity
```

The induction hypothesis contains an application of `lists`. Using a monotone function in the inductive definition always has this effect. The subgoal may look uninviting, but fortunately `lists` distributes over intersection:

$$lists\ (A \cap B) = lists\ A \cap lists\ B \qquad\qquad (lists\_Int\_eq)$$

Thanks to this default simplification rule, the induction hypothesis is quickly replaced by its two parts:

```
            args ∈ lists (well_formed_gterm' arity)
            args ∈ lists (well_formed_gterm arity)
```

Invoking the rule `well_formed_gterm.step` completes the proof. The call to `auto` does all this work.

This example is typical of how monotone functions can be used. In particular, many of them distribute over intersection. Monotonicity implies one direction of this set equality; we have this theorem:

$$mono\ f \implies f\ (A \cap B) \subseteq f\ A \cap f\ B \qquad\qquad (mono\_Int)$$

7.3.4 Another Example of Rule Inversion

Does `gterms` distribute over intersection? We have proved that this function is monotone, so `mono_Int` gives one of the inclusions. The opposite inclusion asserts that if t is a ground term over both of the sets F and G then it is also a ground term over their intersection, $F \cap G$.

```
lemma gterms_IntI:
     "t ∈ gterms F ⟹ t ∈ gterms G ⟶ t ∈ gterms (F∩G)"
```

Attempting this proof, we get the assumption `Apply f args ∈ gterms G`, which cannot be broken down. It looks like a job for rule inversion:

```
inductive_cases gterm_Apply_elim [elim!]: "Apply f args ∈ gterms F"
```

Here is the result.

```
⟦Apply f args ∈ gterms F;
  ⟦∀t∈set args. t ∈ gterms F; f ∈ F⟧ ⟹ P⟧
⟹ P                                           (gterm_Apply_elim)
```

This rule replaces an assumption about `Apply f args` by assumptions about `f` and `args`. No cases are discarded (there was only one to begin with) but the rule applies specifically to the pattern `Apply f args`. It can be applied repeatedly as an elimination rule without looping, so we have given the `elim!` attribute.

Now we can prove the other half of that distributive law.

```
lemma gterms_IntI [rule_format, intro!]:
    "t ∈ gterms F ⟹ t ∈ gterms G ⟶ t ∈ gterms (F∩G)"
apply (erule gterms.induct)
apply blast
done
```

The proof begins with rule induction over the definition of *gterms*, which leaves a single subgoal:

```
1. ⋀args f.
    [∀t∈set args. t ∈ gterms F ∧
                  (t ∈ gterms G ⟶ t ∈ gterms (F ∩ G));
     f ∈ F]
    ⟹ Apply f args ∈ gterms G ⟶ Apply f args ∈ gterms (F ∩ G)
```

To prove this, we assume `Apply f args ∈ gterms G`. Rule inversion, in the form of `gterm_Apply_elim`, infers that every element of `args` belongs to `gterms G`; hence (by the induction hypothesis) it belongs to `gterms (F ∩ G)`. Rule inversion also yields `f ∈ G` and hence `f ∈ F ∩ G`. All of this reasoning is done by `blast`.

Our distributive law is a trivial consequence of previously-proved results:

```
theorem gterms_Int_eq [simp]:
    "gterms (F∩G) = gterms F ∩ gterms G"
by (blast intro!: mono_Int monoI gterms_mono)
```

Exercise 7.3.1 A function mapping function symbols to their types is called a **signature**. Given a type ranging over type symbols, we can represent a function's type by a list of argument types paired with the result type. Complete this inductive definition:

```
consts well_typed_gterm:: "('f ⇒ 't list * 't) ⇒ ('f gterm * 't)set"
inductive "well_typed_gterm sig"
```

7.4 Case Study: A Context Free Grammar

Grammars are nothing but shorthands for inductive definitions of nonterminals which represent sets of strings. For example, the production $A \to Bc$ is short for

$$w \in B \Longrightarrow wc \in A$$

This section demonstrates this idea with an example due to Hopcroft and Ullman, a grammar for generating all words with an equal number of a's and b's:

$$
\begin{aligned}
S &\to \epsilon \mid bA \mid aB \\
A &\to aS \mid bAA \\
B &\to bS \mid aBB
\end{aligned}
$$

At the end we say a few words about the relationship between the original proof [12, p. 81] and our formal version.

We start by fixing the alphabet, which consists only of a's and b's:

datatype alfa = a | b

For convenience we include the following easy lemmas as simplification rules:

lemma *[simp]:* *"(x ≠ a) = (x = b) ∧ (x ≠ b) = (x = a)"*
by *(case_tac x, auto)*

Words over this alphabet are of type alfa list, and the three nonterminals are declared as sets of such words:

consts S :: *"alfa list set"*
          A :: *"alfa list set"*
          B :: *"alfa list set"*

The productions above are recast as a *mutual* inductive definition of S, A and B:

inductive S A B
intros
  "[] ∈ S"
  "w ∈ A ⟹ b#w ∈ S"
  "w ∈ B ⟹ a#w ∈ S"

  "w ∈ S   ⟹ a#w ∈ A"
  "⟦ v∈A; w∈A ⟧ ⟹ b#v@w ∈ A"

  "w ∈ S   ⟹ b#w ∈ B"
  "⟦ v ∈ B; w ∈ B ⟧ ⟹ a#v@w ∈ B"

First we show that all words in S contain the same number of a's and b's. Since the definition of S is by mutual induction, so is the proof: we show at the same time that all words in A contain one more a than b and all words in B contains one more b than a.

lemma *correctness:*
  "(w ∈ S ⟶ size[x∈w. x=a] = size[x∈w. x=b])   ∧
   (w ∈ A ⟶ size[x∈w. x=a] = size[x∈w. x=b] + 1) ∧
   (w ∈ B ⟶ size[x∈w. x=b] = size[x∈w. x=a] + 1)"

These propositions are expressed with the help of the predefined *filter* function on lists, which has the convenient syntax [x∈xs. P x], the list of all elements x in xs such that P x holds. Remember that on lists *size* and *length* are synonymous.

The proof itself is by rule induction and afterwards automatic:

by *(rule S_A_B.induct, auto)*

This may seem surprising at first, and is indeed an indication of the power of inductive definitions. But it is also quite straightforward. For example, consider the production $A \rightarrow bAA$: if $v, w \in A$ and the elements of A contain one more a than b's, then bvw must again contain one more a than b's.

As usual, the correctness of syntactic descriptions is easy, but completeness is hard: does S contain *all* words with an equal number of a's and b's? It turns out that this proof requires the following lemma: every string with two more a's than b's can be cut somewhere such that each half has one more a than b. This is best seen by imagining counting the difference between the number of a's and b's starting at the left end of the word. We start with 0 and end (at the right end) with 2. Since each move to the right increases or decreases the difference by 1, we must have passed through 1 on our way from 0 to 2. Formally, we appeal to the following discrete intermediate value theorem `nat0_intermed_int_val`

$$\llbracket \forall i.\ i < n \longrightarrow |f\ (i + 1) - f\ i| \leq 1;\ f\ 0 \leq k;\ k \leq f\ n \rrbracket$$
$$\implies \exists i.\ i \leq n \wedge f\ i = k$$

where `f` is of type `nat` $\Rightarrow$ `int`, `int` are the integers, $|.|$ is the absolute value function[2], and `1` is the integer 1 (see Sect. 8.1).

First we show that our specific function, the difference between the numbers of a's and b's, does indeed only change by 1 in every move to the right. At this point we also start generalizing from a's and b's to an arbitrary property `P`. Otherwise we would have to prove the desired lemma twice, once as stated above and once with the roles of a's and b's interchanged.

lemma *step1:* `"`$\forall$ `i < size w.`
`  |(int(size[x`$\in$`take (i+1) w. P x])-int(size[x`$\in$`take (i+1) w. ¬P x]))`
`   - (int(size[x`$\in$`take i w. P x])-int(size[x`$\in$`take i w. ¬P x]))| ≤ 1"`

The lemma is a bit hard to read because of the coercion function `int :: nat` $\Rightarrow$ `int`. It is required because `size` returns a natural number, but subtraction on type `nat` will do the wrong thing. Function `take` is predefined and `take i xs` is the prefix of length `i` of `xs`; below we also need `drop i xs`, which is what remains after that prefix has been dropped from `xs`.

The proof is by induction on `w`, with a trivial base case, and a not so trivial induction step. Since it is essentially just arithmetic, we do not discuss it.

apply`(induct_tac w)`
 apply`(simp)`
by`(force simp add: zabs_def take_Cons split: nat.split if_splits)`

Finally we come to the above-mentioned lemma about cutting in half a word with two more elements of one sort than of the other sort:

lemma *part1:*
`  "size[x`$\in$`w. P x] = size[x`$\in$`w. ¬P x]+2` $\implies$
`  `$\exists$`i`$\leq$`size w. size[x`$\in$`take i w. P x] = size[x`$\in$`take i w. ¬P x]+1"`

---

[2] See Table A.1 in the Appendix for the correct ASCII syntax.

This is proved by *force* with the help of the intermediate value theorem, instantiated appropriately and with its first premise disposed of by lemma *step1*:

apply(*insert nat0_intermed_int_val[OF step1, of "P" "w" "1"]*)
by *force*

Lemma *part1* tells us only about the prefix *take i w*. An easy lemma deals with the suffix *drop i w*:

lemma *part2*:
    "⟦size[x∈take i w @ drop i w. P x] =
    size[x∈take i w @ drop i w. ¬P x]+2;
    size[x∈take i w. P x] = size[x∈take i w. ¬P x]+1⟧
    ⟹ size[x∈drop i w. P x] = size[x∈drop i w. ¬P x]+1"
by(*simp del: append_take_drop_id*)

In the proof we have disabled the normally useful lemma

take n xs @ drop n xs = xs   (*append_take_drop_id*)

to allow the simplifier to apply the following lemma instead:

    [x∈xs@ys. P x] = [x∈xs. P x] @ [x∈ys. P x]

To dispose of trivial cases automatically, the rules of the inductive definition are declared simplification rules:

declare *S_A_B.intros[simp]*

This could have been done earlier but was not necessary so far.

The completeness theorem tells us that if a word has the same number of a's and b's, then it is in *S*, and similarly for *A* and *B*:

theorem *completeness*:
    "(size[x∈w. x=a] = size[x∈w. x=b]   ⟶ w ∈ S) ∧
    (size[x∈w. x=a] = size[x∈w. x=b] + 1 ⟶ w ∈ A) ∧
    (size[x∈w. x=b] = size[x∈w. x=a] + 1 ⟶ w ∈ B)"

The proof is by induction on *w*. Structural induction would fail here because, as we can see from the grammar, we need to make bigger steps than merely appending a single letter at the front. Hence we induct on the length of *w*, using the induction rule *length_induct*:

apply(*induct_tac w rule: length_induct*)

The *rule* parameter tells *induct_tac* explicitly which induction rule to use. For details see Sect. 9.3.2 below. In this case the result is that we may assume the lemma already holds for all words shorter than *w*.

The proof continues with a case distinction on *w*, on whether *w* is empty or not.

apply(*case_tac w*)
 apply(*simp_all*)

Simplification disposes of the base case and leaves only a conjunction of two step cases to be proved: if `w = a # v` and

$$\text{length } [x \in v \ . \ x = a] = \text{length } [x \in v \ . \ x = b] + 2$$

then `b # v ∈ A`, and similarly for `w = b # v`. We only consider the first case in detail.

After breaking the conjunction up into two cases, we can apply `part1` to the assumption that `w` contains two more `a`'s than `b`'s.

apply(rule conjI)
 apply(clarify)
 apply(frule part1[of "λx. x=a", simplified])
 apply(clarify)

This yields an index $i \le$ `length v` such that

$$\text{length } [x \in \text{take } i \ v \ . \ x = a] = \text{length } [x \in \text{take } i \ v \ . \ x = b] + 1$$

With the help of `part2` it follows that

$$\text{length } [x \in \text{drop } i \ v \ . \ x = a] = \text{length } [x \in \text{drop } i \ v \ . \ x = b] + 1$$

 apply(drule part2[of "λx. x=a", simplified])
  apply(assumption)

Now it is time to decompose `v` in the conclusion `b # v ∈ A` into `take i v @ drop i v`,

 apply(rule_tac n1=i and t=v in subst[OF append_take_drop_id])

(the variables `n1` and `t` are the result of composing the theorems `subst` and `append_take_drop_id`) after which the appropriate rule of the grammar reduces the goal to the two subgoals `take i v ∈ A` and `drop i v ∈ A`:

 apply(rule S_A_B.intros)

Both subgoals follow from the induction hypothesis because both `take i v` and `drop i v` are shorter than `w`:

  apply(force simp add: min_less_iff_disj)
 apply(force split add: nat_diff_split)

The case `w = b # v` is proved analogously:

apply(clarify)
apply(frule part1[of "λx. x=b", simplified])
apply(clarify)
apply(drule part2[of "λx. x=b", simplified])
 apply(assumption)
apply(rule_tac n1=i and t=v in subst[OF append_take_drop_id])
apply(rule S_A_B.intros)

```
apply(force simp add: min_less_iff_disj)
by(force simp add: min_less_iff_disj split add: nat_diff_split)
```

We conclude this section with a comparison of our proof with Hopcroft and Ullman's [12, p. 81]. For a start, the textbook grammar, for no good reason, excludes the empty word, thus complicating matters just a little bit: they have 8 instead of our 7 productions.

More importantly, the proof itself is different: rather than separating the two directions, they perform one induction on the length of a word. This deprives them of the beauty of rule induction, and in the easy direction (correctness) their reasoning is more detailed than our `auto`. For the hard part (completeness), they consider just one of the cases that our `simp_all` disposes of automatically. Then they conclude the proof by saying about the remaining cases: "We do this in a manner similar to our method of proof for part (1); this part is left to the reader". But this is precisely the part that requires the intermediate value theorem and thus is not at all similar to the other cases (which are automatic in Isabelle). The authors are at least cavalier about this point and may even have overlooked the slight difficulty lurking in the omitted cases. Such errors are found in many pen-and-paper proofs when they are scrutinized formally.

Part III

Advanced Material

8. More about Types

So far we have learned about a few basic types (for example `bool` and `nat`), type abbreviations (**types**) and recursive datatypes (**datatype**). This chapter will introduce more advanced material:

- More about basic types: numbers (Sect. 8.1), pairs (Sect. 8.2) and records (Sect. 8.3), and how to reason about them.
- Type classes: how to specify and reason about axiomatic collections of types (Sect. 8.4).
- Introducing your own types: how to introduce new types that cannot be constructed with any of the basic methods (Sect. 8.5).

The material in this section goes beyond the needs of most novices. Serious users should at least skim the sections on basic types and on type classes. The latter material is fairly advanced; read the beginning to understand what it is about, but consult the rest only when necessary.

8.1 Numbers

Until now, our numerical examples have used the type of **natural numbers**, `nat`. This is a recursive datatype generated by the constructors zero and successor, so it works well with inductive proofs and primitive recursive function definitions. HOL also provides the type `int` of **integers**, which lack induction but support true subtraction. The integers are preferable to the natural numbers for reasoning about complicated arithmetic expressions, even for some expressions whose value is non-negative. The logic HOL-Real also has the type `real` of real numbers. Isabelle has no subtyping, so the numeric types are distinct and there are functions to convert between them. Fortunately most numeric operations are overloaded: the same symbol can be used at all numeric types. Table A.2 in the appendix shows the most important operations, together with the priorities of the infix symbols.

Many theorems involving numeric types can be proved automatically by Isabelle's arithmetic decision procedure, the method `arith`. Linear arithmetic comprises addition, subtraction and multiplication by constant factors; subterms involving other operators are regarded as variables. The procedure can be slow, especially if the subgoal to be proved involves subtraction over type *nat*, which causes case splits.

The simplifier reduces arithmetic expressions in other ways, such as dividing through by common factors. For problems that lie outside the scope of automation, HOL provides hundreds of theorems about multiplication, division, etc., that can be brought to bear. You can locate them using Proof General's Find button. A few lemmas are given below to show what is available.

8.1.1 Numeric Literals

The constants *0* and *1* are overloaded. They denote zero and one, respectively, for all numeric types. Other values are expressed by numeric literals, which consist of one or more decimal digits optionally preceeded by a minus sign (-). Examples are *2*, *-3* and *441223334678*. Literals are available for the types of natural numbers, integers and reals; they denote integer values of arbitrary size.

Literals look like constants, but they abbreviate terms representing the number in a two's complement binary notation. Isabelle performs arithmetic on literals by rewriting rather than using the hardware arithmetic. In most cases arithmetic is fast enough, even for large numbers. The arithmetic operations provided for literals include addition, subtraction, multiplication, integer division and remainder. Fractions of literals (expressed using division) are reduced to lowest terms.

! The arithmetic operators are overloaded, so you must be careful to ensure that
• each numeric expression refers to a specific type, if necessary by inserting type constraints. Here is an example of what can go wrong:

lemma *"2 * m = m + m"*

Carefully observe how Isabelle displays the subgoal:

    1. (2::'a) * m = m + m

The type *'a* given for the literal 2 warns us that no numeric type has been specified. The problem is underspecified. Given a type constraint such as *nat*, *int* or *real*, it becomes trivial.

! Numeric literals are not constructors and therefore must not be used in pat-
• terns. For example, this declaration is rejected:

recdef *h "{}"*
"h 3 = 2"
"h i = i"

You should use a conditional expression instead:

"h i = (if i = 3 then 2 else i)"

8.1.2 The Type of Natural Numbers, nat

This type requires no introduction: we have been using it from the beginning. Hundreds of theorems about the natural numbers are proved in the theories *Nat*, *NatArith* and *Divides*. Only in exceptional circumstances should you resort to induction.

Literals. The notational options for the natural numbers are confusing. Recall that an overloaded constant can be defined independently for each type; the definition of 1 for type nat is

$$1 \equiv Suc \ 0 \qquad\qquad\qquad\qquad (One\_nat\_def)$$

This is installed as a simplification rule, so the simplifier will replace every occurrence of 1::nat by *Suc 0*. Literals are obviously better than nested *Suc*s at expressing large values. But many theorems, including the rewrite rules for primitive recursive functions, can only be applied to terms of the form *Suc n*.

The following default simplification rules replace small literals by zero and successor:

$$2 + n = Suc \ (Suc \ n) \qquad\qquad\qquad (add\_2\_eq\_Suc)$$
$$n + 2 = Suc \ (Suc \ n) \qquad\qquad\qquad (add\_2\_eq\_Suc')$$

It is less easy to transform *100* into *Suc 99* (for example), and the simplifier will normally reverse this transformation. Novices should express natural numbers using *0* and *Suc* only.

Typical lemmas. Inequalities involving addition and subtraction alone can be proved automatically. Lemmas such as these can be used to prove inequalities involving multiplication and division:

$$[\![i \leq j; \ k \leq l]\!] \Longrightarrow i * k \leq j * l \qquad\qquad (mult\_le\_mono)$$
$$[\![i < j; \ 0 < k]\!] \Longrightarrow i * k < j * k \qquad\qquad (mult\_less\_mono1)$$
$$m \leq n \Longrightarrow m \ div \ k \leq n \ div \ k \qquad\qquad (div\_le\_mono)$$

Various distributive laws concerning multiplication are available:

$$(m + n) * k = m * k + n * k \qquad\qquad\quad (add\_mult\_distrib)$$
$$(m - n) * k = m * k - n * k \qquad\qquad\quad (diff\_mult\_distrib)$$
$$(m \ mod \ n) * k = (m * k) \ mod \ (n * k) \qquad (mod\_mult\_distrib)$$

Division. The infix operators *div* and *mod* are overloaded. Isabelle/HOL provides the basic facts about quotient and remainder on the natural numbers:

$$m \ mod \ n = (if \ m < n \ then \ m \ else \ (m - n) \ mod \ n) \qquad (mod\_if)$$
$$m \ div \ n * n + m \ mod \ n = m \qquad\qquad\qquad (mod\_div\_equality)$$

Many less obvious facts about quotient and remainder are also provided. Here is a selection:

```
a * b div c = a * (b div c) + a * (b mod c) div c        (div_mult1_eq)
a * b mod c = a * (b mod c) mod c                         (mod_mult1_eq)
a div (b*c) = a div b div c                               (div_mult2_eq)
a mod (b*c) = b * (a div b mod c) + a mod b               (mod_mult2_eq)
0 < c ⟹ (c * a) div (c * b) = a div b                     (div_mult_mult1)
```

Surprisingly few of these results depend upon the divisors' being nonzero. That is because division by zero yields zero:

```
a div 0 = 0                                   (DIVISION_BY_ZERO_DIV)
a mod 0 = a                                   (DIVISION_BY_ZERO_MOD)
```

As a concession to convention, these equations are not installed as default simplification rules. In `div_mult_mult1` above, one of the two divisors (namely `c`) must still be nonzero.

The **divides** relation has the standard definition, which is overloaded over all numeric types:

```
m dvd n ≡ ∃k. n = m * k                                       (dvd_def)
```

Section 5.17 discusses proofs involving this relation. Here are some of the facts proved about it:

```
⟦m dvd n; n dvd m⟧ ⟹ m = n                             (dvd_anti_sym)
⟦k dvd m; k dvd n⟧ ⟹ k dvd (m + n)                          (dvd_add)
```

Simplifier Tricks. The rule `diff_mult_distrib` shown above is one of the few facts about $m - n$ that is not subject to the condition $n \leq m$. Natural number subtraction has few nice properties; often you should remove it by simplifying with this split rule:

```
P(a-b) = ((a<b ⟶ P 0) ∧ (∀d. a = b+d ⟶ P d))        (nat_diff_split)
```

For example, splitting helps to prove the following fact:

lemma `"(n - 2) * (n + 2) = n * n - (4::nat)"`
apply `(simp split: nat_diff_split, clarify)`
  1. ⋀d. ⟦n < 2; n * n = 4 + d⟧ ⟹ d = 0

The result lies outside the scope of linear arithmetic, but it is easily found if we explicitly split `n<2` as `n=0` or `n=1`:

apply `(subgoal_tac "n=0 | n=1", force, arith)`
done

Suppose that two expressions are equal, differing only in associativity and commutativity of addition. Simplifying with the following equations sorts the terms and groups them to the right, making the two expressions identical:

```
m + n + k = m + (n + k)          .                           (add_assoc)
m + n = n + m                                              (add_commute)
x + (y + z) = y + (x + z)                            (add_left_commute)
```

The name `add_ac` refers to the list of all three theorems; similarly there is `mult_ac`. Here is an example of the sorting effect. Start with this goal:

  1. Suc (i + j * l * k + m * n) = f (n * m + i + k * j * l)

Simplify using `add_ac` and `mult_ac`:

apply *(simp add: add_ac mult_ac)*

Here is the resulting subgoal:

  1. Suc (i + (m * n + j * (k * 1))) = f (i + (m * n + j * (k * 1)))

8.1.3 The Type of Integers, int

Reasoning methods resemble those for the natural numbers, but induction and the constant `Suc` are not available. HOL provides many lemmas for proving inequalities involving integer multiplication and division, similar to those shown above for type `nat`.

The absolute value function `abs` is overloaded for the numeric types. It is defined for the integers; we have for example the obvious law

$$|x * y| = |x| * |y| \qquad\qquad \text{(abs\_mult)}$$

! The absolute value bars shown above cannot be typed on a keyboard. They can
• be entered using the X-symbol package. In ASCII, type `abs x` to get $|x|$.

The `arith` method can prove facts about `abs` automatically, though as it does so by case analysis, the cost can be exponential.

lemma "abs (x+y) $\leq$ abs x + abs (y :: int)"
by `arith`

Concerning simplifier tricks, we have no need to eliminate subtraction: it is well-behaved. As with the natural numbers, the simplifier can sort the operands of sums and products. The name `zadd_ac` refers to the associativity and commutativity theorems for integer addition, while `zmult_ac` has the analogous theorems for multiplication. The prefix `z` in many theorem names recalls the use of $\mathbb{Z}$ to denote the set of integers.

For division and remainder, the treatment of negative divisors follows mathematical practice: the sign of the remainder follows that of the divisor:

0 < b $\Longrightarrow$ 0 $\leq$ a mod b	(pos_mod_sign)
0 < b $\Longrightarrow$ a mod b < b	(pos_mod_bound)
b < 0 $\Longrightarrow$ a mod b $\leq$ 0	(neg_mod_sign)
b < 0 $\Longrightarrow$ b < a mod b	(neg_mod_bound)

ML treats negative divisors in the same way, but most computer hardware treats signed operands using the same rules as for multiplication. Many facts about quotients and remainders are provided:

```
(a + b) div c =
a div c + b div c + (a mod c + b mod c) div c        (zdiv_zadd1_eq)
(a + b) mod c = (a mod c + b mod c) mod c             (zmod_zadd1_eq)

(a * b) div c = a * (b div c) + a * (b mod c) div c   (zdiv_zmult1_eq)
(a * b) mod c = a * (b mod c) mod c                   (zmod_zmult1_eq)
```

```
0 < c ⟹ a div (b*c) = a div b div c                (zdiv_zmult2_eq)
0 < c ⟹ a mod (b*c) = b*(a div b mod c) + a mod b  (zmod_zmult2_eq)
```

The last two differ from their natural number analogues by requiring c to be positive. Since division by zero yields zero, we could allow c to be zero. However, c cannot be negative: a counterexample is $a = 7$, $b = 2$ and $c = -3$, when the left-hand side of `zdiv_zmult2_eq` is -2 while the right-hand side is -1.

8.1.4 The Type of Real Numbers, `real`

The real numbers enjoy two significant properties that the integers lack. They are **dense**: between every two distinct real numbers there lies another. This property follows from the division laws, since if $x < y$ then between them lies $(x + y)/2$. The second property is that they are **complete**: every set of reals that is bounded above has a least upper bound. Completeness distinguishes the reals from the rationals, for which the set $\{x \mid x^2 < 2\}$ has no least upper bound. (It could only be $\sqrt{2}$, which is irrational.) The formalization of completeness is complicated; rather than reproducing it here, we refer you to the theory `RComplete` in directory `Real`. Density, however, is trivial to express:

```
x < y ⟹ ∃r. x < r ∧ r < y                          (real_dense)
```

Here is a selection of rules about the division operator. The following are installed as default simplification rules in order to express combinations of products and quotients as rational expressions:

```
x * (y / z) = x * y / z                        (real_times_divide1_eq)
y / z * x = y * x / z                          (real_times_divide2_eq)
x / (y / z) = x * z / y                        (real_divide_divide1_eq)
x / y / z = x / (y * z)                        (real_divide_divide2_eq)
```

Signs are extracted from quotients in the hope that complementary terms can then be cancelled:

```
- x / y = - (x / y)                            (real_minus_divide_eq)
x / - y = - (x / y)                            (real_divide_minus_eq)
```

The following distributive law is available, but it is not installed as a simplification rule.

```
(x + y) / z = x / z + y / z                    (real_add_divide_distrib)
```

As with the other numeric types, the simplifier can sort the operands of addition and multiplication. The name `real_add_ac` refers to the associativity and commutativity theorems for addition, while similarly `real_mult_ac` contains those properties for multiplication.

The absolute value function `abs` is defined for the reals, along with many theorems such as this one about exponentiation:

```
|r ^ n| = |r| ^ n                                  (realpow_abs)
```

Numeric literals for type *real* have the same syntax as those for type *int* and only express integral values. Fractions expressed using the division operator are automatically simplified to lowest terms:

```
1. P ((3 / 4) * (8 / 15))
apply simp
1. P (2 / 5)
```

Exponentiation can express floating-point values such as *2 * 10^6*, but at present no special simplification is performed.

! Type *real* is only available in the logic HOL-Real, which is HOL extended with
• a definitional development of the real numbers. Base your theory upon theory *Real*, not the usual *Main*. Launch Isabelle using the command

```
Isabelle -l HOL-Real
```

Also distributed with Isabelle is HOL-Hyperreal, whose theory *Hyperreal* defines the type *hypreal* of non-standard reals. These **hyperreals** include infinitesimals, which represent infinitely small and infinitely large quantities; they facilitate proofs about limits, differentiation and integration [8]. The development defines an infinitely large number, *omega* and an infinitely small positive number, *epsilon*. The relation $x \approx y$ means "x is infinitely close to y." Theory *Hyperreal* also defines transcendental functions such as sine, cosine, exponential and logarithm — even the versions for type *real*, because they are defined using nonstandard limits.

8.2 Pairs and Tuples

Ordered pairs were already introduced in Sect. 2.5.2, but only with a minimal repertoire of operations: pairing and the two projections *fst* and *snd*. In any non-trivial application of pairs you will find that this quickly leads to unreadable nests of projections. This section introduces syntactic sugar to overcome this problem: pattern matching with tuples.

8.2.1 Pattern Matching with Tuples

Tuples may be used as patterns in λ-abstractions, for example $\lambda(x,y,z).x+y+z$ and $\lambda((x,y),z).x+y+z$. In fact, tuple patterns can be used in most variable binding constructs, and they can be nested. Here are some typical examples:

```
let (x, y) = f z in (y, x)
case xs of [] ⇒ 0 | (x, y) # zs ⇒ x + y
∀ (x,y)∈A. x=y
{(x,y,z). x=z}
⋃ (x, y)∈A. {x + y}
```

The intuitive meanings of these expressions should be obvious. Unfortunately, we need to know in more detail what the notation really stands for once we have to reason about it. Abstraction over pairs and tuples is merely a convenient shorthand for a more complex internal representation. Thus the internal and external form of a term may differ, which can affect proofs. If you want to avoid this complication, stick to *fst* and *snd* and write λp. *fst* p + *snd* p instead of λ(x,y). x+y. These terms are distinct even though they denote the same function.

Internally, λ(x, y). t becomes *split* (λx y. t), where *split* is the uncurrying function of type ('a ⇒ 'b ⇒ 'c) ⇒ 'a × 'b ⇒ 'c defined as

$$split \equiv \lambda c\ p.\ c\ (fst\ p)\ (snd\ p) \hspace{2cm} (split\_def)$$

Pattern matching in other variable binding constructs is translated similarly. Thus we need to understand how to reason about such constructs.

8.2.2 Theorem Proving

The most obvious approach is the brute force expansion of *split*:

lemma "(λ(x,y).x) p = fst p"
by(simp add: split_def)

This works well if rewriting with *split_def* finishes the proof, as it does above. But if it does not, you end up with exactly what we are trying to avoid: nests of *fst* and *snd*. Thus this approach is neither elegant nor very practical in large examples, although it can be effective in small ones.

If we consider why this lemma presents a problem, we quickly realize that we need to replace the variable p by some pair (a, b). Then both sides of the equation would simplify to a by the simplification rules *split* c (a, b) = c a b and *fst* (a, b) = a. To reason about tuple patterns requires some way of converting a variable of product type into a pair.

In case of a subterm of the form *split* f p this is easy: the split rule *split_split* replaces p by a pair:

lemma "(λ(x,y).y) p = snd p"
apply(split split_split)

1. ∀x y. p = (x, y) ⟶ y = snd p

This subgoal is easily proved by simplification. Thus we could have combined simplification and splitting in one command that proves the goal outright:

by(simp split: split_split)

Let us look at a second example:

lemma "let (x,y) = p in fst p = x"
apply(simp only: Let_def)

1. (λ(x, y). fst p = x) p

A paired `let` reduces to a paired λ-abstraction, which can be split as above. The same is true for paired set comprehension:

lemma "p ∈ {(x,y). x=y} ⟶ fst p = snd p"
apply *simp*

1. `split op = p ⟶ fst p = snd p`

Again, simplification produces a term suitable for `split_split` as above. If you are worried about the strange form of the premise: `split op =` is short for λ(x,y). x=y. The same proof procedure works for

lemma "p ∈ {(x,y). x=y} ⟹ fst p = snd p"

except that we now have to use `split_split_asm`, because `split` occurs in the assumptions.

However, splitting `split` is not always a solution, as no `split` may be present in the goal. Consider the following function:

consts swap :: "'a × 'b ⟹ 'b × 'a"
primrec
  "swap (x,y) = (y,x)"

Note that the above **primrec** definition is admissible because × is a datatype. When we now try to prove

lemma "swap(swap p) = p"

simplification will do nothing, because the defining equation for `swap` expects a pair. Again, we need to turn p into a pair first, but this time there is no `split` in sight. In this case the only thing we can do is to split the term by hand:

apply (case_tac p)

1. ⋀a b. p = (a, b) ⟹ swap (swap p) = p

Again, `case_tac` is applicable because × is a datatype. The subgoal is easily proved by `simp`.

Splitting by `case_tac` also solves the previous examples and may thus appear preferable to the more arcane methods introduced first. However, see the warning about `case_tac` in Sect. 2.4.5.

In case the term to be split is a quantified variable, there are more options. You can split *all* ⋀-quantified variables in a goal with the rewrite rule `split_paired_all`:

lemma "⋀p q. swap(swap p) = q ⟶ p = q"
apply (simp only: split_paired_all)

1. ⋀a b aa ba.
      swap (swap (a, b)) = (aa, ba) ⟶ (a, b) = (aa, ba)

apply *simp*
done

Note that we have intentionally included only *split_paired_all* in the first simplification step, and then we simplify again. This time the reason was not merely pedagogical: *split_paired_all* may interfere with other functions of the simplifier. The following command could fail (here it does not) where two separate *simp* applications succeed.

apply *(simp add: split_paired_all)*

Finally, the simplifier automatically splits all $\forall$ and $\exists$-quantified variables:

lemma *"$\forall p. \exists q. swap\ p = swap\ q$"*
by *simp*

To turn off this automatic splitting, just disable the responsible simplification rules:

$(\forall x.\ P\ x) = (\forall a\ b.\ P\ (a,\ b))$ $(split\_paired\_All)$
$(\exists x.\ P\ x) = (\exists a\ b.\ P\ (a,\ b))$ $(split\_paired\_Ex)$

8.3 Records

Records are familiar from programming languages. A record of n fields is essentially an n-tuple, but the record's components have names, which can make expressions easier to read and reduces the risk of confusing one field for another.

A record of Isabelle/HOL covers a collection of fields, with select and update operations. Each field has a specified type, which may be polymorphic. The field names are part of the record type, and the order of the fields is significant — as it is in Pascal but not in Standard ML. If two different record types have field names in common, then the ambiguity is resolved in the usual way, by qualified names.

Record types can also be defined by extending other record types. Extensible records make use of the reserved pseudo-field *more*, which is present in every record type. Generic record operations work on all possible extensions of a given type scheme; polymorphism takes care of structural sub-typing behind the scenes. There are also explicit coercion functions between fixed record types.

8.3.1 Record Basics

Record types are not primitive in Isabelle and have a delicate internal representation [19], based on nested copies of the primitive product type. A

record declaration introduces a new record type scheme by specifying its fields, which are packaged internally to hold up the perception of the record as a distinguished entity. Here is a simple example:

```
record point =
  Xcoord :: int
  Ycoord :: int
```

Records of type *point* have two fields named *Xcoord* and *Ycoord*, both of type *int*. We now define a constant of type *point*:

```
constdefs
  pt1 :: point
  "pt1 ≡ (| Xcoord = 999, Ycoord = 23 |)"
```

We see above the ASCII notation for record brackets. You can also use the symbolic brackets (| and |). Record type expressions can be also written directly with individual fields. The type name above is merely an abbreviation.

```
constdefs
  pt2 :: "(|Xcoord :: int, Ycoord :: int|)"
  "pt2 ≡ (|Xcoord = -45, Ycoord = 97|)"
```

For each field, there is a *selector* function of the same name. For example, if p has type *point* then *Xcoord p* denotes the value of the *Xcoord* field of p. Expressions involving field selection of explicit records are simplified automatically:

```
lemma "Xcoord (|Xcoord = a, Ycoord = b|) = a"
  by simp
```

The *update* operation is functional. For example, p(|Xcoord := 0|) is a record whose *Xcoord* value is zero and whose *Ycoord* value is copied from p. Updates of explicit records are also simplified automatically:

```
lemma "(|Xcoord = a, Ycoord = b|)(|Xcoord := 0|) =
  (|Xcoord = 0, Ycoord = b|)"
  by simp
```

!• Field names are declared as constants and can no longer be used as variables. It would be unwise, for example, to call the fields of type *point* simply x and y.

8.3.2 Extensible Records and Generic Operations

Now, let us define coloured points (type *cpoint*) to be points extended with a field *col* of type *colour*:

datatype *colour* = *Red* | *Green* | *Blue*

record *cpoint* = *point* +
  col :: *colour*

The fields of this new type are *Xcoord*, *Ycoord* and *col*, in that order.

constdefs
  cpt1 :: *cpoint*
  "*cpt1* ≡ (|*Xcoord* = 999, *Ycoord* = 23, *col* = *Green*|)"

We can define generic operations that work on arbitrary instances of a record scheme, e.g. covering *point*, *cpoint*, and any further extensions. Every record structure has an implicit pseudo-field, *more*, that keeps the extension as an explicit value. Its type is declared as completely polymorphic: '*a*. When a fixed record value is expressed using just its standard fields, the value of *more* is implicitly set to (), the empty tuple, which has type *unit*. Within the record brackets, you can refer to the *more* field by writing "..." (three dots):

lemma "*Xcoord* (|*Xcoord* = a, *Ycoord* = b, ... = p|) = a"
  by *simp*

This lemma applies to any record whose first two fields are *Xcoord* and *Ycoord*. Note that (|*Xcoord* = a, *Ycoord* = b, ... = ()|) is exactly the same as (|*Xcoord* = a, *Ycoord* = b|). Selectors and updates are always polymorphic wrt. the *more* part of a record scheme, its value is just ignored (for select) or copied (for update).

The *more* pseudo-field may be manipulated directly as well, but the identifier needs to be qualified:

lemma "*point.more* cpt1 = (|*col* = *Green*|)"
  by (*simp add: cpt1_def*)

We see that the colour part attached to this *point* is a rudimentary record in its own right, namely (|*col* = *Green*|). In order to select or update *col*, this fragment needs to be put back into the context of the parent type scheme, say as *more* part of another *point*.

To define generic operations, we need to know a bit more about records. Our definition of *point* above has generated two type abbreviations:

    point = (|*Xcoord* :: *int*, *Ycoord* :: *int*|)
    '*a point_scheme* = (|*Xcoord* :: *int*, *Ycoord* :: *int*, ... :: '*a*|)

Type *point* is for fixed records having exactly the two fields *Xcoord* and *Ycoord*, while the polymorphic type '*a point_scheme* comprises all possible extensions to those two fields. Note that *unit point_scheme* coincides with *point*, and (|*col* :: *colour*|) *point_scheme* with *cpoint*.

In the following example we define two operations — methods, if we regard records as objects — to get and set any point's *Xcoord* field.

constdefs
```
getX :: "'a point_scheme ⇒ int"
"getX r ≡ Xcoord r"
setX :: "'a point_scheme ⇒ int ⇒ 'a point_scheme"
"setX r a ≡ r(|Xcoord := a|)"
```

Here is a generic method that modifies a point, incrementing its `Xcoord` field. The `Ycoord` and `more` fields are copied across. It works for any record type scheme derived from `point` (including `cpoint` etc.):

constdefs
```
incX :: "'a point_scheme ⇒ 'a point_scheme"
"incX r ≡
    (|Xcoord = Xcoord r + 1, Ycoord = Ycoord r, ... = point.more r|)"
```

Generic theorems can be proved about generic methods. This trivial lemma relates `incX` to `getX` and `setX`:

lemma `"incX r = setX r (getX r + 1)"`
  by `(simp add: getX_def setX_def incX_def)`

!• If you use the symbolic record brackets (| and |), then you must also use the symbolic ellipsis, "…", rather than three consecutive periods, "...". Mixing the ASCII and symbolic versions causes a syntax error. (The two versions are more distinct on screen than they are on paper.)

8.3.3 Record Equality

Two records are equal if all pairs of corresponding fields are equal. Concrete record equalities are simplified automatically:

lemma `"((|Xcoord = a, Ycoord = b|) = (|Xcoord = a', Ycoord = b'|)) =`
   `(a = a' ∧ b = b')"`
  by `simp`

The following equality is similar, but generic, in that `r` can be any instance of `'a point_scheme`:

lemma `"r(|Xcoord := a, Ycoord := b|) = r(|Ycoord := b, Xcoord := a|)"`
  by `simp`

We see above the syntax for iterated updates. We could equivalently have written the left-hand side as `r(|Xcoord := a|)(|Ycoord := b|)`.

Record equality is *extensional*: a record is determined entirely by the values of its fields.

lemma `"r = (|Xcoord = Xcoord r, Ycoord = Ycoord r|)"`
  by `simp`

The generic version of this equality includes the pseudo-field *more*:

lemma *"r = (|Xcoord = Xcoord r, Ycoord = Ycoord r,... = point.more r|)"*
  by *simp*

The simplifier can prove many record equalities automatically, but general equality reasoning can be tricky. Consider proving this obvious fact:

lemma *"r(|Xcoord := a|) = r(|Xcoord := a'|) ⟹ a = a'"*
  apply *simp?*
  oops

Here the simplifier can do nothing, since general record equality is not eliminated automatically. One way to proceed is by an explicit forward step that applies the selector *Xcoord* to both sides of the assumed record equality:

lemma *"r(|Xcoord := a|) = r(|Xcoord := a'|) ⟹ a = a'"*
  apply *(drule_tac f = Xcoord in arg_cong)*

1. *Xcoord (r(|Xcoord := a|)) = Xcoord (r(|Xcoord := a'|)) ⟹ a = a'*

Now, *simp* will reduce the assumption to the desired conclusion.

  apply *simp*
  done

The *cases* method is preferable to such a forward proof. We state the desired lemma again:

lemma *"r(|Xcoord := a|) = r(|Xcoord := a'|) ⟹ a = a'"*

The *cases* method adds an equality to replace the named record term by an explicit record expression, listing all fields. It even includes the pseudo-field *more*, since the record equality stated here is generic for all extensions.

  apply *(cases r)*

1. ⋀*Xcoord Ycoord more.*
    [r(|Xcoord := a|) = r(|Xcoord := a'|);
      r = (|Xcoord = Xcoord, Ycoord = Ycoord, ... = more|)]
    ⟹ a = a'

Again, *simp* finishes the proof. Because *r* is now represented as an explicit record construction, the updates can be applied and the record equality can be replaced by equality of the corresponding fields (due to injectivity).

  apply *simp*
  done

The generic cases method does not admit references to locally bound parameters of a goal. In longer proof scripts one might have to fall back on the primitive *rule_tac* used together with the internal field representation rules of records. The above use of *(cases r)* would become *(rule_tac r = r in point.cases_scheme)*.

8.3.4 Extending and Truncating Records

Each record declaration introduces a number of derived operations to refer collectively to a record's fields and to convert between fixed record types. They can, for instance, convert between types *point* and *cpoint*. We can add a colour to a point or convert a *cpoint* to a *point* by forgetting its colour.

- Function *make* takes as arguments all of the record's fields (including those inherited from ancestors). It returns the corresponding record.
- Function *fields* takes the record's very own fields and returns a record fragment consisting of just those fields. This may be filled into the *more* part of the parent record scheme.
- Function *extend* takes two arguments: a record to be extended and a record containing the new fields.
- Function *truncate* takes a record (possibly an extension of the original record type) and returns a fixed record, removing any additional fields.

These functions provide useful abbreviations for standard record expressions involving constructors and selectors. The definitions, which are *not* unfolded by default, are made available by the collective name of *defs* (*point.defs*, *cpoint.defs*, etc.).

For example, here are the versions of those functions generated for record *point*. We omit *point.fields*, which happens to be the same as *point.make*.

```
point.make Xcoord Ycoord ≡ (|Xcoord = Xcoord, Ycoord = Ycoord|)
point.extend r more ≡
(|Xcoord = Xcoord r, Ycoord = Ycoord r, ... = more|)
point.truncate r ≡ (|Xcoord = Xcoord r, Ycoord = Ycoord r|)
```

Contrast those with the corresponding functions for record *cpoint*. Observe *cpoint.fields* in particular.

```
cpoint.make Xcoord Ycoord col ≡
(|Xcoord = Xcoord, Ycoord = Ycoord, col = col|)
cpoint.fields col ≡ (|col = col|)
cpoint.extend r more ≡
(|Xcoord = Xcoord r, Ycoord = Ycoord r, col = col r, ... = more|)
cpoint.truncate r ≡
(|Xcoord = Xcoord r, Ycoord = Ycoord r, col = col r|)
```

To demonstrate these functions, we declare a new coloured point by extending an ordinary point. Function *point.extend* augments *pt1* with a colour value, which is converted into an appropriate record fragment by *cpoint.fields*.

constdefs
```
cpt2 :: cpoint
"cpt2 ≡ point.extend pt1 (cpoint.fields Green)"
```

The coloured points *cpt1* and *cpt2* are equal. The proof is trivial, by unfolding all the definitions. We deliberately omit the definition of *pt1* in order to reveal the underlying comparison on type *point*.

lemma *"cpt1 = cpt2"*
  apply *(simp add: cpt1_def cpt2_def point.defs cpoint.defs)*

  1. Xcoord pt1 = 999 ∧ Ycoord pt1 = 23

  apply *(simp add: pt1_def)*
  done

In the example below, a coloured point is truncated to leave a point. We use the *truncate* function of the target record.

lemma *"point.truncate cpt2 = pt1"*
  by *(simp add: pt1_def cpt2_def point.defs)*

Exercise 8.3.1 Extend record *cpoint* to have a further field, *intensity*, of type *nat*. Experiment with generic operations (using polymorphic selectors and updates) and explicit coercions (using *extend*, *truncate* etc.) among the three record types.

Exercise 8.3.2 (For Java programmers.) Model a small class hierarchy using records.

8.4 Axiomatic Type Classes

The programming language Haskell has popularized the notion of type classes. In its simplest form, a type class is a set of types with a common interface: all types in that class must provide the functions in the interface. Isabelle offers the related concept of an **axiomatic type class**. Roughly speaking, an axiomatic type class is a type class with axioms, i.e. an axiomatic specification of a class of types. Thus we can talk about a type τ being in a class C, which is written $\tau :: C$. This is the case if τ satisfies the axioms of C. Furthermore, type classes can be organized in a hierarchy. Thus there is the notion of a class D being a **subclass** of a class C, written $D < C$. This is the case if all axioms of C are also provable in D. We introduce these concepts by means of a running example, ordering relations.

8.4.1 Overloading

We start with a concept that is required for type classes but already useful on its own: *overloading*. Isabelle allows overloading: a constant may have multiple definitions at non-overlapping types.

An Initial Example. If we want to introduce the notion of an *inverse* for arbitrary types we give it a polymorphic type

```
consts inverse :: "'a ⇒ 'a"
```

and provide different definitions at different instances:

defs (**overloaded**)
```
inverse_bool: "inverse(b::bool) ≡ ¬ b"
inverse_set:  "inverse(A::'a set) ≡ -A"
inverse_pair: "inverse(p) ≡ (inverse(fst p), inverse(snd p))"
```

Isabelle will not complain because the three definitions do not overlap: no two of the three types `bool`, `'a set` and `'a × 'b` have a common instance. What is more, the recursion in `inverse_pair` is benign because the type of `inverse` becomes smaller: on the left it is `'a × 'b ⇒ 'a × 'b` but on the right `'a ⇒ 'a` and `'b ⇒ 'b`. The annotation (**overloaded**) tells Isabelle that the definitions do intentionally define `inverse` only at instances of its declared type `'a ⇒ 'a` — this merely suppresses warnings to that effect.

However, there is nothing to prevent the user from forming terms such as `inverse []` and proving theorems such as `inverse [] = inverse []` when inverse is not defined on lists. Proving theorems about unspecified constants does not endanger soundness, but it is pointless. To prevent such terms from even being formed requires the use of type classes.

Controlled Overloading with Type Classes. We now start with the theory of ordering relations, which we shall phrase in terms of the two binary symbols `<<` and `<<=` to avoid clashes with `<` and `<=` in theory `Main`. To restrict the application of `<<` and `<<=` we introduce the class `ordrel`:

axclass `ordrel < type`

This introduces a new class `ordrel` and makes it a subclass of the predefined class `type`, which is the class of all HOL types. This is a degenerate form of axiomatic type class without any axioms. Its sole purpose is to restrict the use of overloaded constants to meaningful instances:

```
consts less :: "('a::ordrel) ⇒ 'a ⇒ bool"    (infixl "<<"  50)
       le   :: "('a::ordrel) ⇒ 'a ⇒ bool"    (infixl "<<=" 50)
```

Note that only one occurrence of a type variable in a type needs to be constrained with a class; the constraint is propagated to the other occurrences automatically.

So far there are no types of class `ordrel`. To breathe life into `ordrel` we need to declare a type to be an **instance** of `ordrel`:

instance `bool :: ordrel`

Command **instance** actually starts a proof, namely that `bool` satisfies all axioms of `ordrel`. There are none, but we still need to finish that proof, which we do by invoking the `intro_classes` method:

by `intro_classes`

More interesting **instance** proofs will arise below in the context of proper axiomatic type classes.

Although terms like `False <<= P` are now legal, we still need to say what the relation symbols actually mean at type `bool`:

defs (overloaded)
```
le_bool_def:   "P <<= Q ≡ P ⟶ Q"
less_bool_def: "P << Q ≡ ¬P ∧ Q"
```

Now `False <<= P` is provable:

lemma `"False <<= P"`
by(`simp add: le_bool_def`)

At this point, `[] <<= []` is not even well-typed. To make it well-typed, we need to make lists a type of class `ordrel`:

instance `list :: (type)ordrel`
by `intro_classes`

This **instance** declaration can be read like the declaration of a function on types. The constructor `list` maps types of class `type` (all HOL types), to types of class `ordrel`; in other words, if `ty :: type` then `ty list :: ordrel`. Of course we should also define the meaning of `<<=` and `<<` on lists:

defs (overloaded)
```
prefix_def:
  "xs <<= (ys::'a::ordrel list)  ≡  ∃zs. ys = xs@zs"
strict_prefix_def:
  "xs << (ys::'a::ordrel list)   ≡  xs <<= ys ∧ xs ≠ ys"
```

Of course this is not the only possible definition of the two relations. Componentwise comparison of lists of equal length also makes sense. This time the elements of the list must also be of class `ordrel` to permit their comparison:

instance `list :: (ordrel)ordrel`
by `intro_classes`

defs (overloaded)
```
le_list_def: "xs <<= (ys::'a::ordrel list) ≡
              size xs = size ys ∧ (∀i<size xs. xs!i <<= ys!i)"
```

The infix function `!` yields the nth element of a list.

! A type constructor can be instantiated in only one way to a given type class. For example, our two instantiations of `list` must reside in separate theories with disjoint scopes.

Predefined Overloading. HOL comes with a number of overloaded constants and corresponding classes. The most important ones are listed in Table A.2 in the appendix. They are defined on all numeric types and sometimes on other types as well, for example − and ≤ on sets.

In addition there is a special input syntax for bounded quantifiers:

$$\forall x \leq y.\ P\ x \quad \rightharpoonup \quad \forall x.\ x \leq y \longrightarrow P\ x$$
$$\exists x \leq y.\ P\ x \quad \rightharpoonup \quad \exists x.\ x \leq y \wedge P\ x$$

And analogously for < instead of ≤. The form on the left is translated into the one on the right upon input. For technical reasons, it is not translated back upon output.

8.4.2 Axioms

Attaching axioms to our classes lets us reason on the level of classes. The results will be applicable to all types in a class, just as in axiomatic mathematics. These ideas are demonstrated by means of our ordering relations.

Partial Orders. A *partial order* is a subclass of `ordrel` where certain axioms need to hold:

```
axclass parord < ordrel
refl:     "x <<= x"
trans:    "[ x <<= y; y <<= z ] ⟹ x <<= z"
antisym:  "[ x <<= y; y <<= x ] ⟹ x = y"
less_le:  "x << y = (x <<= y ∧ x ≠ y)"
```

The first three axioms are the familiar ones, and the final one requires that << and <<= are related as expected. Note that behind the scenes, Isabelle has restricted the axioms to class *parord*. For example, the axiom *refl* really is `(?x::?'a::parord) <<= ?x`.

We have not made `less_le` a global definition because it would fix once and for all that << is defined in terms of <<= and never the other way around. Below you will see why we want to avoid this asymmetry. The drawback of our choice is that we need to define both <<= and << for each instance.

We can now prove simple theorems in this abstract setting, for example that << is not symmetric:

lemma *[simp]*: `"(x::'a::parord) << y ⟹ (¬ y << x) = True"`

The conclusion is not just ¬ y << x because the simplifier's preprocessor (see Sect. 9.1.2) would turn it into `(y << x) = False`, yielding a nonterminating rewrite rule. (It would be used to try to prove its own precondition *ad infinitum*.) In the form above, the rule is useful. The type constraint is necessary because otherwise Isabelle would only assume `'a::ordrel` (as required in the type of <<), when the proposition is not a theorem. The proof is easy:

by *(simp add: less_le antisym)*

We could now continue in this vein and develop a whole theory of results about partial orders. Eventually we will want to apply these results to concrete types, namely the instances of the class. Thus we first need to prove that the types in question, for example *bool*, are indeed instances of *parord*:

instance *bool* :: *parord*
apply *intro_classes*

This time *intro_classes* leaves us with the four axioms, specialized to type *bool*, as subgoals:

1. $\bigwedge x{::}bool.\ x \mathrel{<<=} x$
2. $\bigwedge (x{::}bool)\ (y{::}bool)\ z{::}bool.\ [\![x \mathrel{<<=} y;\ y \mathrel{<<=} z]\!] \implies x \mathrel{<<=} z$
3. $\bigwedge (x{::}bool)\ y{::}bool.\ [\![x \mathrel{<<=} y;\ y \mathrel{<<=} x]\!] \implies x = y$
4. $\bigwedge (x{::}bool)\ y{::}bool.\ (x \mathrel{<<} y) = (x \mathrel{<<=} y \land x \neq y)$

Fortunately, the proof is easy for *blast* once we have unfolded the definitions of << and <<= at type *bool*:

apply (*simp_all* (*no_asm_use*) *only: le_bool_def less_bool_def*)
by (*blast, blast, blast, blast*)

Can you figure out why we have to include (*no_asm_use*)?

We can now apply our single lemma above in the context of booleans:

lemma "(*P*::*bool*) << *Q* $\implies$ ¬(*Q* << *P*)"
by *simp*

The effect is not stunning, but it demonstrates the principle. It also shows that tools like the simplifier can deal with generic rules. The main advantage of the axiomatic method is that theorems can be proved in the abstract and freely reused for each instance.

Linear Orders. If any two elements of a partial order are comparable it is a **linear** or **total** order:

axclass *linord* < *parord*
linear: "*x* <<= *y* $\lor$ *y* <<= *x*"

By construction, *linord* inherits all axioms from *parord*. Therefore we can show that linearity can be expressed in terms of << as follows:

lemma "$\bigwedge x{::}'a{::}linord.\ x \mathrel{<<} y \lor x = y \lor y \mathrel{<<} x$"
apply (*simp add: less_le*)
apply (*insert linear*)
apply *blast*
done

Linear orders are an example of subclassing by construction, which is the most common case. Subclass relationships can also be proved. This is the topic of the following paragraph.

Strict Orders. An alternative axiomatization of partial orders takes `<<`
rather than `<<=` as the primary concept. The result is a **strict** order:

```
axclass strord < ordrel
irrefl:      "¬ x << x"
less_trans:  "⟦ x << y; y << z ⟧ ⟹ x << z"
le_less:     "x <<= y = (x << y ∨ x = y)"
```

It is well known that partial orders are the same as strict orders. Let us prove
one direction, namely that partial orders are a subclass of strict orders.

```
instance parord < strord
apply intro_classes
```

```
1. ⋀x::'a. ¬ x << x
2. ⋀(x::'a) (y::'a) z::'a. ⟦x << y; y << z⟧ ⟹ x << z
3. ⋀(x::'a) y::'a. (x <<= y) = (x << y ∨ x = y)
type variables:
  'a :: parord
```

Assuming `'a :: parord`, the three axioms of class `strord` are easily proved:

```
  apply(simp_all (no_asm_use) add: less_le)
 apply(blast intro: trans antisym)
apply(blast intro: refl)
done
```

The subclass relation must always be acyclic. Therefore Isabelle will complain if you also prove the relationship `strord < parord`.

Multiple Inheritance and Sorts. A class may inherit from more than
one direct superclass. This is called **multiple inheritance**. For example, we
could define the classes of well-founded orderings and well-orderings:

```
axclass wford < parord
wford: "wf {(y,x). y << x}"
```

```
axclass wellord < linord, wford
```

The last line expresses the usual definition: a well-ordering is a linear well-
founded ordering. The result is the subclass diagram in Figure 8.1.

Since class `wellord` does not introduce any new axioms, it can simply be
viewed as the intersection of the two classes `linord` and `wford`. Such intersections need not be given a new name but can be created on the fly: the
expression $\{C_1, \ldots, C_n\}$, where the C_i are classes, represents the intersection of the C_i. Such an expression is called a **sort**, and sorts can appear in
most places where we have only shown classes so far, for example in type
constraints: `'a::{linord,wford}`. In fact, `'a::C` is short for `'a::{C}`. However,
we do not pursue this rarefied concept further.

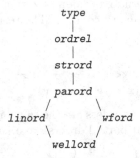

Fig. 8.1. Subclass Diagram

This concludes our demonstration of type classes based on orderings. We remind our readers that `Main` contains a theory of orderings phrased in terms of the usual $\leq$ and $<$. If possible, base your own ordering relations on this theory.

Inconsistencies. The reader may be wondering what happens if we attach an inconsistent set of axioms to a class. So far we have always avoided to add new axioms to HOL for fear of inconsistencies and suddenly it seems that we are throwing all caution to the wind. So why is there no problem?

The point is that by construction, all type variables in the axioms of an **axclass** are automatically constrained with the class being defined (as shown for axiom `refl` above). These constraints are always carried around and Isabelle takes care that they are never lost, unless the type variable is instantiated with a type that has been shown to belong to that class. Thus you may be able to prove `False` from your axioms, but Isabelle will remind you that this theorem has the hidden hypothesis that the class is non-empty.

Even if each individual class is consistent, intersections of (unrelated) classes readily become inconsistent in practice. Now we know this need not worry us.

8.5 Introducing New Types

For most applications, a combination of predefined types like `bool` and $\Rightarrow$ with recursive datatypes and records is quite sufficient. Very occasionally you may feel the need for a more advanced type. If you are certain that your type is not definable by any of the standard means, then read on.

! Types in HOL must be non-empty; otherwise the quantifier rules would be unsound, because $\exists x.\ x = x$ is a theorem.

8.5.1 Declaring New Types

The most trivial way of introducing a new type is by a **type declaration**:

typedecl *my_new_type*

This does not define *my_new_type* at all but merely introduces its name. Thus we know nothing about this type, except that it is non-empty. Such declarations without definitions are useful if that type can be viewed as a parameter of the theory. A typical example is given in Sect. 6.6, where we define a transition relation over an arbitrary type of states.

In principle we can always get rid of such type declarations by making those types parameters of every other type, thus keeping the theory generic. In practice, however, the resulting clutter can make types hard to read.

If you are looking for a quick and dirty way of introducing a new type together with its properties: declare the type and state its properties as axioms. Example:

axioms
just_one: "∃x::my_new_type. ∀y. x = y"

However, we strongly discourage this approach, except at explorative stages of your development. It is extremely easy to write down contradictory sets of axioms, in which case you will be able to prove everything but it will mean nothing. In the example above, the axiomatic approach is unnecessary: a one-element type called *unit* is already defined in HOL.

8.5.2 Defining New Types

Now we come to the most general means of safely introducing a new type, the **type definition**. All other means, for example **datatype**, are based on it. The principle is extremely simple: any non-empty subset of an existing type can be turned into a new type. More precisely, the new type is specified to be isomorphic to some non-empty subset of an existing type.

Let us work a simple example, the definition of a three-element type. It is easily represented by the first three natural numbers:

typedef *three* = "{0::nat, 1, 2}"

In order to enforce that the representing set on the right-hand side is non-empty, this definition actually starts a proof to that effect:

1. ∃x. x ∈ {0, 1, 2}

Fortunately, this is easy enough to show, even *auto* could do it. In general, one has to provide a witness, in our case 0:

apply(*rule_tac x = 0 in exI*)
by *simp*

This type definition introduces the new type *three* and asserts that it is a copy of the set *{0, 1, 2}*. This assertion is expressed via a bijection between the *type* *three* and the *set* *{0, 1, 2}*. To this end, the command declares the following constants behind the scenes:

$$
\begin{array}{rcl}
\text{three} & :: & \text{nat set} \\
\text{Rep\_three} & :: & \text{three} \Rightarrow \text{nat} \\
\text{Abs\_three} & :: & \text{nat} \Rightarrow \text{three}
\end{array}
$$

where constant *three* is explicitly defined as the representing set:

three ≡ {0, 1, 2}   (three_def)

The situation is best summarized with the help of the following diagram, where squares denote types and the irregular region denotes a set:

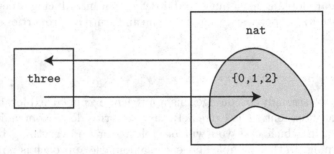

Finally, **typedef** asserts that *Rep_three* is surjective on the subset *three* and *Abs_three* and *Rep_three* are inverses of each other:

$$
\begin{array}{ll}
\text{Rep\_three } x \in \text{three} & (\text{Rep\_three}) \\
\text{Abs\_three (Rep\_three } x) = x & (\text{Rep\_three\_inverse}) \\
y \in \text{three} \implies \text{Rep\_three (Abs\_three } y) = y & (\text{Abs\_three\_inverse})
\end{array}
$$

From this example it should be clear what **typedef** does in general given a name (here *three*) and a set (here *{0, 1, 2}*).

Our next step is to define the basic functions expected on the new type. Although this depends on the type at hand, the following strategy works well:

– define a small kernel of basic functions that can express all other functions you anticipate.
– define the kernel in terms of corresponding functions on the representing type using *Abs* and *Rep* to convert between the two levels.

In our example it suffices to give the three elements of type *three* names:

constdefs
```
  A:: three
 "A ≡ Abs_three 0"
  B:: three
 "B ≡ Abs_three 1"
```

```
  C :: three
"C ≡ Abs_three 2"
```

So far, everything was easy. But it is clear that reasoning about `three` will be hell if we have to go back to `nat` every time. Thus our aim must be to raise our level of abstraction by deriving enough theorems about type `three` to characterize it completely. And those theorems should be phrased in terms of A, B and C, not `Abs_three` and `Rep_three`. Because of the simplicity of the example, we merely need to prove that A, B and C are distinct and that they exhaust the type.

In processing our **typedef** declaration, Isabelle proves several helpful lemmas. The first two express injectivity of `Rep_three` and `Abs_three`:

$$(Rep\_three\ x = Rep\_three\ y) = (x = y) \qquad (Rep\_three\_inject)$$
$$\begin{array}{l} [\![x \in three;\ y \in three\ ]\!] \\ \implies (Abs\_three\ x = Abs\_three\ y) = (x = y) \end{array} \qquad (Abs\_three\_inject)$$

The following ones allow to replace some $x::three$ by $Abs\_three(y::nat)$, and conversely y by $Rep\_three\ x$:

$$[\![y \in three;\ \bigwedge x.\ y = Rep\_three\ x \implies P]\!] \implies P \qquad (Rep\_three\_cases)$$
$$(\bigwedge y.\ [\![x = Abs\_three\ y;\ y \in three]\!] \implies P) \implies P \qquad (Abs\_three\_cases)$$
$$[\![y \in three;\ \bigwedge x.\ P\ (Rep\_three\ x)]\!] \implies P\ y \qquad (Rep\_three\_induct)$$
$$(\bigwedge y.\ y \in three \implies P\ (Abs\_three\ y)) \implies P\ x \qquad (Abs\_three\_induct)$$

These theorems are proved for any type definition, with `three` replaced by the name of the type in question.

Distinctness of A, B and C follows immediately if we expand their definitions and rewrite with the injectivity of `Abs_three`:

lemma "A ≠ B ∧ B ≠ A ∧ A ≠ C ∧ C ≠ A ∧ B ≠ C ∧ C ≠ B"
by(simp add: Abs_three_inject A_def B_def C_def three_def)

Of course we rely on the simplifier to solve goals like $0 \neq 1$.

The fact that A, B and C exhaust type `three` is best phrased as a case distinction theorem: if you want to prove $P\ x$ (where x is of type `three`) it suffices to prove $P\ A$, $P\ B$ and $P\ C$:

lemma three_cases: "[P A; P B; P C] ⟹ P x"

Again this follows easily from a pre-proved general theorem:

apply(induct_tac x rule: Abs_three_induct)

1. $\bigwedge y.$ [P A; P B; P C; y ∈ three] ⟹ P (Abs_three y)

Simplification with `three_def` leads to the disjunction $y = 0 \lor y = 1 \lor y = 2$ which `auto` separates into three subgoals, each of which is easily solved by simplification:

apply(auto simp add: three_def A_def B_def C_def)
done

This concludes the derivation of the characteristic theorems for type *three*.

The attentive reader has realized long ago that the above lengthy definition can be collapsed into one line:

```
datatype better_three = A | B | C
```

In fact, the **datatype** command performs internally more or less the same derivations as we did, which gives you some idea what life would be like without **datatype**.

Although *three* could be defined in one line, we have chosen this example to demonstrate **typedef** because its simplicity makes the key concepts particularly easy to grasp. If you would like to see a non-trivial example that cannot be defined more directly, we recommend the definition of *finite multisets* in the Library [4].

Let us conclude by summarizing the above procedure for defining a new type. Given some abstract axiomatic description P of a type ty in terms of a set of functions F, this involves three steps:

1. Find an appropriate type τ and subset A which has the desired properties P, and make a type definition based on this representation.
2. Define the required functions F on ty by lifting analogous functions on the representation via Abs_ty and Rep_ty.
3. Prove that P holds for ty by lifting P from the representation.

You can now forget about the representation and work solely in terms of the abstract functions F and properties P.

9. Advanced Simplification, Recursion, and Induction

Although we have already learned a lot about simplification, recursion and induction, there are some advanced proof techniques that we have not covered yet and which are worth learning. The three sections of this chapter are almost independent of each other and can be read in any order. Only the notion of *congruence rules*, introduced in the section on simplification, is required for parts of the section on recursion.

9.1 Simplification

This section describes features not covered until now. It also outlines the simplification process itself, which can be helpful when the simplifier does not do what you expect of it.

9.1.1 Advanced Features

Congruence Rules. While simplifying the conclusion Q of $P \implies Q$, it is legal use the assumption P. For $\implies$ this policy is hardwired, but contextual information can also be made available for other operators. For example, $xs = []$ $\longrightarrow$ xs @ $xs = xs$ simplifies to $True$ because we may use $xs = []$ when simplifying xs @ $xs = xs$. The generation of contextual information during simplification is controlled by so-called **congruence rules**. This is the one for $\longrightarrow$:

$$[\![P = P'; \ P' \implies Q = Q']\!] \implies (P \longrightarrow Q) = (P' \longrightarrow Q')$$

It should be read as follows: In order to simplify $P \longrightarrow Q$ to $P' \longrightarrow Q'$, simplify P to P' and assume P' when simplifying Q to Q'.

Here are some more examples. The congruence rules for bounded quantifiers supply contextual information about the bound variable:

$$[\![A = B; \ \bigwedge x. \ x \in B \implies P \ x = Q \ x]\!]$$
$$\implies (\forall x \in A. \ P \ x) = (\forall x \in B. \ Q \ x)$$

One congruence rule for conditional expressions supplies contextual information for simplifying the $then$ and $else$ cases:

T. Nipkow, L.C. Paulson, and M. Wenzel: Isabelle/HOL, LNCS 2283, pp. 175–193, 2002.
© Springer-Verlag Berlin Heidelberg 2002

$$[b = c; \ c \implies x = u; \ \neg \ c \implies y = v]$$
$$\implies \text{(if } b \text{ then } x \text{ else } y) = \text{(if } c \text{ then } u \text{ else } v)$$

An alternative congruence rule for conditional expressions actually *prevents* simplification of some arguments:

$$b = c \implies \text{(if } b \text{ then } x \text{ else } y) = \text{(if } c \text{ then } x \text{ else } y)$$

Only the first argument is simplified; the others remain unchanged. This makes simplification much faster and is faithful to the evaluation strategy in programming languages, which is why this is the default congruence rule for `if`. Analogous rules control the evaluation of `case` expressions.

You can declare your own congruence rules with the attribute `cong`, either globally, in the usual manner,

declare *theorem-name* `[cong]`

or locally in a `simp` call by adding the modifier

`cong:` *list of theorem names*

The effect is reversed by `cong del` instead of `cong`.

! The congruence rule `conj_cong`

$$[P = P'; \ P' \implies Q = Q'] \implies (P \land Q) = (P' \land Q')$$

is occasionally useful but is not a default rule; you have to declare it explicitly.

Permutative Rewrite Rules. An equation is a **permutative rewrite rule** if the left-hand side and right-hand side are the same up to renaming of variables. The most common permutative rule is commutativity: $x + y = y + x$. Other examples include $x - y - z = x - z - y$ in arithmetic and `insert x (insert y A) = insert y (insert x A)` for sets. Such rules are problematic because once they apply, they can be used forever. The simplifier is aware of this danger and treats permutative rules by means of a special strategy, called **ordered rewriting**: a permutative rewrite rule is only applied if the term becomes smaller with respect to a fixed lexicographic ordering on terms. For example, commutativity rewrites $b + a$ to $a + b$, but then stops because $a + b$ is strictly smaller than $b + a$. Permutative rewrite rules can be turned into simplification rules in the usual manner via the `simp` attribute; the simplifier recognizes their special status automatically.

Permutative rewrite rules are most effective in the case of associative-commutative functions. (Associativity by itself is not permutative.) When dealing with an AC-function f, keep the following points in mind:

- The associative law must always be oriented from left to right, namely $f(f(x, y), z) = f(x, f(y, z))$. The opposite orientation, if used with commutativity, can lead to nontermination.

– To complete your set of rewrite rules, you must add not just associativity (A) and commutativity (C) but also a derived rule, **left-commutativity** (LC): $f(x, f(y, z)) = f(y, f(x, z))$.

Ordered rewriting with the combination of A, C, and LC sorts a term lexicographically:

$$f(f(b, c), a) \overset{A}{\leadsto} f(b, f(c, a)) \overset{C}{\leadsto} f(b, f(a, c)) \overset{LC}{\leadsto} f(a, f(b, c))$$

Note that ordered rewriting for + and * on numbers is rarely necessary because the built-in arithmetic prover often succeeds without such tricks.

9.1.2 How the Simplifier Works

Roughly speaking, the simplifier proceeds bottom-up: subterms are simplified first. A conditional equation is only applied if its condition can be proved, again by simplification. Below we explain some special features of the rewriting process.

Higher-Order Patterns. So far we have pretended the simplifier can deal with arbitrary rewrite rules. This is not quite true. For reasons of feasibility, the simplifier expects the left-hand side of each rule to be a so-called *higher-order pattern* [21]. This restricts where unknowns may occur. Higher-order patterns are terms in β-normal form. (This means there are no subterms of the form $(\lambda x.M)(N)$.) Each occurrence of an unknown is of the form $?f\ x_1\ \dots\ x_n$, where the x_i are distinct bound variables. Thus all ordinary rewrite rules, where all unknowns are of base type, for example `?m + ?n + ?k = ?m + (?n + ?k)`, are acceptable: if an unknown is of base type, it cannot have any arguments. Additionally, the rule `(∀x. ?P x ∧ ?Q x) = ((∀x. ?P x) ∧ (∀x. ?Q x))` is also acceptable, in both directions: all arguments of the unknowns `?P` and `?Q` are distinct bound variables.

If the left-hand side is not a higher-order pattern, all is not lost. The simplifier will still try to apply the rule provided it matches directly: without much λ-calculus hocus pocus. For example, `(?f ?x ∈ range ?f) = True` rewrites `g a ∈ range g` to `True`, but will fail to match `g(h b) ∈ range(λx. g(h x))`. However, you can eliminate the offending subterms — those that are not patterns — by adding new variables and conditions. In our example, we eliminate `?f ?x` and obtain `?y = ?f ?x ⟹ (?y ∈ range ?f) = True`, which is fine as a conditional rewrite rule since conditions can be arbitrary terms. However, this trick is not a panacea because the newly introduced conditions may be hard to solve.

There is no restriction on the form of the right-hand sides. They may not contain extraneous term or type variables, though.

The Preprocessor. When a theorem is declared a simplification rule, it need not be a conditional equation already. The simplifier will turn it into a set of conditional equations automatically. For example, $f\ x = g\ x \wedge h\ x = k\ x$ becomes the two separate simplification rules $f\ x = g\ x$ and $h\ x = k\ x$. In general, the input theorem is converted as follows:

$$
\begin{array}{rcl}
\neg P & \mapsto & P = \mathtt{False} \\
P \longrightarrow Q & \mapsto & P \Longrightarrow Q \\
P \wedge Q & \mapsto & P, Q \\
\forall x.\ P\ x & \mapsto & P\ ?x \\
\forall x \in A.\ P\ x & \mapsto & ?x \in A \Longrightarrow P\ ?x \\
\mathtt{if}\ P\ \mathtt{then}\ Q\ \mathtt{else}\ R & \mapsto & P \Longrightarrow Q,\ \neg P \Longrightarrow R
\end{array}
$$

Once this conversion process is finished, all remaining non-equations P are turned into trivial equations $P = \mathtt{True}$. For example, the formula

$$(p \longrightarrow t = u \wedge \neg\ r) \wedge s$$

is converted into the three rules

$$p \Longrightarrow t = u, \quad p \Longrightarrow r = \mathtt{False}, \quad s = \mathtt{True}.$$

9.2 Advanced Forms of Recursion

This section introduces advanced forms of **recdef**: how to establish termination by means other than measure functions, how to define recursive functions over nested recursive datatypes and how to deal with partial functions.

If, after reading this section, you feel that the definition of recursive functions is overly complicated by the requirement of totality, you should ponder the alternatives. In a logic of partial functions, recursive definitions are always accepted. But there are many such logics, and no clear winner has emerged. And in all of these logics you are (more or less frequently) required to reason about the definedness of terms explicitly. Thus one shifts definedness arguments from definition time to proof time. In HOL you may have to work hard to define a function, but proofs can then proceed unencumbered by worries about undefinedness.

9.2.1 Beyond Measure

So far, all recursive definitions were shown to terminate via measure functions. Sometimes this can be inconvenient or impossible. Fortunately, **recdef** supports much more general definitions. For example, termination of Ackermann's function can be shown by means of the lexicographic product `<*lex*>`:

```
consts ack :: "nat×nat ⇒ nat"
recdef ack "measure(λm. m) <*lex*> measure(λn. n)"
  "ack(0,n)        = Suc n"
  "ack(Suc m,0)    = ack(m, 1)"
  "ack(Suc m,Suc n) = ack(m,ack(Suc m,n))"
```

The lexicographic product decreases if either its first component decreases (as in the second equation and in the outer call in the third equation) or its first component stays the same and the second component decreases (as in the inner call in the third equation).

In general, **recdef** supports termination proofs based on arbitrary well-founded relations as introduced in Sect. 6.4. This is called **well-founded recursion**. A function definition is total if and only if the set of all pairs (r, l), where l is the argument on the left-hand side of an equation and r the argument of some recursive call on the corresponding right-hand side, induces a well-founded relation. For a systematic account of termination proofs via well-founded relations see, for example, Baader and Nipkow [3].

Each **recdef** definition should be accompanied (after the function's name) by a well-founded relation on the function's argument type. Isabelle/HOL formalizes some of the most important constructions of well-founded relations (see Sect. 6.4). For example, `measure f` is always well-founded. The lexicographic product of two well-founded relations is again well-founded, which we relied on when defining Ackermann's function above. Of course the lexicographic product can also be iterated:

```
consts contrived :: "nat × nat × nat ⇒ nat"
recdef contrived
  "measure(λi. i) <*lex*> measure(λj. j) <*lex*> measure(λk. k)"
"contrived(i,j,Suc k) = contrived(i,j,k)"
"contrived(i,Suc j,0) = contrived(i,j,j)"
"contrived(Suc i,0,0) = contrived(i,i,i)"
"contrived(0,0,0)    = 0"
```

Lexicographic products of measure functions already go a long way. Furthermore, you may embed a type in an existing well-founded relation via the inverse image construction `inv_image`. All these constructions are known to **recdef**. Thus you will never have to prove well-foundedness of any relation composed solely of these building blocks. But of course the proof of termination of your function definition — that the arguments decrease with every recursive call — may still require you to provide additional lemmas.

It is also possible to use your own well-founded relations with **recdef**. For example, the greater-than relation can be made well-founded by cutting it off at a certain point. Here is an example of a recursive function that calls itself with increasing values up to ten:

consts f :: "nat ⇒ nat"
recdef f "{(i,j). j<i ∧ i ≤ (10::nat)}"
"f i = (if 10 ≤ i then 0 else i * f(Suc i))"

Since **recdef** is not prepared for the relation supplied above, Isabelle rejects the definition. We should first have proved that our relation was well-founded:

lemma wf_greater: "wf {(i,j). j<i ∧ i ≤ (N::nat)}"

The proof is by showing that our relation is a subset of another well-founded relation: one given by a measure function.

apply (rule wf_subset [of "measure (λk::nat. N-k)"], blast)

> 1. {(i, j). j < i ∧ i ≤ N} ⊆ measure (op - N)

The inclusion remains to be proved. After unfolding some definitions, we are left with simple arithmetic:

apply (clarify, simp add: measure_def inv_image_def)

> 1. ⋀a b. [b < a; a ≤ N] ⟹ N - a < N - b

And that is dispatched automatically:

by arith

Armed with this lemma, we use the *recdef_wf* attribute to attach a crucial hint to our definition:

(**hints** recdef_wf: wf_greater)

Alternatively, we could have given *measure (λk::nat. 10-k)* for the well-founded relation in our **recdef**. However, the arithmetic goal in the lemma above would have arisen instead in the **recdef** termination proof, where we have less control. A tailor-made termination relation makes even more sense when it can be used in several function declarations.

9.2.2 Recursion over Nested Datatypes

In Sect. 3.4.2 we defined the datatype of terms

datatype ('a,'b)"term" = Var 'a | App 'b "('a,'b)term list"

and closed with the observation that the associated schema for the definition of primitive recursive functions leads to overly verbose definitions. Moreover, if you have worked exercise 3.4.3 you will have noticed that you needed to declare essentially the same function as *rev* and prove many standard properties of list reversal all over again. We will now show you how **recdef** can simplify definitions and proofs about nested recursive datatypes. As an example we choose exercise 3.4.3:

consts *trev* :: *"('a,'b)term* ⇒ *('a,'b)term"*

Although the definition of *trev* below is quite natural, we will have to overcome a minor difficulty in convincing Isabelle of its termination. It is precisely this difficulty that is the *raison d'être* of this subsection.

Defining *trev* by **recdef** rather than **primrec** simplifies matters because we are now free to use the recursion equation suggested at the end of Sect. 3.4.2:

recdef *trev "measure size"*
  "trev (Var x)   = Var x"
  "trev (App f ts) = App f (rev(map trev ts))"

Remember that function *size* is defined for each **datatype**. However, the definition does not succeed. Isabelle complains about an unproved termination condition

$$t \in set\ ts \longrightarrow size\ t < Suc\ (term\_list\_size\ ts)$$

where *set* returns the set of elements of a list and *term_list_size* :: *term list* ⇒ *nat* is an auxiliary function automatically defined by Isabelle (while processing the declaration of *term*). Why does the recursive call of *trev* lead to this condition? Because **recdef** knows that *map* will apply *trev* only to elements of *ts*. Thus the condition expresses that the size of the argument *t* ∈ *set ts* of any recursive call of *trev* is strictly less than *size (App f ts)*, which equals *Suc (term_list_size ts)*. We will now prove the termination condition and continue with our definition. Below we return to the question of how **recdef** knows about *map*.

The termination condition is easily proved by induction:

lemma *[simp]: "t* ∈ *set ts* ⟶ *size t < Suc(term_list_size ts)"*
by*(induct_tac ts, auto)*

By making this theorem a simplification rule, **recdef** applies it automatically and the definition of *trev* succeeds now. As a reward for our effort, we can now prove the desired lemma directly. We no longer need the verbose induction schema for type *term* and can use the simpler one arising from *trev*:

lemma *"trev(trev t) = t"*
apply*(induct_tac t rule: trev.induct)*

```
1. ⋀x. trev (trev (Var x)) = Var x
2. ⋀f ts.
      ∀x. x ∈ set ts ⟶ trev (trev x) = x ⟹
      trev (trev (App f ts)) = App f ts
```

Both the base case and the induction step fall to simplification:

`by(simp_all add: rev_map sym[OF map_compose] cong: map_cong)`

If the proof of the induction step mystifies you, we recommend that you go through the chain of simplification steps in detail; you will probably need the help of `trace_simp`. Theorem `map_cong` is discussed below.

The definition of `trev` above is superior to the one in Sect. 3.4.2 because it uses `rev` and lets us use existing facts such as `rev (rev xs) = xs`. Thus this proof is a good example of an important principle:

> *Chose your definitions carefully*
> *because they determine the complexity of your proofs.*

Let us now return to the question of how **recdef** can come up with sensible termination conditions in the presence of higher-order functions like `map`. For a start, if nothing were known about `map`, then `map trev ts` might apply `trev` to arbitrary terms, and thus **recdef** would try to prove the unprovable `size t < Suc (term_list_size ts)`, without any assumption about `t`. Therefore **recdef** has been supplied with the congruence theorem `map_cong`:

$$[\![\textit{xs} = \textit{ys}; \; \bigwedge x. \; x \in \textit{set ys} \implies f \; x = g \; x]\!]$$
$$\implies \textit{map} \; f \; \textit{xs} = \textit{map} \; g \; \textit{ys}$$

Its second premise expresses that in `map f xs`, function `f` is only applied to elements of list `xs`. Congruence rules for other higher-order functions on lists are similar. If you get into a situation where you need to supply **recdef** with new congruence rules, you can append a hint after the end of the recursion equations:

(**hints** `recdef_cong: map_cong`)

Or you can declare them globally by giving them the `recdef_cong` attribute:

declare `map_cong[recdef_cong]`

The `cong` and `recdef_cong` attributes are intentionally kept apart because they control different activities, namely simplification and making recursive definitions.

9.2.3 Partial Functions

Throughout this tutorial, we have emphasized that all functions in HOL are total. We cannot hope to define truly partial functions, but must make them total. A straightforward method is to lift the result type of the function from τ to τ `option` (see 2.5.3), where `None` is returned if the function is applied to an argument not in its domain. Function `assoc` in Sect. 3.4.4 is a simple example. We do not pursue this schema further because it should be clear how it works. Its main drawback is that the result of such a lifted function has to be unpacked first before it can be processed further. Its main advantage is that you can distinguish if the function was applied to an argument in its domain or not. If you do not need to make this distinction, for example because the function is never used outside its domain, it is easier to work with *underdefined* functions: for certain arguments we only know that a result exists, but we do not know what it is. When defining functions that are normally considered partial, underdefinedness turns out to be a very reasonable alternative.

We have already seen an instance of underdefinedness by means of non-exhaustive pattern matching: the definition of `last` in Sect. 3.5.1. The same is allowed for **primrec**

```
consts hd :: "'a list ⇒ 'a"
primrec "hd (x#xs) = x"
```

although it generates a warning. Even ordinary definitions allow underdefinedness, this time by means of preconditions:

```
constdefs minus :: "nat ⇒ nat ⇒ nat"
"n ≤ m ⟹ minus m n ≡ m - n"
```

The rest of this section is devoted to the question of how to define partial recursive functions by other means than non-exhaustive pattern matching.

Guarded Recursion. Neither **primrec** nor **recdef** allow to prefix an equation with a condition in the way ordinary definitions do (see `minus` above). Instead we have to move the condition over to the right-hand side of the equation. Given a partial function f that should satisfy the recursion equation $f(x) = t$ over its domain $dom(f)$, we turn this into the **recdef**

```
f x = (if x ∈ dom f then t else arbitrary)
```

where `arbitrary` is a predeclared constant of type `'a` which has no definition. Thus we know nothing about its value, which is ideal for specifying underdefined functions on top of it.

As a simple example we define division on `nat`:

```
consts divi :: "nat × nat ⇒ nat"
recdef divi "measure(λ(m,n). m)"
  "divi(m,0) = arbitrary"
  "divi(m,n) = (if m < n then 0 else divi(m-n,n)+1)"
```

Of course we could also have defined `divi (m, 0)` to be some specific number, for example 0. The latter option is chosen for the predefined `div` function, which simplifies proofs at the expense of deviating from the standard mathematical division function.

As a more substantial example we consider the problem of searching a graph. For simplicity our graph is given by a function f of type `'a ⇒ 'a` which maps each node to its successor; the graph has out-degree 1. The task is to find the end of a chain, modelled by a node pointing to itself. Here is a first attempt:

```
find (f, x) = (if f x = x then x else find (f, f x))
```

This may be viewed as a fixed point finder or as the second half of the well known *Union-Find* algorithm. The snag is that it may not terminate if f has non-trivial cycles. Phrased differently, the relation

constdefs *step1* :: "('a ⇒ 'a) ⇒ ('a × 'a)set"
  "*step1 f* ≡ {(y,x). y = f x ∧ y ≠ x}"

must be well-founded. Thus we make the following definition:

consts *find* :: "('a ⇒ 'a) × 'a ⇒ 'a"
recdef *find* "*same_fst* (λf. wf(step1 f)) step1"
  "*find(f,x) = (if wf(step1 f)*
                then if f x = x then x else find(f, f x)
                else arbitrary)"
(**hints** *recdef_simp: step1_def*)

The recursion equation itself should be clear enough: it is our aborted first attempt augmented with a check that there are no non-trivial loops. To express the required well-founded relation we employ the predefined combinator *same_fst* of type

$$('a \Rightarrow bool) \Rightarrow ('a \Rightarrow ('b \times 'b)set) \Rightarrow (('a \times 'b) \times ('a \times 'b))set$$

defined as

  same_fst P R ≡ {((x', y'), x, y). x' = x ∧ P x ∧ (y', y) ∈ R x}

This combinator is designed for recursive functions on pairs where the first component of the argument is passed unchanged to all recursive calls. Given a constraint on the first component and a relation on the second component, *same_fst* builds the required relation on pairs. The theorem

  (⋀x. P x ⟹ wf (R x)) ⟹ wf (same_fst P R)

is known to the well-foundedness prover of **recdef**. Thus well-foundedness of the relation given to **recdef** is immediate. Furthermore, each recursive call descends along that relation: the first argument stays unchanged and the second one descends along *step1 f*. The proof requires unfolding the definition of *step1*, as specified in the **hints** above.

Normally you will then derive the following conditional variant from the recursion equation:

lemma *[simp]:*
  "*wf(step1 f) ⟹ find(f,x) = (if f x = x then x else find(f, f x))*"
by *simp*

Then you should disable the original recursion equation:

declare *find.simps[simp del]*

Reasoning about such underdefined functions is like that for other recursive functions. Here is a simple example of recursion induction:

```
lemma "wf(step1 f) ⟶ f(find(f,x)) = find(f,x)"
apply(induct_tac f x rule: find.induct)
apply simp
done
```

The while Combinator. If the recursive function happens to be tail recursive, its definition becomes a triviality if based on the predefined `while` combinator. The latter lives in the Library theory `While_Combinator`.

Constant `while` is of type $('a \Rightarrow bool) \Rightarrow ('a \Rightarrow 'a) \Rightarrow 'a$ and satisfies the recursion equation

```
while b c s = (if b s then while b c (c s) else s)
```

That is, `while b c s` is equivalent to the imperative program

```
x := s; while b(x) do x := c(x); return x
```

In general, *s* will be a tuple or record. As an example consider the following definition of function *find*:

```
constdefs find2 :: "('a ⇒ 'a) ⇒ 'a ⇒ 'a"
  "find2 f x ≡
   fst(while (λ(x,x'). x' ≠ x) (λ(x,x'). (x',f x')) (x,f x))"
```

The loop operates on two "local variables" *x* and *x'* containing the "current" and the "next" value of function *f*. They are initialized with the global *x* and *f x*. At the end *fst* selects the local *x*.

Although the definition of tail recursive functions via `while` avoids termination proofs, there is no free lunch. When proving properties of functions defined by `while`, termination rears its ugly head again. Here is `while_rule`, the well known proof rule for total correctness of loops expressed with `while`:

$$[P \; s; \; \bigwedge s. \; [P \; s; \; b \; s] \implies P \; (c \; s);$$
$$\bigwedge s. \; [P \; s; \; \neg b \; s] \implies Q \; s; \; wf \; r;$$
$$\bigwedge s. \; [P \; s; \; b \; s] \implies (c \; s, \; s) \in r]$$
$$\implies Q \; (while \; b \; c \; s)$$

P needs to be true of the initial state *s* and invariant under *c* (premises 1 and 2). The post-condition *Q* must become true when leaving the loop (premise 3). And each loop iteration must descend along a well-founded relation *r* (premises 4 and 5).

Let us now prove that *find2* does indeed find a fixed point. Instead of induction we apply the above while rule, suitably instantiated. Only the final premise of `while_rule` is left unproved by `auto` but falls to `simp`:

```
lemma lem: "wf(step1 f) ⟹
  ∃y. while (λ(x,x'). x' ≠ x) (λ(x,x'). (x',f x')) (x,f x) = (y,y) ∧
      f y = y"
```

```
apply(rule_tac P = "λ(x,x'). x' = f x" and
                r = "inv_image (step1 f) fst" in while_rule)
apply auto
apply(simp add: inv_image_def step1_def)
done
```

The theorem itself is a simple consequence of this lemma:

```
theorem "wf(step1 f) ⟹ f(find2 f x) = find2 f x"
apply(drule_tac x = x in lem)
apply(auto simp add: find2_def)
done
```

Let us conclude this section on partial functions by a discussion of the merits of the `while` combinator. We have already seen that the advantage of not having to provide a termination argument when defining a function via `while` merely puts off the evil hour. On top of that, tail recursive functions tend to be more complicated to reason about. So why use `while` at all? The only reason is executability: the recursion equation for `while` is a directly executable functional program. This is in stark contrast to guarded recursion as introduced above which requires an explicit test $x \in dom\ f$ in the function body. Unless `dom` is trivial, this leads to a definition that is impossible to execute or prohibitively slow. Thus, if you are aiming for an efficiently executable definition of a partial function, you are likely to need `while`.

9.3 Advanced Induction Techniques

Now that we have learned about rules and logic, we take another look at the finer points of induction. We consider two questions: what to do if the proposition to be proved is not directly amenable to induction (Sect. 9.3.1), and how to utilize (Sect. 9.3.2) and even derive (Sect. 9.3.3) new induction schemas. We conclude with an extended example of induction (Sect. 9.3.4).

9.3.1 Massaging the Proposition

Often we have assumed that the theorem to be proved is already in a form that is amenable to induction, but sometimes it isn't. Here is an example. Since `hd` and `last` return the first and last element of a non-empty list, this lemma looks easy to prove:

```
lemma "xs ≠ [] ⟹ hd(rev xs) = last xs"
apply(induct_tac xs)
```

But induction produces the warning

```
    Induction variable occurs also among premises!
```

and leads to the base case

```
1. xs ≠ [] ⟹ hd (rev []) = last []
```

Simplification reduces the base case to this:

```
1. xs ≠ [] ⟹ hd [] = last []
```

We cannot prove this equality because we do not know what `hd` and `last` return when applied to `[]`.

We should not have ignored the warning. Because the induction formula is only the conclusion, induction does not affect the occurrence of `xs` in the premises. Thus the case that should have been trivial becomes unprovable. Fortunately, the solution is easy:[1]

> Pull all occurrences of the induction variable into the conclusion using ⟶.

Thus we should state the lemma as an ordinary implication (⟶), letting `rule_format` (Sect. 5.14) convert the result to the usual ⟹ form:

lemma `hd_rev [rule_format]: "xs ≠ [] ⟶ hd(rev xs) = last xs"`

This time, induction leaves us with a trivial base case:

```
1. [] ≠ [] ⟶ hd (rev []) = last []
```

And `auto` completes the proof.

If there are multiple premises $A_1, \ldots, A_n$ containing the induction variable, you should turn the conclusion C into

$$A_1 \longrightarrow \cdots A_n \longrightarrow C.$$

Additionally, you may also have to universally quantify some other variables, which can yield a fairly complex conclusion. However, `rule_format` can remove any number of occurrences of ∀ and ⟶.

A second reason why your proposition may not be amenable to induction is that you want to induct on a complex term, rather than a variable. In general, induction on a term t requires rephrasing the conclusion C as

$$\forall y_1 \ldots y_n.\ x = t \longrightarrow C. \tag{9.1}$$

where $y_1 \ldots y_n$ are the free variables in t and x is a new variable. Now you can perform induction on x. An example appears in Sect. 9.3.2 below.

The very same problem may occur in connection with rule induction. Remember that it requires a premise of the form $(x_1, \ldots, x_k) \in R$, where R is some inductively defined set and the x_i are variables. If instead we have a premise $t \in R$, where t is not just an n-tuple of variables, we replace it with $(x_1, \ldots, x_k) \in R$, and rephrase the conclusion C as

---

[1] A similar heuristic applies to rule inductions; see Sect. 7.2.

$$\forall y_1 \ldots y_n. \ (x_1, \ldots, x_k) = t \longrightarrow C.$$

For an example see Sect. 9.3.4 below.

Of course, all premises that share free variables with t need to be pulled into the conclusion as well, under the $\forall$, again using $\longrightarrow$ as shown above.

Readers who are puzzled by the form of statement (9.1) above should remember that the transformation is only performed to permit induction. Once induction has been applied, the statement can be transformed back into something quite intuitive. For example, applying wellfounded induction on x (w.r.t. $\prec$) to (9.1) and transforming the result a little leads to the goal

$$\bigwedge \overline{y}. \ \forall \overline{z}. \ t\,\overline{z} \prec t\,\overline{y} \ \longrightarrow \ C\,\overline{z} \implies C\,\overline{y}$$

where $\overline{y}$ stands for $y_1 \ldots y_n$ and the dependence of t and C on the free variables of t has been made explicit. Unfortunately, this induction schema cannot be expressed as a single theorem because it depends on the number of free variables in t — the notation $\overline{y}$ is merely an informal device.

9.3.2 Beyond Structural and Recursion Induction

So far, inductive proofs were by structural induction for primitive recursive functions and recursion induction for total recursive functions. But sometimes structural induction is awkward and there is no recursive function that could furnish a more appropriate induction schema. In such cases a general-purpose induction schema can be helpful. We show how to apply such induction schemas by an example.

Structural induction on `nat` is usually known as mathematical induction. There is also **complete** induction, where you prove $P(n)$ under the assumption that $P(m)$ holds for all $m < n$. In Isabelle, this is the theorem `nat_less_induct`:

$$(\bigwedge n. \ \forall m. \ m < n \longrightarrow P\,m \implies P\,n) \implies P\,n$$

As an application, we prove a property of the following function:

```
consts f :: "nat ⇒ nat"
axioms f_ax: "f(f(n)) < f(Suc(n))"
```

! We discourage the use of axioms because of the danger of inconsistencies. Ax-
• iom `f_ax` does not introduce an inconsistency because, for example, the identity function satisfies it. Axioms can be useful in exploratory developments, say when you assume some well-known theorems so that you can quickly demonstrate some point about methodology. If your example turns into a substantial proof development, you should replace axioms by theorems.

The axiom for `f` implies $n \le$ `f n`, which can be proved by induction on `f n`. Following the recipe outlined above, we have to phrase the proposition as follows to allow induction:

lemma *f_incr_lem:* "∀ i. k = f i ⟶ i ≤ f i"

To perform induction on k using *nat_less_induct*, we use the same general induction method as for recursion induction (see Sect. 3.5.4):

apply(*induct_tac k rule: nat_less_induct*)

We get the following proof state:

1. ⋀n. ∀m. m < n ⟶ (∀ i. m = f i ⟶ i ≤ f i) ⟹
      ∀ i. n = f i ⟶ i ≤ f i

After stripping the ∀ i, the proof continues with a case distinction on i. The case i = 0 is trivial and we focus on the other case:

apply(*rule allI*)
apply(*case_tac i*)
 apply(*simp*)

1. ⋀n i nat.
     ⟦∀m. m < n ⟶ (∀ i. m = f i ⟶ i ≤ f i); i = Suc nat⟧
     ⟹ n = f i ⟶ i ≤ f i

by(*blast intro!: f_ax Suc_leI intro: le_less_trans*)

If you find the last step puzzling, here are the two lemmas it employs:

m < n ⟹ Suc m ≤ n	(Suc_leI)
⟦i ≤ j; j < k⟧ ⟹ i < k	(le_less_trans)

The proof goes like this (writing j instead of *nat*). Since i = Suc j it suffices to show j < f (Suc j), by *Suc_leI*. This is proved as follows. From *f_ax* we have f (f j) < f (Suc j) (1) which implies f j ≤ f (f j) by the induction hypothesis. Using (1) once more we obtain f j < f (Suc j) (2) by the transitivity rule *le_less_trans*. Using the induction hypothesis once more we obtain j ≤ f j which, together with (2) yields j < f (Suc j) (again by *le_less_trans*).

This last step shows both the power and the danger of automatic proofs. They will usually not tell you how the proof goes, because it can be hard to translate the internal proof into a human-readable format. Automatic proofs are easy to write but hard to read and understand.

The desired result, i ≤ f i, follows from *f_incr_lem*:

lemmas *f_incr = f_incr_lem[rule_format, OF refl]*

The final *refl* gets rid of the premise ?k = f ?i. We could have included this derivation in the original statement of the lemma:

lemma *f_incr[rule_format, OF refl]:* "∀ i. k = f i ⟶ i ≤ f i"

Exercise 9.3.1 From the axiom and lemma for f, show that f is the identity function.

Method `induct_tac` can be applied with any rule r whose conclusion is of the form $?P\ ?x_1 \dots ?x_n$, in which case the format is

apply (`induct_tac` $y_1 \dots y_n$ `rule:` r)

where $y_1, \dots, y_n$ are variables in the first subgoal. The conclusion of r can even be an (iterated) conjunction of formulae of the above form in which case the application is

apply (`induct_tac` $y_1 \dots y_n$ `and` $\dots$ `and` $z_1 \dots z_m$ `rule:` r)

A further useful induction rule is `length_induct`, induction on the length of a list

$$(\bigwedge \texttt{xs.}\ \forall \texttt{ys.}\ \texttt{length ys < length xs} \longrightarrow P\ \texttt{ys} \implies P\ \texttt{xs}) \implies P\ \texttt{xs}$$

which is a special case of `measure_induct`

$$(\bigwedge \texttt{x.}\ \forall \texttt{y.}\ \texttt{f y < f x} \longrightarrow P\ \texttt{y} \implies P\ \texttt{x}) \implies P\ \texttt{a}$$

where `f` may be any function into type `nat`.

9.3.3 Derivation of New Induction Schemas

Induction schemas are ordinary theorems and you can derive new ones whenever you wish. This section shows you how, using the example of `nat_less_induct`. Assume we only have structural induction available for `nat` and want to derive complete induction. We must generalize the statement as shown:

lemma `induct_lem`: `"(`$\bigwedge$`n::nat.` $\forall$`m<n.` `P m` $\implies$ `P n)` $\implies$ $\forall$`m<n.` `P m"`
apply (`induct_tac n`)

The base case is vacuously true. For the induction step (`m < Suc n`) we distinguish two cases: case `m < n` is true by induction hypothesis and case `m = n` follows from the assumption, again using the induction hypothesis:

 apply (`blast`)
by (`blast elim: less_SucE`)

The elimination rule `less_SucE` expresses the case distinction:

$$\llbracket \texttt{m < Suc n; m < n} \implies P;\ \texttt{m = n} \implies P \rrbracket \implies P$$

Now it is straightforward to derive the original version of `nat_less_induct` by manipulating the conclusion of the above lemma: instantiate `n` by `Suc n` and `m` by `n` and remove the trivial condition `n < Suc n`. Fortunately, this happens automatically when we add the lemma as a new premise to the desired goal:

theorem `nat_less_induct`: `"(`$\bigwedge$`n::nat.` $\forall$`m<n.` `P m` $\implies$ `P n)` $\implies$ `P n"`
by (`insert induct_lem, blast`)

HOL already provides the mother of all inductions, well-founded induction (see Sect. 6.4). For example theorem `nat_less_induct` is a special case of `wf_induct` where r is < on `nat`. The details can be found in theory `Wellfounded_Recursion`.

9.3.4 CTL Revisited

The purpose of this section is twofold: to demonstrate some of the induction principles and heuristics discussed above and to show how inductive definitions can simplify proofs. In Sect. 6.6.2 we gave a fairly involved proof of the correctness of a model checker for CTL. In particular the proof of the `infinity_lemma` on the way to `AF_lemma2` is not as simple as one might expect, due to the `SOME` operator involved. Below we give a simpler proof of `AF_lemma2` based on an auxiliary inductive definition.

Let us call a (finite or infinite) path A-*avoiding* if it does not touch any node in the set A. Then `AF_lemma2` says that if no infinite path from some state s is A-avoiding, then $s \in lfp$ (`af` A). We prove this by inductively defining the set `Avoid` s A of states reachable from s by a finite A-avoiding path:

```
consts Avoid :: "state ⇒ state set ⇒ state set"
inductive "Avoid s A"
intros "s ∈ Avoid s A"
     "⟦ t ∈ Avoid s A; t ∉ A; (t,u) ∈ M ⟧ ⟹ u ∈ Avoid s A"
```

It is easy to see that for any infinite A-avoiding path f with $f\ 0 \in$ `Avoid` s A there is an infinite A-avoiding path starting with s because (by definition of `Avoid`) there is a finite A-avoiding path from s to $f\ 0$. The proof is by induction on $f\ 0 \in$ `Avoid` s A. However, this requires the following reformulation, as explained in Sect. 9.3.1 above; the `rule_format` directive undoes the reformulation after the proof.

```
lemma ex_infinite_path[rule_format]:
  "t ∈ Avoid s A ⟹
   ∀f∈Paths t. (∀i. f i ∉ A) ⟶ (∃p∈Paths s. ∀i. p i ∉ A)"
apply(erule Avoid.induct)
 apply(blast)
apply(clarify)
apply(drule_tac x = "λi. case i of 0 ⇒ t | Suc i ⇒ f i" in bspec)
apply(simp_all add: Paths_def split: nat.split)
done
```

The base case ($t = s$) is trivial and proved by `blast`. In the induction step, we have an infinite A-avoiding path f starting from u, a successor of t. Now we simply instantiate the $\forall f \in$ `Paths` t in the induction hypothesis by the path starting with t and continuing with f. That is what the above λ-term expresses. Simplification shows that this is a path starting with t and that the instantiated induction hypothesis implies the conclusion.

Now we come to the key lemma. Assuming that no infinite A-avoiding path starts from s, we want to show s ∈ lfp (af A). For the inductive proof this must be generalized to the statement that every point t "between" s and A, in other words all of Avoid s A, is contained in lfp (af A):

lemma *Avoid_in_lfp[rule_format(no_asm)]:*
  "∀p∈Paths s. ∃i. p i ∈ A ⟹ t ∈ Avoid s A ⟶ t ∈ lfp(af A)"

The proof is by induction on the "distance" between t and A. Remember that *lfp (af A) = A ∪ M⁻¹ '' lfp (af A)*. If t is already in A, then *t ∈ lfp (af A)* is trivial. If t is not in A but all successors are in *lfp (af A)* (induction hypothesis), then *t ∈ lfp (af A)* is again trivial.

The formal counterpart of this proof sketch is a well-founded induction on M restricted to *Avoid s A - A*, roughly speaking:

$$\{(y, x).\ (x, y) \in M \wedge x \in Avoid\ s\ A \wedge x \notin A\}$$

As we shall see presently, the absence of infinite A-avoiding paths starting from s implies well-foundedness of this relation. For the moment we assume this and proceed with the induction:

apply(*subgoal_tac "wf{(y,x). (x,y) ∈ M ∧ x ∈ Avoid s A ∧ x ∉ A}"*)
  apply(*erule_tac a = t in wf_induct*)
  apply(*clarsimp*)

1. ⋀t. ⟦∀p∈Paths s. ∃i. p i ∈ A; t ∈ Avoid s A;
       ∀y. (t, y) ∈ M ∧ t ∉ A ⟶
           y ∈ Avoid s A ⟶ y ∈ lfp (af A)⟧
     ⟹ t ∈ lfp (af A)
2. ∀p∈Paths s. ∃i. p i ∈ A ⟹
     wf {(y, x). (x, y) ∈ M ∧ x ∈ Avoid s A ∧ x ∉ A}

Now the induction hypothesis states that if t ∉ A then all successors of t that are in *Avoid s A* are in *lfp (af A)*. Unfolding *lfp* in the conclusion of the first subgoal once, we have to prove that t is in A or all successors of t are in *lfp (af A)*. But if t is not in A, the second *Avoid*-rule implies that all successors of t are in *Avoid s A*, because we also assume t ∈ Avoid s A. Hence, by the induction hypothesis, all successors of t are indeed in *lfp (af A)*. Mechanically:

  apply(*subst lfp_unfold[OF mono_af]*)
  apply(*simp (no_asm) add: af_def*)
  apply(*blast intro: Avoid.intros*)

Having proved the main goal, we return to the proof obligation that the relation used above is indeed well-founded. This is proved by contradiction: if the relation is not well-founded then there exists an infinite A-avoiding path all in *Avoid s A*, by theorem *wf_iff_no_infinite_down_chain*:

$$wf\ r = (\neg\ (\exists f.\ \forall i.\ (f\ (Suc\ i),\ f\ i) \in r))$$

From lemma *ex_infinite_path* the existence of an infinite *A*-avoiding path starting in *s* follows, contradiction.

apply(*erule contrapos_pp*)
apply(*simp add: wf_iff_no_infinite_down_chain*)
apply(*erule exE*)
apply(*rule ex_infinite_path*)
apply(*auto simp add: Paths_def*)
done

The (*no_asm*) modifier of the *rule_format* directive in the statement of the lemma means that the assumption is left unchanged; otherwise the $\forall p$ would be turned into a $\bigwedge p$, which would complicate matters below. As it is, *Avoid_in_lfp* is now

$$[\![\forall p \in Paths\ s.\ \exists i.\ p\ i \in A;\ t \in Avoid\ s\ A]\!] \Longrightarrow t \in lfp\ (af\ A)$$

The main theorem is simply the corollary where *t* = *s*, when the assumption $t \in Avoid\ s\ A$ is trivially true by the first *Avoid*-rule. Isabelle confirms this:

theorem *AF_lemma2:*   "{*s.* $\forall p \in Paths\ s.\ \exists i.\ p\ i \in A$} $\subseteq$ *lfp(af A)*"
by(*auto elim: Avoid_in_lfp intro: Avoid.intros*)

10. Case Study: Verifying a Security Protocol

Communications security is an ancient art. Julius Caesar is said to have encrypted his messages, shifting each letter three places along the alphabet. Mary Queen of Scots was convicted of treason after a cipher used in her letters was broken. Today's postal system incorporates security features. The envelope provides a degree of *secrecy*. The signature provides *authenticity* (proof of origin), as do departmental stamps and letterheads.

Networks are vulnerable: messages pass through many computers, any of which might be controlled by an adversary, who thus can capture or redirect messages. People who wish to communicate securely over such a network can use cryptography, but if they are to understand each other, they need to follow a *protocol*: a pre-arranged sequence of message formats.

Protocols can be attacked in many ways, even if encryption is unbreakable. A *splicing attack* involves an adversary's sending a message composed of parts of several old messages. This fake message may have the correct format, fooling an honest party. The adversary might be able to masquerade as somebody else, or he might obtain a secret key.

Nonces help prevent splicing attacks. A typical nonce is a 20-byte random number. Each message that requires a reply incorporates a nonce. The reply must include a copy of that nonce, to prove that it is not a replay of a past message. The nonce in the reply must be cryptographically protected, since otherwise an adversary could easily replace it by a different one. You should be starting to see that protocol design is tricky!

Researchers are developing methods for proving the correctness of security protocols. The Needham-Schroeder public-key protocol [20] has become a standard test case. Proposed in 1978, it was found to be defective nearly two decades later [16]. This toy protocol will be useful in demonstrating how to verify protocols using Isabelle.

10.1 The Needham-Schroeder Public-Key Protocol

This protocol uses public-key cryptography. Each person has a private key, known only to himself, and a public key, known to everybody. If Alice wants to send Bob a secret message, she encrypts it using Bob's public key (which

T. Nipkow, L.C. Paulson, and M. Wenzel: Isabelle/HOL, LNCS 2283, pp. 195–205, 2002.
© Springer-Verlag Berlin Heidelberg 2002

everybody knows), and sends it to Bob. Only Bob has the matching private key, which is needed in order to decrypt Alice's message.

The core of the Needham-Schroeder protocol consists of three messages:

$$1. \quad A \to B : \{Na, A\}_{Kb}$$
$$2. \quad B \to A : \{Na, Nb\}_{Ka}$$
$$3. \quad A \to B : \{Nb\}_{Kb}$$

First, let's understand the notation. In the first message, Alice sends Bob a message consisting of a nonce generated by Alice (Na) paired with Alice's name (A) and encrypted using Bob's public key (Kb). In the second message, Bob sends Alice a message consisting of Na paired with a nonce generated by Bob (Nb), encrypted using Alice's public key (Ka). In the last message, Alice returns Nb to Bob, encrypted using his public key.

When Alice receives Message 2, she knows that Bob has acted on her message, since only he could have decrypted $\{Na, A\}_{Kb}$ and extracted Na. That is precisely what nonces are for. Similarly, message 3 assures Bob that Alice is active. But the protocol was widely believed [6] to satisfy a further property: that Na and Nb were secrets shared by Alice and Bob. (Many protocols generate such shared secrets, which can be used to lessen the reliance on slow public-key operations.) Lowe found this claim to be false: if Alice runs the protocol with someone untrustworthy (Charlie say), then he can start a new run with another agent (Bob say). Charlie uses Alice as an oracle, masquerading as Alice to Bob [16].

$$1. \quad A \to C : \{Na, A\}_{Kc} \qquad 1'. \quad C \to B : \{Na, A\}_{Kb}$$
$$2. \quad B \to A : \{Na, Nb\}_{Ka}$$
$$3. \quad A \to C : \{Nb\}_{Kc} \qquad 3'. \quad C \to B : \{Nb\}_{Kb}$$

In messages 1 and 3, Charlie removes the encryption using his private key and re-encrypts Alice's messages using Bob's public key. Bob is left thinking he has run the protocol with Alice, which was not Alice's intention, and Bob is unaware that the "secret" nonces are known to Charlie. This is a typical man-in-the-middle attack launched by an insider.

Whether this counts as an attack has been disputed. In protocols of this type, we normally assume that the other party is honest. To be honest means to obey the protocol rules, so Alice's running the protocol with Charlie does not make her dishonest, just careless. After Lowe's attack, Alice has no grounds for complaint: this protocol does not have to guarantee anything if you run it with a bad person. Bob does have grounds for complaint, however: the protocol tells him that he is communicating with Alice (who is honest) but it does not guarantee secrecy of the nonces.

Lowe also suggested a correction, namely to include Bob's name in message 2:

1. $A \rightarrow B : \{Na, A\}_{Kb}$
2. $B \rightarrow A : \{Na, Nb, B\}_{Ka}$
3. $A \rightarrow B : \{Nb\}_{Kb}$

If Charlie tries the same attack, Alice will receive the message $\{Na, Nb, B\}_{Ka}$ when she was expecting to receive $\{Na, Nb, C\}_{Ka}$. She will abandon the run, and eventually so will Bob. Below, we shall look at parts of this protocol's correctness proof.

In ground-breaking work, Lowe [16] showed how such attacks could be found automatically using a model checker. An alternative, which we shall examine below, is to prove protocols correct. Proofs can be done under more realistic assumptions because our model does not have to be finite. The strategy is to formalize the operational semantics of the system and to prove security properties using rule induction.

10.2 Agents and Messages

All protocol specifications refer to a syntactic theory of messages. Datatype `agent` introduces the constant `Server` (a trusted central machine, needed for some protocols), an infinite population of friendly agents, and the `Spy`:

datatype *agent* = *Server* | *Friend* nat | *Spy*

Keys are just natural numbers. Function `invKey` maps a public key to the matching private key, and vice versa:

types *key* = nat
consts *invKey* :: "key=>key"

Datatype `msg` introduces the message forms, which include agent names, nonces, keys, compound messages, and encryptions.

datatype
    msg = *Agent* *agent*
        | *Nonce* nat
        | *Key*   key
        | *MPair* msg msg
        | *Crypt* key msg

The notation $\{X_1, \ldots X_{n-1}, X_n\}$ abbreviates $\mathtt{MPair}\, X_1 \ldots (\mathtt{MPair}\, X_{n-1}\, X_n)$.

Since datatype constructors are injective, we have the theorem

Crypt K X = Crypt K' X' $\implies$ *K=K'* $\land$ *X=X'*.

A ciphertext can be decrypted using only one key and can yield only one plaintext. In the real world, decryption with the wrong key succeeds but yields garbage. Our model of encryption is realistic if encryption adds some redundancy to the plaintext, such as a checksum, so that garbage can be detected.

10.3 Modelling the Adversary

The spy is part of the system and must be built into the model. He is a malicious user who does not have to follow the protocol. He watches the network and uses any keys he knows to decrypt messages. Thus he accumulates additional keys and nonces. These he can use to compose new messages, which he may send to anybody.

Two functions enable us to formalize this behaviour: `analz` and `synth`. Each function maps a sets of messages to another set of messages. The set `analz H` formalizes what the adversary can learn from the set of messages H. The closure properties of this set are defined inductively.

```
consts   analz    :: "msg set => msg set"
inductive "analz H"
  intros
    Inj [intro,simp] : "X ∈ H ⟹ X ∈ analz H"
    Fst:       "{|X,Y|} ∈ analz H ⟹ X ∈ analz H"
    Snd:       "{|X,Y|} ∈ analz H ⟹ Y ∈ analz H"
    Decrypt [dest]:
              "[|Crypt K X ∈ analz H; Key(invKey K): analz H|]
               ⟹ X ∈ analz H"
```

Note the `Decrypt` rule: the spy can decrypt a message encrypted with key K if he has the matching key, K^{-1}. Properties proved by rule induction include the following:

$$G{\subseteq}H \implies \mathtt{analz}(G) \subseteq \mathtt{analz}(H) \hspace{3cm} (\mathtt{analz\_mono})$$
$$\mathtt{analz\ (analz\ }H) = \mathtt{analz\ }H \hspace{3cm} (\mathtt{analz\_idem})$$

The set of fake messages that an intruder could invent starting from H is `synth(analz H)`, where `synth H` formalizes what the adversary can build from the set of messages H.

```
consts   synth    :: "msg set => msg set"
inductive "synth H"
  intros
    Inj    [intro]: "X ∈ H ⟹ X ∈ synth H"
    Agent  [intro]: "Agent agt ∈ synth H"
    MPair  [intro]:
              "[|X ∈ synth H;   Y ∈ synth H|] ⟹ {|X,Y|} ∈ synth H"
    Crypt  [intro]:
              "[|X ∈ synth H;   Key K ∈ H|] ⟹ Crypt K X ∈ synth H"
```

The set includes all agent names. Nonces and keys are assumed to be unguessable, so none are included beyond those already in H. Two elements of `synth` H can be combined, and an element can be encrypted using a key present in H.

Like `analz`, this set operator is monotone and idempotent. It also satisfies an interesting equation involving `analz`:

$$\mathtt{analz\ (synth\ }H) = \mathtt{analz\ }H \cup \mathtt{synth\ }H \hspace{3cm} (\mathtt{analz\_synth})$$

Rule inversion plays a major role in reasoning about *synth*, through declarations such as this one:

inductive_cases *Nonce_synth [elim!]: "Nonce n ∈ synth H"*

The resulting elimination rule replaces every assumption of the form *Nonce n ∈ synth H* by *Nonce n ∈ H*, expressing that a nonce cannot be guessed.

A third operator, *parts*, is useful for stating correctness properties. The set *parts H* consists of the components of elements of *H*. This set includes *H* and is closed under the projections from a compound message to its immediate parts. Its definition resembles that of *analz* except in the rule corresponding to the constructor *Crypt*:

$$Crypt\ K\ X\ \in\ parts\ H \implies X \in parts\ H$$

The body of an encrypted message is always regarded as part of it. We can use *parts* to express general well-formedness properties of a protocol, for example, that an uncompromised agent's private key will never be included as a component of any message.

10.4 Event Traces

The system's behaviour is formalized as a set of traces of *events*. The most important event, *Says A B X*, expresses $A \to B : X$, which is the attempt by A to send B the message X. A trace is simply a list, constructed in reverse using *#*. Other event types include reception of messages (when we want to make it explicit) and an agent's storing a fact.

Sometimes the protocol requires an agent to generate a new nonce. The probability that a 20-byte random number has appeared before is effectively zero. To formalize this important property, the set *used evs* denotes the set of all items mentioned in the trace *evs*. The function *used* has a straightforward recursive definition. Here is the case for *Says* event:

$$used\ ((Says\ A\ B\ X)\ \#\ evs) = parts\ \{X\} \cup (used\ evs)$$

The function *knows* formalizes an agent's knowledge. Mostly we only care about the spy's knowledge, and *knows Spy evs* is the set of items available to the spy in the trace *evs*. Already in the empty trace, the spy starts with some secrets at his disposal, such as the private keys of compromised users. After each *Says* event, the spy learns the message that was sent:

$$knows\ Spy\ ((Says\ A\ B\ X)\ \#\ evs) = parts\ \{X\} \cup (knows\ Spy\ evs)$$

Combinations of functions express other important sets of messages derived from *evs*:

– *analz (knows Spy evs)* is everything that the spy could learn by decryption
– *synth (analz (knows Spy evs))* is everything that the spy could generate

The function *pubK* maps agents to their public keys. The function *priK* maps agents to their private keys. It is defined in terms of *invKey* and *pubK* by a translation; therefore *priK* is not a proper constant, so we declare it using **syntax** (cf. Sect. 4.1.4).

```
consts pubK      :: "agent => key"
syntax priK      :: "agent => key"
translations    "priK x" ⇌ "invKey(pubK x)"
```

The set *bad* consists of those agents whose private keys are known to the spy.

Two axioms are asserted about the public-key cryptosystem. No two agents have the same public key, and no private key equals any public key.

```
axioms
  inj_pubK:        "inj pubK"
  priK_neq_pubK:   "priK A ≠ pubK B"
```

10.5 Modelling the Protocol

Let us formalize the Needham-Schroeder public-key protocol, as corrected by Lowe:

1. $A \rightarrow B : \{Na, A\}_{Kb}$
2. $B \rightarrow A : \{Na, Nb, B\}_{Ka}$
3. $A \rightarrow B : \{Nb\}_{Kb}$

Each protocol step is specified by a rule of an inductive definition. An event trace has type *event list*, so we declare the constant *ns_public* to be a set of such traces.

```
consts ns_public :: "event list set"
```

Figure 10.1 presents the inductive definition. The *Nil* rule introduces the empty trace. The *Fake* rule models the adversary's sending a message built from components taken from past traffic, expressed using the functions *synth* and *analz*. The next three rules model how honest agents would perform the three protocol steps.

Here is a detailed explanation of rule *NS2*. A trace containing an event of the form

Says A' B (Crypt (pubK B) {|Nonce NA, Agent A|})

may be extended by an event of the form

Says B A (Crypt (pubK A) {|Nonce NA, Nonce NB, Agent B|})

where *NB* is a fresh nonce: *Nonce NB ∉ used evs2*. Writing the sender as *A'* indicates that *B* does not know who sent the message. Calling the trace variable *evs2* rather than simply *evs* helps us know where we are in a proof after many case-splits: every subgoal mentioning *evs2* involves message 2 of the protocol.

```
inductive ns_public
  intros

  Nil:  "[] ∈ ns_public"


  Fake: "⟦evsf ∈ ns_public; X ∈ synth (analz (knows Spy evsf))⟧
         ⟹ Says Spy B X # evsf ∈ ns_public"


  NS1:  "⟦evs1 ∈ ns_public; Nonce NA ∉ used evs1⟧
         ⟹ Says A B (Crypt (pubK B) {|Nonce NA, Agent A|})
                # evs1 ∈ ns_public"


  NS2:  "⟦evs2 ∈ ns_public; Nonce NB ∉ used evs2;
          Says A' B (Crypt (pubK B) {|Nonce NA, Agent A|}) ∈ set evs2⟧
         ⟹ Says B A (Crypt (pubK A) {|Nonce NA, Nonce NB, Agent B|})
                # evs2 ∈ ns_public"


  NS3:  "⟦evs3 ∈ ns_public;
          Says A  B (Crypt (pubK B) {|Nonce NA, Agent A|}) ∈ set evs3;
          Says B' A (Crypt (pubK A) {|Nonce NA, Nonce NB, Agent B|})
              ∈ set evs3⟧
         ⟹ Says A B (Crypt (pubK B) (Nonce NB)) # evs3 ∈ ns_public"
```

Fig. 10.1. An Inductive Protocol Definition

Benefits of this approach are simplicity and clarity. The semantic model is set theory, proofs are by induction and the translation from the informal notation to the inductive rules is straightforward.

10.6 Proving Elementary Properties

Secrecy properties can be hard to prove. The conclusion of a typical secrecy theorem is $X \notin$ analz (knows Spy evs). The difficulty arises from having to reason about analz, or less formally, showing that the spy can never learn X. Much easier is to prove that X can never occur at all. Such *regularity* properties are typically expressed using parts rather than analz.

The following lemma states that A's private key is potentially known to the spy if and only if A belongs to the set bad of compromised agents. The statement uses parts: the very presence of A's private key in a message, whether protected by encryption or not, is enough to confirm that A is compromised. The proof, like nearly all protocol proofs, is by induction over traces.

lemma Spy_see_priK [simp]:
    "evs ∈ ns_public

$\Longrightarrow$ *(Key (priK A) $\in$ parts (knows Spy evs)) = (A $\in$ bad)"*
apply *(erule ns_public.induct, simp_all)*

The induction yields five subgoals, one for each rule in the definition of
ns_public. The idea is to prove that the protocol property holds initially
(rule *Nil*), is preserved by each of the legitimate protocol steps (rules *NS1*–
3), and even is preserved in the face of anything the spy can do (rule *Fake*).

The proof is trivial. No legitimate protocol rule sends any keys at all,
so only *Fake* is relevant. Indeed, simplification leaves only the *Fake* case, as
indicated by the variable name *evsf*:

```
1. ⋀X evsf.
     ⟦evsf ∈ ns_public;
         (Key (priK A) ∈ parts (knows Spy evsf)) = (A ∈ bad);
         X ∈ synth (analz (knows Spy evsf))⟧
     ⟹ (Key (priK A) ∈ parts (insert X (knows Spy evsf))) =
         (A ∈ bad)
```
by *blast*

The *Fake* case is proved automatically. If *priK A* is in the extended trace
then either (1) it was already in the original trace or (2) it was generated by
the spy, who must have known this key already. Either way, the induction
hypothesis applies.

Unicity lemmas are regularity lemmas stating that specified items can
occur only once in a trace. The following lemma states that a nonce cannot
be used both as *Na* and as *Nb* unless it is known to the spy. Intuitively,
it holds because honest agents always choose fresh values as nonces; only
the spy might reuse a value, and he doesn't know this particular value. The
proof script is short: induction, simplification, *blast*. The first line uses the
rule *rev_mp* to prepare the induction by moving two assumptions into the
induction formula.

lemma *no_nonce_NS1_NS2*:
    *"⟦Crypt (pubK C) ⦃NA', Nonce NA, Agent D⦄ ∈ parts (knows Spy evs);
     Crypt (pubK B) ⦃Nonce NA, Agent A⦄ ∈ parts (knows Spy evs);
     evs ∈ ns_public⟧*
     $\Longrightarrow$ *Nonce NA ∈ analz (knows Spy evs)"*
apply *(erule rev_mp, erule rev_mp)*
apply *(erule ns_public.induct, simp_all)*
apply *(blast intro: analz_insertI)+*
done

The following unicity lemma states that, if *NA* is secret, then its appearance in any instance of message 1 determines the other components. The
proof is similar to the previous one.

lemma *unique_NA*:
    *"⟦Crypt(pubK B) ⦃Nonce NA, Agent A ⦄ ∈ parts(knows Spy evs);
     Crypt(pubK B') ⦃Nonce NA, Agent A'⦄ ∈ parts(knows Spy evs);
     Nonce NA ∉ analz (knows Spy evs); evs ∈ ns_public⟧*
     $\Longrightarrow$ *A=A' ∧ B=B'"*

10.7 Proving Secrecy Theorems

The secrecy theorems for Bob (the second participant) are especially important because they fail for the original protocol. The following theorem states
that if Bob sends message 2 to Alice, and both agents are uncompromised,
then Bob's nonce will never reach the spy.

theorem *Spy_not_see_NB [dest]:*
"⟦*Says B A (Crypt (pubK A) ⦃Nonce NA, Nonce NB, Agent B⦄)* ∈ *set evs;*
   A ∉ *bad; B* ∉ *bad; evs* ∈ *ns_public*⟧
 ⟹ *Nonce NB* ∉ *analz (knows Spy evs)"*

To prove it, we must formulate the induction properly (one of the assumptions
mentions *evs*), apply induction, and simplify:

apply (*erule rev_mp, erule ns_public.induct, simp_all*)

The proof states are too complicated to present in full. Let's examine the
simplest subgoal, that for message 1. The following event has just occurred:

$$1. \quad A' \to B' : \{Na', A'\}_{Kb'}$$

The variables above have been primed because this step belongs to a different
run from that referred to in the theorem statement — the theorem refers to a
past instance of message 2, while this subgoal concerns message 1 being sent
just now. In the Isabelle subgoal, instead of primed variables like B' and Na'
we have *Ba* and *NAa*:

1. ⋀*Ba NAa evs1.*
    ⟦*A* ∉ *bad; B* ∉ *bad; evs1* ∈ *ns_public;*
       Says B A (Crypt (pubK A) ⦃Nonce NA, Nonce NB, Agent B⦄)
       ∈ *set evs1* ⟶
       Nonce NB ∉ *analz (knows Spy evs1);*
       Nonce NAa ∉ *used evs1*⟧
    ⟹ *Ba* ∈ *bad* ⟶
       Says B A (Crypt (pubK A) ⦃Nonce NA, Nonce NB, Agent B⦄)
       ∈ *set evs1* ⟶
       NB ≠ *NAa*

The simplifier has used a default simplification rule that does a case analysis
for each encrypted message on whether or not the decryption key is compromised.

analz (insert (Crypt K X) H) =
  (if Key (invKey K) ∈ *analz H*
   then insert (Crypt K X) (anal z (insert X H))
   else insert (Crypt K X) (analz H))   (*analz_Crypt_if*)

The simplifier has also used *Spy_see_priK*, proved in Sect. 10.6) above, to
yield *Ba* ∈ *bad*.

   Recall that this subgoal concerns the case where the last message to be
sent was

$$1. \quad A' \to B' : \{Na', A'\}_{Kb'}.$$

This message can compromise Nb only if $Nb = Na'$ and B' is compromised, allowing the spy to decrypt the message. The Isabelle subgoal says precisely this, if we allow for its choice of variable names. Proving NB $\neq$ NAa is easy: NB was sent earlier, while NAa is fresh; formally, we have the assumption Nonce NAa $\notin$ used evs1.

Note that our reasoning concerned B's participation in another run. Agents may engage in several runs concurrently, and some attacks work by interleaving the messages of two runs. With model checking, this possibility can cause a state-space explosion, and for us it certainly complicates proofs. The biggest subgoal concerns message 2. It splits into several cases, such as whether or not the message just sent is the very message mentioned in the theorem statement. Some of the cases are proved by unicity, others by the induction hypothesis. For all those complications, the proofs are automatic by blast with the theorem no_nonce_NS1_NS2.

The remaining theorems about the protocol are not hard to prove. The following one asserts a form of *authenticity*: if B has sent an instance of message 2 to A and has received the expected reply, then that reply really originated with A. The proof is a simple induction.

theorem B_trusts_NS3:
" ⟦Says B A (Crypt (pubK A) {|Nonce NA, Nonce NB, Agent B|}) ∈ set evs;
   Says A' B (Crypt (pubK B) (Nonce NB)) ∈ set evs;
   A ∉ bad; B ∉ bad; evs ∈ ns_public⟧
 ⟹ Says A B (Crypt (pubK B) (Nonce NB)) ∈ set evs"

From similar assumptions, we can prove that A started the protocol run by sending an instance of message 1 involving the nonce NA. For this theorem, the conclusion is

    Says A B (Crypt (pubK B) {|Nonce NA, Agent A|}) ∈ set evs

Analogous theorems can be proved for A, stating that nonce NA remains secret and that message 2 really originates with B. Even the flawed protocol establishes these properties for A; the flaw only harms the second participant.

Detailed information on this protocol verification technique can be found elsewhere [28], including proofs of an Internet protocol [29]. We must stress that the protocol discussed in this chapter is trivial. There are only three messages; no keys are exchanged; we merely have to prove that encrypted data remains secret. Real world protocols are much longer and distribute many secrets to their participants. To be realistic, the model has to include the possibility of keys being lost dynamically due to carelessness. If those keys have been used to encrypt other sensitive information, there may be cascading losses. We may still be able to establish a bound on the losses and to prove that other protocol runs function correctly [24]. Proofs of real-world protocols follow the strategy illustrated above, but the subgoals can be much bigger and there are more of them.

You know my methods. Apply them!
Sherlock Holmes

A. Appendix

⟦	[I	\<lbrakk>
⟧	I]	\<rbrakk>
⟹	==>	\<Longrightarrow>
⋀	!!	\<And>
≡	==	\<equiv>
⇌	==	\<rightleftharpoons>
⇁	=>	\<rightharpoonup>
↽	<=	\<leftharpoondown>
λ	%	\<lambda>
⇒	=>	\<Rightarrow>
∧	&	\<and>
∨	|	\<or>
⟶	-->	\<longrightarrow>
¬	~	\<not>
≠	~=	\<noteq>
∀	ALL, !	\<forall>
∃	EX, ?	\<exists>
∃!	EX!, ?!	\<exists>!
ε	SOME, @	\<epsilon>
∘	o	\<circ>
||	abs	\<bar> \<bar>
≤	<=	\<le>
×	*	\<times>
∈	:	\<in>
∉	~:	\<notin>
⊆	<=	\<subseteq>
⊂	<	\<subset>
∪	Un	\<union>
∩	Int	\<inter>
⋃	UN, Union	\<Union>
⋂	INT, Inter	\<Inter>
*	^*	\<^sup>*
−1	^-1	\<inverse>

Table A.1. Mathematical Symbols, Their ASCII-Equivalents and Internal Names

Constant	Type	Syntax
0	*'a::zero*	
1	*'a::one*	
+	*('a::plus)* ⇒ *'a* ⇒ *'a*	(infixl 65)
–	*('a::minus)* ⇒ *'a* ⇒ *'a*	(infixl 65)
–	*('a::minus)* ⇒ *'a*	
*	*('a::times)* ⇒ *'a* ⇒ *'a*	(infixl 70)
div	*('a::div)* ⇒ *'a* ⇒ *'a*	(infixl 70)
mod	*('a::div)* ⇒ *'a* ⇒ *'a*	(infixl 70)
dvd	*('a::times)* ⇒ *'a* ⇒ *bool*	(infixl 50)
/	*('a::inverse)* ⇒ *'a* ⇒ *'a*	(infixl 70)
^	*('a::power)* ⇒ *nat* ⇒ *'a*	(infixr 80)
abs	*('a::minus)* ⇒ *'a*	$\|x\|$
≤	*('a::ord)* ⇒ *'a* ⇒ *bool*	(infixl 50)
<	*('a::ord)* ⇒ *'a* ⇒ *bool*	(infixl 50)
min	*('a::ord)* ⇒ *'a* ⇒ *'a*	
max	*('a::ord)* ⇒ *'a* ⇒ *'a*	
Least	*('a::ord* ⇒ *bool)* ⇒ *'a*	*LEAST x. P*

Table A.2. Overloaded Constants in HOL

ALL	BIT	CHR	EX	GREATEST	INT	Int	LEAST	0
OFCLASS	PI	PROP	SIGMA	SOME	THE	TYPE	UN	Un
WRT	case	choose	div	dvd	else	funcset	if	in
let	mem	mod	o	of	op	then		

Table A.3. Reserved Words in HOL Terms

Bibliography

[1] David Aspinall. Proof General. http://www.proofgeneral.org.

[2] David Aspinall. Proof General: A generic tool for proof development. In *Tools and Algorithms for the Construction and Analysis of Systems (TACAS)*, volume 1785 of *Lecture Notes in Computer Science*, pages 38–42. Springer-Verlag, 2000.

[3] Franz Baader and Tobias Nipkow. *Term Rewriting and All That*. Cambridge University Press, 1998.

[4] Gertrud Bauer, Tobias Nipkow, David von Oheimb, Lawrence C Paulson, Thomas M Rasmussen, Christophe Tabacznyj, and Markus Wenzel. The supplemental Isabelle/HOL library. Part of the Isabelle distribution, http://isabelle.in.tum.de/library/HOL/Library/document.pdf, 2002.

[5] Richard Bird. *Introduction to Functional Programming using Haskell*. Prentice-Hall, 1998.

[6] M. Burrows, M. Abadi, and R. M. Needham. A logic of authentication. *Proceedings of the Royal Society of London*, 426:233–271, 1989.

[7] Edmund Clarke, Orna Grumberg, and Doron Peled. *Model Checking*. MIT Press, 1999.

[8] Jacques Fleuriot and Lawrence C. Paulson. Mechanizing nonstandard real analysis. *LMS Journal of Computation and Mathematics*, 3:140–190, 2000. http://www.lms.ac.uk/jcm/3/lms1999-027/.

[9] Jean-Yves Girard. *Proofs and Types*. Cambridge University Press, 1989. Translated by Yves LaFont and Paul Taylor.

[10] M. J. C. Gordon and T. F. Melham, editors. *Introduction to HOL: A Theorem Proving Environment for Higher Order Logic*. Cambridge University Press, 1993.

[11] David Harel, Dexter Kozen, and Jerzy Tiuryn. *Dynamic Logic*. MIT Press, 2000.

[12] John E. Hopcroft and Jeffrey D. Ullman. *Introduction to Automata Theory, Languages, and Computation*. Addison-Wesley, 1979.

[13] Paul Hudak. *The Haskell School of Expression*. Cambridge University Press, 2000.

[14] Michael Huth and Mark Ryan. *Logic in Computer Science. Modelling and reasoning about systems*. Cambridge University Press, 2000.

T. Nipkow, L.C. Paulson, and M. Wenzel: Isabelle/HOL, LNCS 2283, pp. 209–211, 2002.
© Springer-Verlag Berlin Heidelberg 2002

[15] Donald E. Knuth. *The Art of Computer Programming, Volume 3: Sorting and Searching*. Addison-Wesley, 1975.

[16] Gavin Lowe. Breaking and fixing the Needham-Schroeder public-key protocol using CSP and FDR. In T. Margaria and B. Steffen, editors, *Tools and Algorithms for the Construction and Analysis of Systems: second international workshop, TACAS '96*, LNCS 1055, pages 147–166. Springer, 1996.

[17] Robin Milner, Mads Tofte, and Robert Harper. *The Definition of Standard ML*. MIT Press, 1990.

[18] Olaf Müller, Tobias Nipkow, David von Oheimb, and Oscar Slotosch. HOLCF = HOL + LCF. *Journal of Functional Programming*, 9:191–223, 1999.

[19] Wolfgang Naraschewski and Markus Wenzel. Object-oriented verification based on record subtyping in higher-order logic. In Jim Grundy and Malcóm Newey, editors, *Theorem Proving in Higher Order Logics: TPHOLs '98*, LNCS 1479, 1998.

[20] Roger M. Needham and Michael D. Schroeder. Using encryption for authentication in large networks of computers. *Communications of the ACM*, 21(12):993–999, December 1978.

[21] Tobias Nipkow. Functional unification of higher-order patterns. In M. Vardi, editor, *Eighth Annual Symposium on Logic in Computer Science*, pages 64–74. IEEE Computer Society Press, 1993.

[22] Tobias Nipkow, Lawrence C. Paulson, and Markus Wenzel. *Isabelle's Logics: HOL*. http://isabelle.in.tum.de/doc/logics-HOL.pdf.

[23] Lawrence C. Paulson. *The Isabelle Reference Manual*. http://isabelle.in.tum.de/doc/ref.pdf.

[24] Lawrence C. Paulson. Relations between secrets: Two formal analyses of the Yahalom protocol. *Journal of Computer Security*. in press.

[25] Lawrence C. Paulson. *Logic and Computation: Interactive proof with Cambridge LCF*. Cambridge University Press, 1987.

[26] Lawrence C. Paulson. *Isabelle: A Generic Theorem Prover*. Springer, 1994. LNCS 828.

[27] Lawrence C. Paulson. *ML for the Working Programmer*. Cambridge University Press, 2nd edition, 1996.

[28] Lawrence C. Paulson. The inductive approach to verifying cryptographic protocols. *Journal of Computer Security*, 6:85–128, 1998.

[29] Lawrence C. Paulson. Inductive analysis of the Internet protocol TLS. *ACM Transactions on Information and System Security*, 2(3):332–351, August 1999.

[30] F. J. Pelletier. Seventy-five problems for testing automatic theorem provers. *Journal of Automated Reasoning*, 2:191–216, 1986. Errata, JAR 4 (1988), 235–236 and JAR 18 (1997), 135.

[31] Kenneth H. Rosen. *Discrete Mathematics and Its Applications*. McGraw-Hill, 1998.

[32] Simon Thompson. *Haskell: The Craft of Functional Programming.* Addison-Wesley, 1999.

[33] Markus Wenzel. *The Isabelle/Isar Reference Manual.* http://isabelle.in. tum.de/doc/isar-ref.pdf.

[34] Markus Wenzel. *Isabelle/Isar — a versatile environment for human-readable formal proof documents.* PhD thesis, Institut für Informatik, Technische Universität München, 2002.

[35] Markus Wenzel and Stefan Berghofer. *The Isabelle System Manual.* http://isabelle.in.tum.de/doc/system.pdf.

Index

Lecture Notes in Computer Science

For information about Vols. 1–2228
please contact your bookseller or Springer-Verlag